THE GEOGRAPHY OF POWER
IN MEDIEVAL JAPAN

THE GEOGRAPHY OF POWER
IN MEDIEVAL JAPAN

Thomas Keirstead

PRINCETON UNIVERSITY PRESS

PRINCETON, NEW JERSEY

LIBRARY OF CONGRESS CATALOGING-IN-PUBLICATION DATA

KEIRSTEAD, THOMAS, 1958–

THE GEOGRAPHY OF POWER IN MEDIEVAL JAPAN / THOMAS KEIRSTEAD

P.   CM.

INCLUDES BIBLIOGRAPHICAL REFERENCES AND INDEX

ISBN 0-691-03183-5

1. MANORS—JAPAN—HISTORY.   2. PEASANTRY—JAPAN—HISTORY

3. JAPAN—HISTORY—TO 1600

HD914.K4 1992   91-32067   305.5′0591′0902—DC20

PUBLICATION OF THIS BOOK HAS BEEN ASSISTED BY
A GRANT FROM THE JAPAN FOUNDATION

THIS BOOK HAS BEEN COMPOSED IN LINOTRON PALATINO

PRINCETON UNIVERSITY PRESS BOOKS ARE PRINTED
ON ACID-FREE PAPER AND MEET THE GUIDELINES FOR
PERMANENCE AND DURABILITY OF THE COMMITTEE ON
PRODUCTION GUIDELINES FOR BOOK LONGEVITY
OF THE COUNCIL ON LIBRARY RESOURCES

PRINTED IN THE UNITED STATES OF AMERICA

1 3 5 7 9 10 8 6 4 2

For Deidre

CONTENTS

ACKNOWLEDGMENTS

EVERY TEXT has its contexts. In this case, the Fulbright-Hays Commission and the Social Science Research Council supported me through nearly two years in Japan conducting research; Professor Kanai of the Historiographical Institute at the University of Tokyo found me space to work and access to their formidable archive. A Whiting fellowship helped turn that research into a first approximation of a manuscript, and a recent ACLS grant allowed me to complete the book. A version of Chapter 4 appeared in the *Journal of Japanese Studies*; I thank the editors for permission to republish it here.

I must also thank Jeffrey Mass, whose thoughtful skepticism and rigorous readings shepherded the manuscript along when it was still a dissertation-to-be. Peter Duus, Nancy Kollmann, Jim Given, and Bin Wong all read various versions of the manuscript; I thank them for their comments and suggestions. My special thanks go to Herman Ooms: he is a model reader and insightful critic, and his friendship and enthusiasm encouraged me to carry this project to fruition.

My most profound debt is also the most personal. Deidre Lynch has steadfastly borne with my obsession, even when I neglected to reciprocate. Throughout she has been my best teacher and critic, a constant source of support and inspiration. Without her, this book would not be.

THE GEOGRAPHY OF POWER

IN MEDIEVAL JAPAN

ONE

IN GO-SANJŌ'S ARCHIVE

DISCOVERING THE SYSTEM OF THE ESTATES

THE DISCOVERY of European historiography in the nineteenth and early twentieth centuries led Japanese historians to discoveries about their own past. Reinterpreting Japanese experience in the light of European models, scholars in the late Meiji era located in their own history analogues to Western historical periods and institutions. This quest for resemblances produced a Japanese history demarcated, along Western lines, into ancient, medieval, and modern eras and distinguished by institutional formations, such as feudalism or, most pertinent for this study, manorialism—concepts of Western provenance. Arraying itself against the assertions of Westernizers (like Fukuzawa Yukichi) who taught that Japan must break with its past in order to modernize, this scholarship seemed to demonstrate startling similarities between Japanese and European history and to promise Japan's future progress along a trail blazed by the West.[1] As Asakawa Kan'ichi, a pioneering student of early Japanese institutions, remarked in describing feudal society in Japan, "I am inclined to think that feudal growth (like social progress itself) is *not* normal; and is, on the whole, a fortunate abnormality that has been the gift of a very few races in the world's history."[2]

This early historiography did not merely fulfill the national mission of salvaging Japan's past for the modernizing nation; it also structured that past by proposing the categories and lines of analysis that defined the modern historiographical endeavor. Molded by the concerns of contemporary European historical practice, this was an objective, "scientific," and, perhaps most generally, systematic, history. It produced a vision of the past defined by the interplay of legal, political, and socioeconomic systems; and among its discoveries was the estate system (*shōensei*). This is not to say that the estate (*shōen* or *shō*) went unnoticed until this time, for it is one of the most profusely documented phenomena in Japanese history;[3] it is merely to note that in the comparative enterprise inspired by the discovery of modern Western historiography the shōen were for the first time accredited the status of a system—recognized as a coherent, organized body and as a proper subject of analysis.

Accordingly, the earliest treatises on the estates qua system drew heavily on European paradigms to evaluate and categorize their subject. Nakada Kaoru's path-breaking explorations of the legal framework of estate holding in Japan, for example, were conspicuously comparative, developing their argument by contrasts to Germanic law and to the principles that underlay Western manorialism.[4] Similarly, Asakawa's studies exploited his extensive knowledge of European feudalism to delineate the differences between Japanese shōen and Western manors and to designate and describe feudal institutions in Japan.[5] But beyond the specific comparisons with European institutions that allowed these scholars to identify and define the subject of their inquiries rests a more basic influence. Their elaborations of the shōen were conditioned by an understanding that the terrain of history came already inscribed with certain patterns—came already organized by legal, economic, and other systems. In other words, an idea that the past can and should be made to yield to some sort of systematic order inhabits and makes possible these scholars' investigations—else Asakawa and Nakada could not have written as they did. And, unavoidably, this understanding orders not only their method, but the subject/object of their study as well. The estate system must be seen, in short, as a discursive as well as a historical product: its condition of possibility not only the estates that dotted the Japanese landscape circa 800 to 1600, but also the nineteenth- and early-twentieth-century refashioning of the discipline.

These circumstances framing the birth of scholarship on the shōen system have had profound consequences (in both Japan and the West) down to the present day. Scholars like Nakada and Asakawa, in effect, produced the field, and their concerns outlined its shape. To be sure, in the decades that have intervened since they drafted their pioneering works much of what they wrote has been contested and superseded. Yet if details of their argument have been disproved or rendered superfluous, their effort to situate Japan's past by reference to a cluster of ostensibly universal categories has provided the framework for research on shōen. Subsequent scholars have thus expended much effort attempting to place the system within these categories—debating, for example, whether the system belongs properly to antiquity or to the medieval epoch (or to some transitional period); disputing whether its institutions should be characterized as feudal or as something else; trying to decide if its peasant subjects are best classified as slaves, serfs, or freemen; and devising classificatory shemes for the patterns of land ownership found within the Japanese counterpart of the "manor."

Such debates have produced a wealth of knowledge about the es-

tates. Patterns of landholding, types of tenure, modes of administration, and rent systems have been exhaustively studied; archives
have been combed for information, and a dazzling amount of material has been made available for study. The picture that has emerged
from these explorations is of a diverse, even chaotic, body. Shōen
have been revealed to encompass just about every kind of holding
imaginable, and to incorporate all manner of economic activity, not
just agriculture. Yet for all the diversity, there has never been any
doubt that the disparate parts formed a coherent whole, that the estates comprised a recognizable socioeconomic formation, a social
system. Despite the many directions shōen studies have taken, and
despite intense controversies, the shōen have from the start been
comprehended as part of a system; "estate" has been used more or
less interchangeably with "estate system." Derived ultimately, I believe, from a historical tradition in which legal, economic, and political systems comprised the basic horizon of analysis, this assumption
has offered a ground of coherence upon which shōen studies could
build. And accepting this premise of systematicity as a starting point,
historians have been able to concentrate on measuring the estate system's deviation from (or conformity to) certain institutional archetypes or on settling its place within history's master narratives; few
have felt called upon to inquire into what precisely it was that allowed one to speak of the shōen as a system, that sanctioned the leap
from the variety of individual estates to the consistency of a system.

This study takes a somewhat different tack. I aim neither to catalog
the features of the Japanese manifestation of manorialism nor to nar-
rate the system's rise and fall. Such an enterprise, though valuable, is
at odds with my main purpose: to view the shōen in its *longue durée*;
not to explicate a succession of types of estates or a series of political and economic turmoils, but to recover the basic structures that
marshaled the diversity of individual estates into the regularity of a
system. While I agree that there is method to the estates, I think there
is value in an approach that takes the premise slightly differently. Instead of regarding it as license to launch other sorts of exploration,
I see a need to redirect attention to the nature, operation, and functioning of the system itself. Shifting emphasis, I believe, can help to
develop a new understanding of the shōen. By focusing on *how* the
system operated before attempting to label it, by investigating the
regularities that ordered its seeming chaos before recounting how it
evolved out of the preceding era or presaged the succeeding one, I
hope to detail how the system can be understood as, in the words of
one prominent medievalist, "the central defining characteristic of the
medieval period."[6]

My approach, accordingly, will be somewhat different from that found in many histories of the estates. I wish to avoid, in particular, the teleology implicit in narrative description—the sense, as François Furet puts it, that "what comes first explains what follows," that institutions or systems must change perceptibly with each passing decade and that those changes fall all in a line, toward "growth" and "maturity" for a "young" institution, toward "decline" and "death" for a system already mature.[7] Much work on the estate system is marked by just such a desire to plot the trajectory of the institution, to find a coherent path that leads ineluctably from the institution's beginning, through its middle or maturity, on to its end.[8] Such a chronological or narrative approach bestows a sense of linear development that in the case of the estate system seems particularly misleading. For what one encounters in the shōen is not the steady evolution of one type of estate from another, but a confused and repetitive movement that cannot be reduced to a temporal succession of archetypes. Any attempt to identify the "typical" eleventh- or thirteenth- or fifteenth-century estate and describe the stages by which one form evolved into the next is bound to be thwarted by the multiplicity of estate histories running contrary or otherwise at variance to the "typical" flow and by the "untimely" (whether late or early) presence of certain institutions or practices.[9] The chief result of such attempts is an impoverished understanding of the estate system; aiming for a persuasive (hi)story of the estate form, this approach tends instead to reduce the variety of individual estate histories to so many archetypes bound to follow a given evolutionary path.

A narrative approach is plagued by other, equally problematic, effects. First, even as the demands of narrative flow create a history that evolves through distinct stages (because the eleventh-century estate *must* demonstrably differ from its thirteenth-century counterpart, etc.), narrative tends to deflect attention away from the very stages it constructs. The main concern of a narrative history will always be the movement from one stage to the next and the causes governing that movement. The stages and types of estate associated with them become, in effect, no more than stations on the way toward a preordained goal—i. e., an economic system in which shōen do not predominate.[10] Estates and the social and cultural formations within which they operated thus cease to be objects of interest in themselves and become worthy of attention only insofar as they serve as markers of change. A chronological approach therefore responds to a manifestly transhistorical interest; its desire is to reach an end point and fulfill a destiny that it knows lies ahead, and not to describe the operation of an institution or culture apart from its fate.[11] Moreover, to the extent that this approach attributes particular value to evidence that "embodies" change, it will restrict the range of materials/subjects available to history: because cause and effect are of such importance, matters that do not lend themselves to causal explanation will inevitably be suppressed as nonhistorical.[12] Everything must first be interrogated for its possible contribution to the evolution of the system. A hierarchy of evidence is thereby created in which artifacts and social practices that seem not to lead anywhere are judged to be of secondary importance, while events which seem to betoken change are promoted in significance. Thus, in most histories of the shōen, estate maps, for instance, or the rituals of daily life, take a backseat to ostensibly more "obvious" harbingers of change: unruly warriors, defiant estate managers, tax revolts, and the like. Impeded in this fashion, a history of the estates will be hard-pressed to recognize the dynamics and contradictions that underlie the reproduction of the mundane, or, conversely, see how peasant uprisings, for example, might comment on the regular operation of the system and not just on its decline.

These reflections suggest that one needs a new strategy to comprehend the estates as a central feature of medieval life and not simply as a stage in the evolution of Japanese landholding. Therefore, this study will not attempt to chart the production, growth, and development of estates through time, but will emphasize the stability, the reproduction at wide removes of time and space, of certain fundamental notions and structures against which the diverse histories of individual estates played themselves out. Here, too, is found my rationale for treating roughly three centuries, from approximately 1100 to 1400, as a single bloc. By no means do I wish to suggest that nothing happened during this period—that, for example, the fourteenth-century economy was no different from that of the twelfth century, or that the political climate remained unchanged. I wish only to emphasize that despite profound changes in high politics or within the economy, the basic structures that defined the estate *system* remained remarkably durable. Embedded in the flows of goods and people which sustained and enabled the system was a communication between proprietors and their estates that carried political as well as economic significance. The constant circulation into the capital and out again to the provinces conveyed a particular organization of the countryside, placed the realm within a network of relationships that shaped and ordered it in certain ways. This network of relationships and the interactions it produced, and by which it, in turn, was reproduced, comprise the subject matter of this study. Embodied in the manner in which estates were conjured out of the natural landscape and organized into a basis of production; discernible in the ways peasants were constituted as subjects of the system; implicit in the codes peasant residents of estates manipulated to make their protests known—are certain ordering principles that composed the system of the estates. This study takes shape, therefore, as a search for the system that allows us to speak, write, even conceive of, an estate system.

Instead, then, of a new typology of estates or a new narrative of the institution's rise and fall, I propose a different starting point and a different set of questions. This study commences not with "Where does the estate system fit in the march of history?" or "What patterns of landholding or administration can be observed on different estates?" but, more basically, with "How did the shōen constitute a social and cultural system?" The central problem, as I see it, is to mark the social, spatial, and other configurations that delimited the realm of the shōen and to register the patterns of interaction that provided for the system's reproduction through time. Addressed specifically to the broad ordering of society, space, and meaning that the system posed, this sort of analysis is intended as a corrective to accounts which unthinkingly conflate individual estates and the system of which they were a part. To understand the system, one must look beyond the estates to the basic structures within which they were constituted.

This procedure will, I hope, show the estate system to be a complex and multileveled social and cultural order, not merely a congeries of landholding patterns. And I further hope that it will counter a tendency of historians to take the system for granted and proceed thence to other questions, instead of probing the premise of systematicity that lies at the root of the knowledge they produce. In this study, I propose to counter this historiographical tradition with a series of analyses of the system's basic conditions of possibility—with a set of inquiries designed to recover the patterns of interaction and the signifying practices that enabled and ordered the system of estates.

Following Anthony Giddens, we may look for the system of this social and cultural edifice in certain basic criteria.[13] First, any social or cultural system occupies and defines a "social space." In the present case, this place is the estate: a site comprising not only the lands within estate boundaries, but also the social realm of the estate's inhabitants and the cultural understanding that recognized the estate as a distinct space. The ability to lay claim to this social space presupposes a second characteristic of systems: in addition to occupying territory, they describe structures of legitimation. The system exists through the assertions that maintain and police its social space, certifying rulers' claims to authority at the same time as they authorize the demands of those groups recognized as the system's subjects. In the case of the estate system, such structures of legitimation are revealed in the assertions that justified a proprietor's expropriation of rents and other levies, but also in the counterclaims of the peasant residents of estates. In these reciprocal claims one begins to discover the assumptions that underwrote the exercise of power and authority in the shōen. That these structures of legitimation may carry force, however, necessitates a third, and extremely important, feature of cultural systems: that they constitute networks of signification; that they, in short, organize meaning. The spatial and social reach of an estate was defined as much by a common consciousness that invested its institutions and practices with particular meanings as by the physical boundary markers that flanked estates or by the signs of status (deeds of investiture, possession of a residence, etc.) that visibly distinguished its residents. The estate system may therefore be seen to exist as a realm of shared understanding, as residing not merely in a certain set of institutions, but also in the constellation of concepts, notions, and assumptions inscribed within these institutions.[14] Running through and unifying the clusters of institutions by which we normally identify systems are certain regularities—in practice, in the structure of everyday life, in the codes which lend meaning to actions. These regularities joined the disparate elements of the shōen— the estates, their resident groups, their proprietors—into a vital cultural system.

To undertake a description of the system of the estates, we must first abandon some of the assumptions implicit in much shōen historiography. The common notion, for example, that the histories of individual estates, if only enough of them are accumulated, can reconstruct the totality of the system, must be replaced by the realization that estate and system are distinct entities. Likewise, the positivist understanding that the system can be discovered in a thorough catalog of the entities (and their variations) with which the estates were populated must yield to a recognition that such a catalog can never register the networks of signification or structures of legitimation that make the system. Instead of attempting to identify the shōen system with a particular configuration of institutions (types of estates, modes of proprietorship, patterns of landholding), we must be concerned with the orders within which those institutions, in all their diversity, were constituted and structured.[15] Along the lines Giddens has set down, we may look for these orders in the concepts that defined the system's physical and social space, in the notions of authority that sanctioned the exercise of power, and in the understandings that interpreted the system to its inhabitants. Rather than seeking the estate system in a chronicle of the birth, growth, and decline of its institutional apparatus, this approach attempts to discover the system in the interactions and ideas that shaped and sustained those institutions and that welded them into a social and cultural order.

Estates and the Estate System

In barest outline, the shōen system consisted in a vast number of landed estates, the rents from which sustained (at the highest levels) a relatively small, centrally located elite of aristocratic houses, Buddhist temples, and Shinto shrines, as well as the imperial household. Although concentrated in the central and western provinces, estates could be found across Japan. Their wide geographical distribution is matched by their temporal dispersal: from the eighth through the sixteenth centuries, holdings known as shōen are a feature of the Japanese landscape. Scattered throughout the country and across the centuries, shōen define a mode of landownership that is a prominent feature of much of Japan's premodern history.

What is most immediately apparent about shōen is the wide variety of landholdings the term encompassed. Ranging in size from a few to several thousand hectares, estates might be loose aggregations of irrigated fields situated on rich plains, or compact holdings clustered in mountain valleys; some were fishing villages, so that the bulk of the holding consisted of a lake or a bay, while others were primarily commercial or trading entrepôts. This variety also marked what the shōen produced. Rice was unquestionably the main crop, but many estates, especially in eastern Japan, paid their rents in silk or linen; others were valued primarily for salt, oil, iron, lacquer wares, even mushrooms.[16] The welter of terms used to designate local tenures and different types of landholdings signals a similar diversity with respect to administration and organization.[17]

The term shōen (Chinese, *sheng yüan*) originated in Tang China, where it designated a noble's villa and park; by the mid-eighth century, the phrase was applied in Japan to tracts of unopened lands granted by the court to temples and elite families who undertook to develop them for cultivation.[18] Although they share with later estates the basic trait of being legally sanctioned forms of private land possession, the early estates differ markedly from their future namesakes. Where, for instance, exemption from taxes and from entry by state officials was a defining characteristic of later estates (guaranteed in their founding charters), the early shōen often possessed only rudimentary, and uncertain, immunities. Moreover, such immunities were often granted only after an estate had been established, rather than being an integral condition of its founding.[19] Befitting the ambiguous status of their immunities, early estates often possessed a comparatively modest managerial structure. Nothing existed at this stage, for example, to rival the complex hierarchies of ranks and specialized councils that governed Tōji's or Tōdaiji's estates in the medieval period.[20] Similarly, the physical structure of early shōen was relatively simple: whereas later estates claimed the broad expanses of territory contained within the estate's marked boundaries—encompassing, indiscriminately, rice paddy, dry field, mountain, forest, and other uncultivated areas—the extent of early estates was generally measured field by field.[21] Nor did early estates possess the group of residents (shōmin) that was so prominent a feature of the estate after the eleventh and twelfth centuries.[22] Many, in fact, possessed no indigenous labor force, relying instead on peasants recruited from nearby public lands to whom plots were rented out on an annual basis.[23]

This inventory of differences between early and mature estates may seem at first glance to invite a chronological reconstruction of the system of the sort against which I cautioned earlier. And indeed the genesis of the estate system is frequently recounted as just that: a story concentrating on changes in the estate form itself, in which the axis of progress is the estate's steady accumulation of tax and other immunities and its development of surer, more sophisticated administrative and managerial techniques. Such advances, it is held, bespeak the increasing stability of the estate form; the estate system is a fait accompli, *the* form of landholding, once these advances have produced an estate that is both secure in its immunities and managerially stable.

Let us rehearse in a little more detail the standard narrative of the emergence of the estate system. As it is typically told, the rise of the system passes through two or three evolutionary stages and culminates in the late-eleventh and twelfth centuries with the advent of "commendation-type" estates (kishin-gata shōen). Created when a local landholder surrendered title to his lands to one of the central elites, who in return undertook to gain tax exemption and immunity from state jurisdiction for the holding, such estates are typically cast as the final stage in the rise of the estate system. Identified by their complete fiscal and judicial autonomy, these estates provide the norms by which the estate system (and retroactively other entities that went by the name shōen) is defined and judged. Their appearance supplies the standard narrative with its capstone.

Proceeding along these lines to generate the system from the internal evolution of estates, one might begin the story in the eighth and early ninth centuries with estates like Tōdaiji's Kuwabara or Tōji's Ōyama. Both estates came into existence as parcels of wasteland granted to the temples, which sought to reclaim them for cultivation. The enormous expense of reclamation work and the difficulty of securing adequate labor generally spelled a quick end to this type of estate.[24] The textbook narrative, however, carries forward with a new type of shōen which appeared around the middle of the tenth century. Known as "exempt-field" (*menden*) estates, these consisted of a core of paddy, mountains, forest, or other lands. The proprietor was granted exclusive right to the revenues these lands generated, but the lands themselves remained within the jurisdiction of the state. Compared to the commendation-type estates, which are regarded as embodying the essence of the estate system, exempt-field shōen seem organizationally indistinct; the fiscal privileges they entailed are divorced from territorial and managerial rights. Still, from these entities to the mature estates that define the shōen system it was only a matter of growth and struggle as estate proprietors worked to commute acknowledged revenue rights into territorial claims and to convert partial tax exemptions into full immunity from state levies and jurisdiction. Thus the tenth and eleventh centuries witnessed intense competition between estate proprietors and provincial bureaucrats over the status of contested holdings. It was a struggle, most accounts agree, the bureaucrats were destined to lose, for by the twelfth century shōen immunities had received widespread sanction. The estate system, in this rendering, is born when a sufficient corpus of estates has been accumulated and when, as a matter of course, all estates enjoy a twin exemption from state taxes and the jurisdiction of state and local officials.

This, for all the intents and purposes of previous historiography, is how the estate system developed—as a narrative unfolding of the estate form. To write the history of the system in such terms, though, involves a specious elision; it confuses content and context, taking the characteristics of individual estates as a definition for the system within which they were deployed. We must maintain a critical distinction between "estates" and the "estate system,"as the two belong properly to discrete levels of analysis. For what distinguished the shōen system was not the growth or development of estates, an internal evolution to be gauged by their acquisition of more stable immunities or more sophisticated organization, but rather a radical reordering of the cultural system within which estates were constituted.

Estates of the twelfth century and beyond rested upon a different basis than their precursors; from the eighth century to the sixteenth, the term "shōen" continued to indicate a large, private landholding which enjoyed at least some measure of fiscal and juridic autonomy. But its social significance, what Foucault would call the "field of use in which it is placed," changed considerably.[25] The estates which rank as "early" in the standard narrative were ensconced within the state-mediated land and tax systems of antiquity. Sometimes consisting of no more than lands from which the taxes, still collected by the state apparatus, were assigned to the estate's proprietor, such estates were administratively and fiscally part of the "public" realm—except that the revenues they produced flowed to private interests rather than the public treasury. The so-called mature estates are products of a systemic shift, of a general recoding of practices and structures that constituted a particular sort of break—not so much a recasting of the basic meaning of shōen, as a rearrangement of the structural connections that underlay estate holding. The commendation-type estates which crown the narrative of estate development speak not merely, or even primarily, of changes in the form or content of estates. They signal something much more important: that the conditions of possibility for landholding had changed drastically. Behind the new type of estate, enabling it, indeed demanding it, is not a history of growing immunities or juridical autonomy, but a reconfiguration of the realm and of the deployment of the estate within it. The system cannot therefore be reduced to the sum of estates; it is a distinct entity, possessed of its own history and demanding its own analysis.

Of the long span covered by the existence of estates, only a portion, commencing well after the first appearance of shōen, in the eleventh and twelfth centuries, and ending sometime in the fifteenth, can be deemed the era of the estate system, an era in which estates comprised not merely an important form of landholding, but a privileged site in the general social topography, a focal point in the discourses that organized society. To write the history of that ordering of society one must concentrate on what is left after the stories of individual estates have been sifted out. For a history of the estate system cannot take as its object the steady accretion of estates or immunities. It is not the story of how an entity continuously growing in quantity and quality became entitled, when it achieved a certain critical mass, to the standing of a "system." The stability of the terminology, in effect, obscures a semantic break. The story of the estate system, therefore, must be that of a distinct break in the context and conceptualization of estate holding. And one begins to tell that story by recognizing the break and attending to the new orders that rewrote the usage of the term.

I have in mind in this study, then, something akin to what Foucault has termed "archaeology": I focus my analysis on the implicit structures that systematized the estates—on the "syntactic" arrangement that regulated their diversity—and not on the specific content of the form. I propose, in particular, to concentrate on the ways in which the daily experience of estate inhabitants shaped and was shaped by the structures of the system. My primary concern will not be the relations among estate elites, but rather the peasant residents of estates and the practices which reveal how their world was figured within the shōen system. But I will examine that perspective in tandem with the view "from above"—inherent in the ways in which the system is represented in the texts and images produced by shōen proprietors. For the system, I contend, cannot be understood as uniquely the product of one or the other vision: it was not something possessed by proprietors and imposed upon peasants, nor again a structure grounded in peasant communities to which elites accommodated their rule, but rather something that arose from, and existed through their interaction. Accordingly, it was afflicted by a sort of double vision. The estate system should not be seen as a realm of unequivocal meanings—its basic terms, including such apparently inarguable realities as the estate, were open to radically different interpretations. And precisely such tensions, I hope to show, describe the enabling conditions of the system; not the commandments of a ruling elite, but the interplay of conflicting practices and representations, produced and reproduced the system of the estates.

Tracing the Break

The advent of the estate system must be viewed in terms of a systemic shift, of a decisive restructuring of the context of estate holding. And we may begin to map out this shift in the massive redrawing of boundaries—the sweeping realignment of the political landscape and the concomitant transformation in the economic undergirding of elite power—that occurred in the late-eleventh and twelfth centuries.

By the beginning of the eleventh century, the early estate was in trouble. On Ōyama Estate, for example, difficulties in obtaining labor had stalled efforts to open up new land, and the uncertain status of the estate's immunities had rendered it vulnerable to attacks by provincial authorities.[26] The significance of these troubles, though, must be sought on a broader register than the individual estate. For the halting development of Ōyama and other estates stands not, I believe, as sign of their formal imperfection as shōen, nor as a sign of the system's immaturity, but indicates rather that the political and economic systems which had fostered and sustained the early estates were faltering. The imperial state conceived in the eighth and ninth centuries was meant to encompass the whole nation. The land and the people—commoners and elites alike—were all considered adjuncts of a unified imperial state. All were to be sustained within its elaborate bureaucratic structure—commoners by periodic distributions of rice land, nobles by a graded system of stipends tied to rank and office, the ecclesiastical elite by grants from the imperial treasury. Within this framework, estates figured as a means either of expanding the realm (tax incentives were offered to open new lands) or of rewarding especially worthy elites (hence the prominence of temples, religious guardians of the realm, among estate holders). Exactly why this conception of the realm began to be replaced in the tenth and eleventh centuries is a matter of sharp dispute; but whatever the causes, Japanese society from about this time onward entered a period of transition during which its political and economic bases were reformulated.[27]

The systematizing of the estates is part and parcel of this reformulation. In place of the unified, "public," bureaucratic framework of antiquity, the estate system was built on multiple, quasi-independent, "private" centers of power.[28] And where the economic base of antiquity lay in a unified imperial domain (which sustained the elites through state taxes), the economic base of the estate system lay in private holdings seen as administratively and juridically distinct from the public domain. The advent of the estate system reconceived the relationship between the imperial state (and the elites who comprised the officials of that state) and the realm it tended. In place of a unitary imperium that acknowledged no split between public and private, the shōen system installed a new notion of the construction of the realm. In sum, the emergence of the estate system predicated a new series of structural links between central proprietors and the countryside, and this restructuring can be traced to a specific historical moment.

That "moment" is the twelfth century (if the limits of that century may be stretched so as to incorporate a movement begun in the last decades of the eleventh century). The era was marked by political turmoil in the capital, and also by important social and economic developments in the provinces. Witness to the revival of imperial fortunes under the aegis of the retired emperors, palace coups in the 1150s, the rise of the Taira clan, and finally the wars that ushered in the Kamakura Bakufu, the age also saw the development of a self-conscious warrior class, important advances in agriculture, and a string of economic crises in the provinces. In the midst of this turbulent environment the number of estates grew at an extraordinary rate. Although precise figures for the country as a whole cannot be known, the evidence available for particular provinces reveals a rapid proliferation of estates. In Noto Province, over half of the land was converted to shōen between 1136 and 1150, and information from Wakasa Province reveals a similar trend: very little growth of estates before the twelfth century; rapid proliferation thereafter.[29] Likewise, the estate portfolios of elites swelled. The bulk of estates held by the Fujiwara Regents House, for instance, date from the second half of the eleventh century and later, and the imperial family alone may have established over one thousand shōen after about 1090.[30]

Of perhaps greater note than their sheer increase in numbers, shōen also secured the twin immunites during the twelfth century—unquestioned exemption from state levies and from entry by state officials—that would define the institution when it became the object of modern historiography. No longer incidental privileges accruing to estates as for earlier shōen, these immunities would henceforth be the mark that conclusively separated estates from the public realm (now defined, in opposition, as that which owed taxes and was administered by provincial officials) and that identified the estate form of landholding.

However, the significance of the twelfth-century "crisis" must be sought on grounds other than the perfection of the estate form. The enormous production of estates cannot be explained solely by developments peculiar to the estates. For the issue, of course, is not what incited the extraordinary growth in numbers (for which an explanation stressing the economic advantages that estate immunities afforded is sufficient), but what enabled, perhaps required, shōen to be the solution to the crisis. What reconception of landholding, and of the realm in general, suddenly (for it happened quite rapidly) mandated the estate form and reconfigured it as part of a new system of landholding? The advent of the estate system cannot be considered apart from a general re-formation of state and society: it must be linked to a process of differentiation which recast a previously unitary realm (at least in theory) into "private" and "public" domains, and to a concomitant disengagement from the stipulations of the imperial bureaucratic codes by which the state and society came to embrace private lands and private networks of administration. The explosion of estates in the twelfth century resulted not merely from the discovery of loopholes in the imperial law or a change in strategies among the elite. It did not come about because a generation of aristocrats decided (or were forced by circumstances) to become tax evaders. The explosion of estates testifies not to developments within an unchanged construction of realm, but to a fundamental reordering of space and society—to broad conceptual shifts that encouraged and underwrote the production of the estate form and legitimated its possibility.

It is this reconception of the realm that defines the rise of the estate system. Estates and their properties do not so much define the system as the other way around: a systemic shift—in fact, a double movement—rearticulated the deployment and use of estates. Demarcating the sphere of the (private) estates entailed a reciprocal recognition of a distinctive public domain (*kokugaryō*). And while the kokugaryō of the twelfth century and beyond bears certain formal affinities to the public domain of antiquity, it displays crucial differences that mark it, too, as a product of a general transformation. As many scholars have noted, the public domain itself became substantially "privatized"—the object of hereditary possession much like the shōen.[31] The medieval public domain, however, did not become merely a duplicate of the shōen. As recent studies have emphasized, the shōen-kokugaryō division also had functional dimensions. Concentrated around ports, rivers, transportation routes, and other nodal points in regional networks, the kokugaryō has, in fact, been likened to the "glue, running between shōen, that binds them together as a region."[32] This symbiotic development of shōen and kokugaryō provides further evidence of the redrawing of boundaries that occurred in Japan in the eleventh and twelfth centuries: the estate system did not arise because certain (now private) holdings were withdrawn from an unaltered public realm, but as the result of a general metamorphosis in the articulation of the land.

Go-Sanjō's Archive

Emperor Go-Sanjō's celebrated attempts at shōen regulation exemplify the dual lines along which this transformation proceeded. Acceding to the throne in 1068 as the first emperor in eight generations without a Fujiwara father-in-law, Go-Sanjō sought to exercise the freedom this accident of birth afforded to rein in the power of the aristocracy. Following the lead of emperors before him, Go-Sanjō, in 1069, issued an edict regulating the growth of estates. All estates founded after 1045 were declared void, while those established be-

fore that date might be confiscated if they were not properly documented (i.e., if the estate's charters contained irregularities, or if their
proprietors claimed privileges not authorized in the founding
grants).[33] A more significant move he made at nearly the same time
was to establish the *kiroku shōen kenkeisho*, or "office for the investigation of estate records" (*kirokujo*, or "records office," for short).
Charged with scrutinizing estate documents for irregularities, the records office seems to have returned a number of estates to the public
domain.[34] But the importance of Go-Sanjō's decree extends beyond
the confiscation of a few estates. By commanding proprietors to document the legality of their claims, the edict in effect legitimated those
estates whose charters were free of blemish and accredited the estate
form of landholding; investigated and certified by state officials, the
estate was substantiated in a trail of official writ.

Go-Sanjō's decree and the apparatus it established may stand
therefore as an emblem of the reordering of the realm that produced
the shōen system, offering a condensed narrative of the institutional
and conceptual refiguring from which the estate system resulted.
In this, Go-Sanjō's project seems kin to the archive as described by
Foucault:

> The archive is first the law of what can be said, the system that governs
> the appearance of statements as unique events. But the archive is also
> that which determines that all these things do not accumulate endlessly
> in an amorphous mass, nor are they inscribed in an unbroken linearity;
> . . . but they are grouped together in distinct figures, composed to-
> gether in accordance with multiple relations, maintained or blurred in
> accordance with specific regularities. . . . It is *the general system of the for-
> mation and transformation of statements.*[35]

The archive in Foucault's usage is thus a metaphor for the structures that underlie knowledge. Go-Sanjō matches this metaphor with
an actual archive, but the effect is the same: the archive's orders prescribe rules for the formation of valid statements; the boundaries it
draws, the regularities it enjoins, delimit what can (legitimately) be
said. And, implicated in the practices of power that sustain the archive itself, statements are given substance, established as things of
value, events of note. Inscribing the estate within an ordered system
of differences, Go-Sanjō's edict (as had, to a lesser extent, the shōen
regulations which preceded it) established a new discourse of landholding. Setting forth a range of possibility for valid statements/
claims about land, it prescribed a systematic structure in which the
estate was a necessary object.

In discussing Go-Sanjō's project, historians typically note its initial success (the confiscations it generated) and its ultimate failure (inability to halt the expansion of estates).[36] But to assess the project in terms of its success or failure at capping the spread of estates is, I believe, to misread it. Seen in another light, the records office achieved precisely its charge to regulate (systematize) the estates. Installed in the archive of official records, deployed within a domain differentiated into public lands and private estates, the shōen system was brought into being in the ordered system of statements inaugurated by Go-Sanjō's decree. Laid out in charters, maps, land surveys, and grants of immunities, the estate was constituted within an array of writ that, charged with the power of the imperium, established a new syntax of landholding. The edict and the work of the records office should not therefore be regarded simply as legitimizing the estates or as a shift in strategies for containing their propagation. Rather, they herald a transformation in the state's construction of its domain. In Go-Sanjō's archive we can perceive the first condition of possibility for the estate system as *system*: an ordering of the corpus of text that gave substance to the estate form.

We may register another aspect of the shift in the fate of the estates confiscated under this decree. Many were converted to "imperial edict fields" (*chokushiden*), lands indistinguishable from shōen except that their revenues flowed to the imperial family rather than into the coffers of the aristocracy. Go-Sanjō's edict therefore marks another important turn—away from a public realm administered by state officials and toward private holdings and privately constituted systems of administration and rent collection as the economic basis of society.

The terminology of land possession offers a telling index of this turn. As Kuroda Toshio has shown, the terms which throughout the middle ages would signify possession—*shoryō, ryōchi, ryōsho, ryōshō,* etc.—first appear in sources during the tenth century.[37] Marking a shift from the (theoretically) undifferentiated public land of antiquity to the parceled landscape of private holdings characteristic of the medieval era, this new language is emblematic of a more general shift in the land and tax strategies of the imperial state. As the economic apparatus of the centralized bureaucratic state unraveled, new methods were sought to shore up state revenues. In part this effort took shape as a drawing of boundaries, an attempt to differentiate lands free of some or all state levies from those fully subject to taxation. The shōen limitation ordinances pursue this strategy, and it is apparent as well, for example, in the court order to prepare standard reference-maps of the provinces. With tax-exempt fields clearly noted, these maps served to identify the status of a given holding and provided a baseline against which changes in that status could be measured. They acknowledge, in short, a realm differentiated into public and private spheres.

In part, then, this reformulation of the realm also involved embracing private holdings. In an attempt to expand the tax base, provincial authorities over the course of the tenth and eleventh centuries encouraged local notables to open up new lands. Offered, in return, clear title to these lands and effective carte blanche to administer them so long as the appropriate taxes were met, influential local families scrambled to assemble extensive private holdings.[38] Some of these local figures, like Fujiwara Sanetō, built up possessions that extended through entire provinces.[39] Notable for stimulating the development of local lordships, the policies that encouraged Sanetō and others to open new lands also underscore a fundamental transformation in the constitution and conception of the state; they place local administration on a new basis, anchored not in bureaucratic codes and public land, but in private holdings and proprietary lordship.

As recent studies have shown, however, this lordship remained vulnerable on many counts.[40] Sources from the eleventh and, especially, the twelfth centuries indicate a widespread crisis in local lordship. Pressed by provincial officials, caught up in wrangles over inheritance, embroiled in boundary disputes, or beset by economic reverses, many of the lordships established in the previous century failed. Thus Fujiwara Sanetō, in surrendering a portion of his holdings to a temple in Kyoto, lamented: "The residents of the district have all died or fled; for decades there has not been a single inhabitant. . . . It has become a garden for boar and deer."[41] Mounting debts, rising arrears in taxes, and a general "deterioration of the district" likewise compelled Fujiwara Naritaka, a prominent landholder in Aki province, to relinquish his lands to Nakahara Moronaga, a Kyoto noble.[42] The crisis in local lordship thus fueled a wave of commendations (kishin), as local holders ceded title to their lands to others more powerful and influential than they and accepted in return investiture, as often as not, as custodian of the newly formed estates. Holders like Sanetō and Naritaka supply the paradigm: seeking the assistance of elites, whose influence could secure a holding from interference—whether by provincial officials or by other local lords—they relinquished title to their holdings to aristocratic families or to the great temples and shrines. These groups, in return, exercised their influence to gain for the holding the privileges that would reconstitute it as an immune estate. It was this tide of commendations that prompted the extraordinary growth of shōen during this period.

Although it has become the textbook example, this sort of transaction between powerful local magnates and Kyoto elites was by no
means the only type of commendation. Similar acts can be found
at all levels of society. To the local notables, then, we must add at
least one group of peasants who jointly commended their holdings
to the abbot of Kanshin'in.[43] And the same Naritaka who commended his holdings to Moronaga acquired at least some of his lands by
transactions that, though lacking the name, seem suspiciously close
to commendations. In one bill of sale, for example, a certain Nagatomo, "harried on all sides" to repay outstanding loans, sold his
holdings to Naritaka, hoping to receive in return "just two or three
places in token of your benevolence."[44] Reaching down as far as
peasants and minor landholders, commendation must also be extended at the upper levels: frequently a minor noble who had been
commended some land might in turn commend the holding to someone of greater stature and influence, adding another layer to the
pyramid.[45]

Exactly how much authority the original holder surrendered in the
chain of commendations is a matter of much debate. Until recently,
historians maintained that the holder relinquished only nominal
rights—title to the land and some income—while retaining administrative control. Later studies, however, have contended that central
proprietors were able to exert considerable influence, and the histories of many shōen bear this out. Regardless of the balance struck in
individual cases, commendation marked a significant restructuring of
the relationship between the central elites and the provinces. In place
of a relationship mediated by a single state bureaucracy, commendation created multiple, parallel hierarchies of interest and patronage.
Rooted in immune estates, these hierarchies would demarcate the
landscape of medieval Japan, redefining networks of affiliation and
redrawing boundaries of competition.[46]

The estate system is part and parcel of this reformation. It may thus
be traced in part to a change in material conditions that induced local
holders to seek new alliances with the elites and prompted elites to
look beyond the state for revenues. But, equally importantly, the system was also built upon a conceptual refiguring that permitted such
alliances to form. The significance of commendation is by no means
exhausted when one has laid bare its economics. It must not be seen
as producing the capstone of a narrative of progress in the maturation
of the estate form, but as enacting a structural shift. In the alliances
that commendation forged, we can perceive a fundamental change in
the conditions of possibility for the estates. These alliances elaborated
a new field for the shōen; they deployed it within a newly articulated

domain, and that domain, consisting in a particular configuration of ideas that define society and space and give meaning to everyday practice, is what I regard as the system of the estates.

.   .   .   .   .

It will be the task of the chapters that follow to explore that domain. Taking as my guiding thread the understanding of social and cultural systems outlined above, this exploration will take a special form. To comprehend the estate system in its full complexity, one must look not merely to the system's empirical traces, but also to the seemingly empty region surrounding these actualities. The rent rolls, land registers, and deeds that document the estate as a tangible monument must be examined for what they say about the system, but also for what they leave unsaid. For the implicit, the unarticulated, the assumed—these also define the system, revealing by their absence from explicit discourse the system's limits and bounds. Giddens's observation that a social system constitutes a realm of shared signification is vital; by calling attention to the implicit operations of power that render certain actions (speech, thoughts) meaningful and others unthinkable, it reminds us that social systems exist as much in what is normally unseen as in what is visible.

Throughout this study I will be concerned with the topography revealed at the system's boundaries—conceived of not only as limits, defining the extent of the system, but also as points of conflict (between neighboring estates, between residents and nonresidents, between everyday practice and the system's structures). For it is at the boundaries, in the zones of fracture they describe, that the plays of power and resistance, the conflicts that shape the system, may be revealed. I am not, therefore, concerned primarily with the "typical" instance, with sifting through all known occurrences of a given formation or action in order to extract the statistical mean that designates the "normal" or "regular." Rather, and this provides the point of departure for the chapters that follow, I seek the atypical instant, the moment of crisis that imperils the normal and confuses boundaries—and in so doing discloses with some clarity the practices that produce both normal and abnormal.

Accordingly, the subsequent sections of this study each broach a fracture point, an instant of conflict that disconcerts, so as to lay out what I consider to be fundamental aspects of the system. In Chapter 2, an examination of the conflict between estate residents and outsiders sheds light on the practices that defined the social realm of the estates. Just as the system divided up space into estates, it recast the peasant as *hyakushō*, or resident of those estates. Producer and payer of rents, the hyakushō was the fundamental identity of the system and the primary subject upon which estate proprietors grounded their rule. But it is an identity possessed of a strange duality. Within official discourse, the hyakushō is a figure bound to the estate, defined foremost by possession of a residence and the obligation to meet certain rents. His antithesis is the wanderer, the person without a stable residence, who acknowledges no proprietor and whose realm is not bound by the estate. On the plane of daily practice, however, these antitheses collapse, the space between the poles eradicated by a seemingly endless traffic across estate and status boundaries. The tensions between everyday experience and the system's rhetoric suggest a much more complex subject than is normally assumed, and by investigating the elements that marked off hyakushō from other inhabitants of Japan's medieval world, I show how this subject was constituted and expose the orders of power involved in its constitution.

Chapter 3, charting the gap between daily economic activity and the system's orders of production, seeks to expose the ways in which the system (pro)claimed a space for its purposes. Land, then, is examined both in its economic aspect, as the basis of production, and as the space gathered within shōen boundaries. Out of the patchwork of smallholdings that comprised the medieval landscape, the system forged the shōen and turned them to productive purposes. Contained in maps, on land registers, within a system of taxation, space was refigured according to the categories of the system. Yet at the boundaries—on the borders where estates conflict, at the sites where the space of everyday life intersects with the places defined by the authority of the system—these categories are called into question. The welter of separate holdings contained within a single estate renders the notion of borders problematic; yet one of the most common crimes of the medieval era was the violation of an estate's boundaries. Set forth in maps and land registers, the estate was an orderly place, a static and uniform realm designed to produce rents; defined by everyday practice, however—by the social networks of estate residents or movement of people to markets, etc.—the estate loses its orderly bounds. In the tension between these sites, we can discern the power relations that outline the system's geography.

Chapter 4 focuses on the interaction between peasants and proprietors as revealed in the charged exchanges of rebellion. Where historians have traditionally viewed uprisings as straightforward contests between the ruled and authority, a form of nascent class struggle, I discern instead an elaborately scripted theater of protest. A reading of the rituals, oaths, and petitions that comprised this script, this chapter seeks to isolate the structures that inform the tropes of peasant rebellion and lend meaning to the gestures of protest. Rebellion here discloses a common, constituting discourse, an underlying dialogue between proprietors and peasants that casts each as the other's guarantor, naming peasants as the subjects (objects) of proprietary authority and proprietors as guarantors of peasant status. And it reveals as well that power functioned not merely in the overt mode of suppression, but was diffused throughout the system, operating silently, through structure, by inciting a dialogue couched in terms that reproduced its validity.

What follows, then, is not so much a history of the shōen system, as a set of focused interpretations of its conditions of existence. I am motivated in this approach both by my understanding of the nature of social systems (as outlined above) and by a broader, theoretical concern. In rejecting a narrative framework, I am of course rejecting the notion of a developmental or evolutionary history for the estate system. But I am signaling as well that I do not wish to "reconstruct" the shōen system in order to reduce its heterogeneity to variations on a theme. I am not offering an analysis that categorizes or taxonomizes the estates, but one that seeks rather to open out the enabling tensions that produced the orderings of society and space, the patterned interactions of ruler and ruled, that characterized the social and cultural system of the shōen. The readings offered here are intended, as H. D. Harootunian has put it, to "re-exoticize" some of the apparently most familiar and least problematic aspects of the system in order to point out the slips, gaps, and dislocations attending its functioning.[47] And I hope, above all, that through this my study will be seen to have something to say about social systems and the operation of power in general, not just in medieval Japan.

TWO

HYAKUSHŌ AND THE RHETORIC OF IDENTITY

WHEN THE PLAINTIFF in a mid-thirteenth-century lawsuit attempted to ridicule his opponents by labeling them "wanderers (*rōnin*) without a jot of land to their names," he was engaging in a rudimentary sort of social classification, drawing a line across his society that set the landed against the landless, the settled peasant against the rootless wanderer.[1] This same logic underlies an order from the great Nara temple of Tōdaiji which prohibited the entry of "outcasts from the various provinces" onto its estates.[2] And another man's pathetic oath, by which he consigned himself to "wander the roads without food or shelter, a beggar . . . bereft of human kindness," should he break his word, rehearses a similar act of ordering and exclusion.[3] In each of these instances we can catch the echo of a refrain found again and again in the rhetoric of the medieval estate system, a rhetoric that divided society as our plaintiff did, posing on the one side a shifting, aimless population of beggars and the like, and on the other side the stable, landed peasant or hyakushō.

In modern typologies of medieval social status, the hyakushō sits squarely at the center, falling in one representative scheme below aristocrats and warriors and ranking above bondsmen/servants and outcasts.[4] The term is usually rendered into English as "peasant" or "cultivator," but these translations, though broadly applicable, seem hardly adequate to describe the place of the hyakushō in the estate system. Nor, despite its prevalence in Japanese historiography, does a vocabulary based on the categories of European feudalism seem to fit the case. The hyakushō should not be confused with the serf. Although enmeshed, like the serf, within an estate-based agrarian regime that exacted land rents and labor services, hyakushō did not belong life and limb to the lord.[5] They were juridically free and could own and alienate land, and their right to leave an estate was established in law.[6] The legal authority of estate holders did not pursue runaway peasants beyond the estate, and no agreements existed between proprietors to force the return of fugitives.[7] But more than that, if the ties of serfdom were essentially "corporal," that is, to a man and not to a tenure, the distinguishing metaphor for the hyakushō (as I will attempt to show) lay elsewhere. Rent-payer and

producer, the hyakushō was the subject upon which estate proprietors founded their rule, the identity that defined the social limits of
the system. It is an identity which I intend to problematize. For
against the image of explicit social boundaries propounded in the
rhetoric of the system and implicit in the examples cited above, we
must set the considerable evidence of social flux, which obscured
distinctions between categories. And against the seemingly time-
less, indigenous quality of the peasant, we must weigh the historical
practices which constrained and constructed the hyakushō as subject. These tensions between a rhetoric of fixity and attachment and
a "reality" of movement force us to examine the determinants of the
status and to comprehend the structures of power that informed it.
We must ask not only "What was a hyakushō—what did the term
signify?" but also "How was the identity constructed?" and "What
were the consequences that proceeded from its specific manner of
constitution?"

Defining the Subject

In 1271, one Sainen appeared on Tara Estate after an absence of more
than forty years. Why he stayed away so long and what he did during
those years remain mysteries, but his return sparked a series of conflicts that lay bare the problematic nature of hyakushō status. At issue
was a holding, Kanshin *myō*, originally worked by Sainen's mother
but assumed by her brother, Kanshin, when she fled the estate sometime in the late 1220s or early 1230s. Yet if land was technically the
issue, the conflict revolved around status—who was eligible to attain
the position of hyakushō and how that was to be determined.
Sainen's quest for recognition reveals the complex of figures from
which the status was constructed, and his progress from Tara
hyakushō to exile and back again to hyakushō highlights as well the
background of physical and social mobility against which the
hyakushō identity was defined.

Sainen's aim in returning to the estate was to claim a holding abandoned by his mother four decades earlier. The exact cause of her
flight is unknown, although many years later it was charged that she
left the estate, taking her son with her, to escape punishment for her
husband's theft of some rice. What is certain, however, is that she
fled during a period of considerable turmoil on the estate. Confiscated from its aristocratic proprietor in the aftermath of the Jōkyū
War (1221), Tara was at the same time subjected to a new jitō, who
exercised a typically unbridled authority.[8] Accusations later leveled

against him and his deputy detail a pattern of arbitrary fines, excessive labor levies, and other offenses, and it seems likely that such threats loomed large in Sainen's mother's decision to abscond.[9] Whatever the cause of her flight, she entrusted the holding to her brother, Kanshin, who was, Sainen later maintained, to relinquish it when Sainen came of age.

Kanshin, however, did nothing of the sort, and that was the burden of Sainen's complaint. Contending that Kanshin had reneged on his vow to surrender the holding, Sainen petitioned the estate's custodian for recognition of his inheritance. His claim lay dormant until Kanshin died in 1273, whereupon the custodian awarded Sainen possession of half of his uncle's holdings; the other half he granted to Shigezane, Kanshin's longtime servant.[10] This decision, far from settling matters, only provoked a new round of discontent. Branding Sainen's appointment illicit, Shigezane and other hyakushō of the estate petitioned repeatedly to have it rescinded. With Sainen's death in 1278 (and with a new custodian) the suit finally met with success: reversing his predecessor's ruling, the current custodian awarded to Shigezane the entirety of Kanshin's holding.[11]

Again, matters did not stop there. Disgruntled with the decision, Sainen's heir, Muneuji, protested directly to Tōji, which, after hearing from both parties, judiciously reinstated the division of the holding that had been in effect since Kanshin's demise.[12] And this, we may judge from later documents which refer to both Muneuji and Shigezane as hyakushō of Tara, is where the matter finally came to rest.[13] But it is not the conclusion of the suit, revealing though it may be of Tōji's judicial temperament, that concerns us here. Rather, the appeals themselves merit closer examination, for in their reasoning we can discern several of the elements that identify the hyakushō.

First, and most generally, each side based its claim on hereditary right: Muneuji traced the rightful descent of the holding to himself from Sainen and Sainen's mother before him; Shigezane claimed it as heir to Kanshin. But lacking a bequest or other documentation that would definitively lend authority to his version, each marshaled in support other forms of "evidence." Muneuji produced both the document from the former custodian appointing Sainen to the myōshu post in 1273 as well as testimony taken from two estate elders (korō hyakushō), who indicated that Sainen's mother had performed the miscellaneous levies (kuji) due from the holding. Muneuji also charged that Shigezane and his confederates were mere "servants" and therefore ineligible to inherit. Shigezane, too, brandished an appointment from the custodian and the support of other residents of Tara, who cosigned his petitions. Muneuji's claim he dismissed as spurious: by fleeing, Sainen had surrendered his title to the holding; as successor to an absconding felon, Muneuji could have no legitimate claim to the land. Decades earlier, the myō, left "without a master," had been awarded to Kanshin, who, Shigezane emphasized, had performed the duties associated with it for "more than seventy years."

The status of hyakushō is thus outlined in Muneuji's petition, obliquely by allusion to its difference from other statuses (a hyakushō is not a servant or criminal) and far more immediately and directly by the execution of certain duties and the sanction of the proprietor. Shigezane constructs his hyakushō along similar lines. He cites Muneuji's tainted lineage, the authority of the estate's custodian and of fellow residents and Kanshin's fulfillment of kuji duties for the myō.

As sketched in this exchange, the hyakushō stands out as an intriguing hybrid. It is a position conceived within a definite hierarchy, and therefore marked in part by its difference from other statuses. Whether or not one accepts as true the allegations made by either party, they are clearly grounded in a common understanding of the hyakushō as a station to which servants and criminals were not to be admitted. The hyakushō is defined here as that which is *not* of servile rank or tainted by criminality. Set, like the wanderers cited at the outset of this chapter, beyond the pale, these others by their marginality circumscribe and establish the core identity. Their tenuous attachment to community and subordinate stature highlight the opposite qualities of the hyakushō and confirm the normative boundaries that mark them as the central subject of the estate. Yet it must be added that the status boundaries were not so rigidly established that Shigezane's assertions could simply be disregarded, nor that a claimant like Sainen, whose long absence and tainted past had estranged him from the resident group, could be dismissed out of hand.

Hyakushō status also seems to arise from the communal setting. The important part played by estate elders, and the solidarity shown by Shigezane and his supporters in the face of the challenges posed first by Sainen and then by Muneuji, seem to place the hyakushō firmly within the province of the local community. These factors serve to distance the hyakushō from any overt ideological or structural imperatives of the system, casting it instead as the product of social and economic forces independent of and anterior to the shōen system. On one level, then, the episode seems to invite a reading organized about the notion of community, a reading that emphasizes supposedly "natural" divisions of outsider and insider or that pits the community of residents against interlopers. This, for example, is the tenor of Amino Yoshihiko's interpretation of the episode.[14]

Amino plots the contest between Shigezane and Muneuji as a struggle between a self-contained and self-regulating peasant community and "outsiders." By casting the dispute in this guise, Amino affirms that this collectivity was foundational, the wellspring of identity: a hyakushō first and foremost was a member of a community, and that community was something distinct from and prior to the estate of which it formed the nucleus.[15] Sainen's threat (hence Muneuji's as well) is seen to lie in his otherness—he represents an alternative formulation of social identity, by ancestry and descent, that would deny the importance of the residence group. The episode thus unfolds as a conflict between contrasting constructions of self. It pits an older, "primitive" form, one based on blood ties and traceable to the first human communities, against another form rooted in common residence and the bonds of place that would find its apotheosis in the Tokugawa village. In either mode, identity emerges, unmediated by the structures of the system, from the seemingly natural ties of kinship or locale.

Proprietor and system are noticeably peripheral in this scheme. Amino's analysis sets the community of hyakushō apart from, locating it prior to and independent of, the estate system. The main competition is played out within the peasant community: Tōji arbitrates the dispute and enacts the compromise which brings it to a close, but the temple stands apart from the controversy, its authority ultimately dependent on its externality. According to Amino, Muneuji by appealing the case to Tōji transferred a decision customarily rendered locally by the custodian and estate residents to the orbit of the proprietor and established the temple as the ultimate arbiter of hyakushō status. A powerful, well-connected outsider, Tōji in effect extended the residents a service by judging and deciding their disputes; in return, the residents accepted Tōji's jurisdiction because it offered a means to still the conflict. The event thus reduces in Amino's scheme into a paradigm of how Tōji insinuated its (alien) mechanisms of control into a peasant community.

While Amino's treatment of the dispute offers a perceptive commentary on the operation of proprietary control, it falls short in its analysis of community and identity within the estates. Tōji's command of the estate sprang not merely from its position in society at large, but from a deeper substrate. Missing from Amino's account is an appreciation of the ways in which the system produced and shaped the hyakushō and the hyakushō community; the insider/outsider model posed in his analysis fails to apprehend how these are loaded terms—not merely natural divisions in society, but also ideological constructs. For the hyakushō that issues from this dispute rests also on foundations manifestly supplied by the system; in the language of the appeals, the hyakushō is betrayed as a construct shot through with the structures of the shōen system. The twin refrains, fundamental to the claims of both parties, of duties faithfully performed and the sanction of higher officials alert us to the constellation of effects out of which identity was constituted. Like Levi-Strauss's *bricoleurs*, the litigants fashioned their cases from a limited sphere of rhetorical possibility, and in the formulations they conceived we catch a glimpse of the broader structures that informed their world. The "community of hyakushō" emerges in this light not so much as a "natural" unit, eternally preexistent and ready to be enfolded within an estate, but as the estate system's central creation. The community simply cannot be separated from the institutional framework that defined its boundaries and produced the oppositions—insider and outsider, peasant and wanderer—that confirmed its solidarity. Regularly penetrated by "outsiders" like Sainen, and riddled with conflict, this community assumed solidity in the rhetoric of the system. And its constituent, the hyakushō, was likewise constituted within a web of rhetorical effects which fixed his place and identity.

The Lineaments of Identity

Prior to all other rhetorical effects of the system was an act of naming that fixed the subject within a particular estate community. Pronouncements from proprietors, invariably addressed to the "hyakushō" of such-and-such estate, propose a social identity that is inseparably linked with the spatial domain of the estate. Thus when Tōji warned the "hyakushō of Yano Estate" to be on guard against marauders, or Tōdaiji directed a claim for delinquent rents to the "hyakushō of Akanabe Estate," the terms by which these proprietors addressed their subjects served notice of the importance of this naming as a condition of communication.[16] Significantly, whether in the arguments and counterarguments of lawsuits or in the statements of grievance they directed so frequently to estate proprietors, peasants referred to themselves in precisely the same terms. It was as hyakushō, then, that Tara peasants pressed for rent relief in 1302 and 1305, or petitioned for the dismissal of rapacious overseers in 1334 and 1357; as hyakushō that residents of Hiranodono Estate protested the outrages committed by brigands from nearby Nara.[17] And in language that reproduces even more clearly the crucial congruities generated here between proprietor, subject, and estate, one resident of Ōyama Estate, in a complaint against the estate's overseer, declared himself to be "entirely a hyakushō of the proprietor" (*ryōke ichien no hyakushō*).[18] Similarly, on Tara Estate in 1363, "hyakushō belonging wholly to the temple" tendered a petition to Tōji in which they complained of hardships caused by provincial authorities.[19]

These commonplace, even banal, phrases are nonetheless noteworthy, for they bespeak an act of identification that was fundamental to the shōen system. In identifying themselves as hyakushō of a given estate, and in being so designated by authority, peasants aligned themselves with the social and spatial confines of the system; a process reminiscent of the "interpellation" designated by Althusser to be ideology's primary mode recruited the peasants and named them as subjects.[20] Hailed as hyakushō of a particular estate, peasants recognized themselves as subjects of the system. The realm of the hyakushō is thus presented as a world of community and of attachment that sharply differentiated it from, to paraphrase a contemporary source, the "unattached" world of "outcasts."[21]

The focal figure of the realm of the hyakushō was the idea that the estate, physically and socially, comprised a unified, delimited (and delimitable) whole. The records of the estate system speak endlessly of boundaries—both material and social. No crime, for example, was more egregious than the violation of an estate's borders, no punishment more severe than expulsion. In lawsuits, as we have seen, hyakushō contrasted themselves to wanderers and servants, stressing by this contrast their own stability, their roots in the estate community. To effect the illusion that the estates contained a system of self-evident physical and social demarcations, the language of the system returns repeatedly to a triple refrain of land, rents, and, especially, residence.

Significantly, these motifs permeate not only the language of authority, but also the language of hyakushō themselves. Even in rebellion, where we might expect to see the rhetoric of the system repudiated, peasants cast their demands—their calls for relief from onerous exactions, for lower rents, for the dismissal of dishonest overseers—in a language that relied on the very categories the system propounded. Thus all that peasant petitions demanded was that "the hyakushō be allowed to fulfill their rent-paying obligations."[22] To add teeth to their complaints, hyakushō threatened to abandon their dwellings until the proprietor responded to their distress. This threat, a conventional motif of peasant protest in the medieval era, is an interesting one, for it creates its effect by an inversion of the attachment to residence that was a cardinal attribute of the hyakushō. The threat to forsake residence stands on its head one of the principal qualities of the hyakushō status. Yet, even while it does this, the threat in no way challenges the centrality ascribed to residence; it inverts, but does not reject, the dominant metaphor. It remains, in sum, bound to the rhetorical frame of the estates.

These tropes of peasant protest find echoes in other areas of estate life. The system's notions of transgression, for instance, placed heavy emphasis on residence. The punishment most frequently meted out to murderers, thieves, and other miscreants was not incarceration or some other punishment enacted on the body, but expulsion from the estate (although, more frequently than not, malefactors seem to have fled before sentence could be served).[23] Thus, one proprietor, for example, held that "expulsion is the customary penalty for thieves and murderers; they should not be incarcerated."[24] And thirteen hyakushō and officials (shōkan) of Ushigahara Estate, who together attacked and murdered another resident and his family, either absconded or were punished with banishment.[25]

Just as critical, and symbolically perhaps more important, however, was the act that accompanied expulsion: burning the criminal's dwelling.[26] One Nara temple held that murderers and arsonists, among others, should be expelled, their assets confiscated, and their dwellings razed to the ground.[27] When hyakushō of Niimi Estate, for instance, set out to avenge the murder of the estate's overseer, their first action was to set fire to the murderer's dwelling; continuing on, they then proceeded to raze the official residence (mandokoro) of the jitō, with whom the offender was closely associated.[28] And in 1249, a resident of Kuroda Estate who was branded a "hated enemy of the Great Buddha" (the proprietor's patron deity) was expelled from the estate, his property and goods confiscated, and his residence burnt to the ground.[29] Sometimes this could have unforeseen consequences, as we learn in a fourteenth-century lament from a man whose residence burned to the ground when sparks from the razing of a neighboring dwelling (which belonged to an accused thief) set his roof on fire.

Tellingly, burning the residence was only the most spectacular of a number of actions centered on the dwelling. A step below burning was dismantling, in which the offender's residence would be ransacked of its belongings and then systematically torn down. Thus on Tara Estate, a woman accused of being a thief (falsely, she claimed) had her house plundered and destroyed.[30] And Gion Shrine periodically assembled groups of attendants to destroy the residences of offenders, such as a monk who had murdered a child, or a man who had failed to pay his rents and who, to compound the crime, had flagrantly disregarded the seals that the shrine had placed on his dwelling in order to sequester his belongings.[31] This last example introduces another variation on the theme, by which delinquent rent-payers might find their houses and fields roped off or staked out with consecrated branches or papers marking the site as taboo—a method not always successful: In one case, a tenant of Kuroda Estate, whose fields and residence were staked with such markers, nevertheless tore out the markers and "willfully harvested the crop." For this, all his possessions were confiscated.[32] In another instance, an exasperated official of Kurami Estate complained of outrages committed by agents attempting to collect an oil levy for Hitoyoshi Shrine. The agent's misdeeds included placing sacred slips of paper on the "houses of the people" (thereby preventing them from entering their dwellings); as a result, the official declared, the hyakushō had all fled and the estate had fallen to ruin.[33]

What is fascinating about these punishments is that the substitution of the dwelling for the body of the criminal establishes an equation between the two, in effect anthropomorphizing the residence and institutionalizing the body. Expelling a murderer from the estate, razing or dismantling a thief's dwelling, or sequestering the fields and house of a tardy rent payer all play upon this close association of the residence with the person: the denial of residence represents also the denial of identity and status, bringing with it the implicit suggestion that to be a hyakushō is to possess a residence and to live in an estate community.

Other facets of the system can be explored to flesh out this exegesis of the hyakushō's institutional profile. Land registers that carefully record a residence plot (yashiki), often equal in size, for each hyakushō provide further evidence of the conflation of residence and hyakushō identity that is apparent in the system's penal techniques.[34] Uprisings organized not to reduce rents but rather to replace lost documents verifying the hyakushō's possession of their dwellings and fields further demonstrate the vital importance of land and residence in forming the hyakushō status.[35] And in disputes where the payment of rents and performance of other duties proved the key to establishing rightful possession of this status, the linkage between rents and hyakushō identity stands out. All these aspects of the estates can be examined with a view to exposing the deep structures that underwrote the system's utterances. But rather than pursuing this course, I would like to consider briefly the following directive issued by Kamakura bakufu in 1259 during a famine,[36] a source that in its silences seems to comment most revealingly on the place and qualities ascribed to the hyakushō: "Because of the famine," the order states, "sufferers from near and far have been driven to the mountains, there to subsist on roots and grasses; or else they have ventured to the sea, in search of fish and seaweeds." The directive further enjoined

Kamakura's followers not to interfere with these foraging attempts, but to assist the displaced "wanderers."

Unstated in the order, but implicit in its phrasing, is the idea that it was somehow legitimate to restrict people's access to "mountain and sea"—which in the idiom of the time could stand for any noncultivated area. Also implied is the notion that it was certainly a transgression for peasants, at least in ordinary times, to seek sustenance in such places. Such a way of life, the directive seems to suggest, was appropriate only to wanderers, only to those who had been displaced from the agrarian communities that were the peasant's proper sphere. Mountains, in medieval lore, were wild, dark, untamed places, gateways to another world;[37] in the eyes of authority, they had the additional connotation of, to borrow a telling phrase from land registers, "masterless waste" (*mushu no kōya*). "Mountain and sea" thus emerge as sites that defy attempts at acculturation or institutionalization. Above all, they emerge as spaces antithetical to the mode of the hyakushō, who is by implication pigeonholed in a world where all land is cultivated (i.e., productive), where stable residence is the rule, and where attachment to some sort of "master" is obligatory.

The language of the system thus constituted the hyakushō within a discursive field, fixed and delimited the status, that is, in a system of rhetorical linkages that allowed certain possibilities but precluded others. Rent and residence, the dominant tropes of the system, are the conditions of the status, the figures that define the hyakushō.

A Wandering State

Any attempt to sketch the social sphere of the hyakushō must, however, also contend with the fluidity that marked—and to many historians is now regarded as the defining characteristic of—medieval Japanese society.[38] The boundaries of the estate community, in theory so impermeable, were in reality ceaselessly penetrated. Economic ties basic to the system (which, after all, relied upon communications and transportation links that united provincial estates with their centrally located proprietors) drew peasants into regional, even cross-regional, exchanges. The hyakushō of one island estate, for instance, rotated among themselves the duty of accompanying the annual rent shipment to Kyoto, and part of the cargo seems to have consisted of items the chosen hyakushō marketed for his own gain.[39] Nor was rent delivery the only form of interregional intercourse in which peasants participated. From a twelfth-century source, we learn that the residents of one estate "came forth in spring and summer to work the fields, but in fall and winter they journeyed to a neighboring province."[40] And hyakushō of Tara Estate are known to have been involved in a system of local and regional markets from at least the middle of the thirteenth century.[41] Such records of the system clearly attest to an endless traffic between center and periphery, and across estate and provincial boundaries—a traffic not restricted to the elite, but in which commoners also energetically participated.

The social networks of hyakushō, too, extended beyond individual estates. A study of marriage ties, for instance, reveals the networks' extent. In one singular case, a man absented himself from an estate for several years in order to travel, so he claimed, to a neighboring province in search of a bride. What is perhaps even more remarkable is that in a dispute occasioned by his prolonged exile his opponents accepted this explanation without demur.[42] This suggests that such journeys and extended absences, though perhaps unusual, were not at all beyond the realm of possibility. In the same vein are the "Martin Guerres" of medieval Japan—men like Sainen, who for one reason or another left an estate only to return, sometimes decades later, having in the meantime lived and worked as hyakushō of other estates. One intriguing case, for it comments on both social and economic boundaries, involved a man sold into servitude by his father to clear a debt. After serving for several years, he announced to his master that a debt moratorium (tokusei) had been proclaimed (the court and bakufu periodically promulgated such decrees) and abruptly wandered off— only to return many years later to lay claim to the goods and property left by his former master (now deceased).[43] Although the claim was ultimately denied, it carried enough force to occasion a long and involved lawsuit.

Significantly, as the last example suggests, the geographic fluidity of medieval Japan extended to the social realm as well. The stories of physical mobility I have just sketched were mirrored by a social mobility that challenged the status boundaries drawn by the estates. Not only did the fluidity of medieval society test the idea of the estate as a set of material boundaries, it also tested the immutable boundaries between categories that the language of the system stressed. The rhetorical dichotomy between the stable and the rootless notwithstanding, the region between these poles was incessantly in flux. Like the margins of medieval scroll paintings which are littered with beggars, gamblers, itinerant peddlers, entertainers, and other "masterless men" (to borrow Christopher Hill's phrase), the margins of the agrarian regime teemed with wanderers whose lives were not tied to the land, and periphery and center often overlapped. Landholding peasants might look askance at landless wanderers, but should the crops fail, they might easily (and often did) find themselves obliged to wander as well; and proprietors regularly turned to these landless individuals to take over abandoned peasant holdings. Unconsciously reproducing the solidity ascribed to community in the normative discourses of the shōen system, historical narrative frequently depicts the estate (i.e., hyakushō) community as given, as the fixed, immutable nucleus of peasant identity. Yet the dichotomies thus engendered—cast in terms of "outsiders" and "insiders" or "central" and "marginal"—describe not absolutes, but relationships. So, too, do the terms hyakushō and rōnin, peasant and wanderer; the demarcation of these categories testifies as much to the modes of interaction specified by the system as to any "natural" division of society.

Belying the rhetoric of exclusion, rōnin figured prominently in the life of the estates. On Hine Estate in 1234, as on Ushigahara Estate in 1132, rōnin comprised the labor force that developed and settled the estate.[44] Likewise, a directive to local officials in Nagato province endowing a prayer site (kitōsho) for the province's Sumiyoshi Shrine called for rōnin to develop the lands set aside for the shrine.[45] Rōnin also frequently supplied the labor to reclaim and settle lands that had fallen out of cultivation, as we see in an order directing rōnin to reclaim wastelands in Aki Province in 1179, or in the Kamakura Bakufu command that the jitō of Awa, Kazusa, and Shimōsa develop the waste fields of those provinces by settling them with rōnin.[46] Indeed, from the formative period of the estate system on, shōen officials, charged with developing the estate, turned regularly to rōnin to accomplish this task. Phrases like "invite and settle rōnin [on the estate]" begin to crop up in officials' reports from the middle of the eleventh century, and the process thereafter became standard procedure.[47] Adjudicating a mid-thirteenth-century dispute about the disposition of vacant holdings on Ishiguro Estate, therefore, the Kamakura Bakufu ordered the contending parties "together to invite and settle rōnin on waste and uncultivated fields vacated by absconding or deceased commoners (heimin)."[48] This, Kamakura asserted, was the customary practice (bōrei). Significantly, the bakufu also stipulated that the holdings should not be assigned to bondsmen (genin), for that would lead to the "neglect of public duties." In another ruling, this one concerning Kunitomi Estate in Wakasa, the bakufu ordered a jitō to stop confiscating the abandoned holdings of absconding hyakushō and, with the proprietor, to settle the properties with rōnin.[49] These judgments do not uphold the structure of barriers that informs the rhetoric of the system, but dictate instead a parity between the statuses of rōnin and hyakushō that reveals the boundaries of the estate to have been easily and regularly transgressed. Indeed, the evidence indicates that the system itself must be regarded as one of the main forces behind this transgression, for its procedures for agricultural development hinged on inviting rōnin to settle as hyakushō on the estates.[50]

The record attests equally to transitions in the opposite direction, from hyakushō to rōnin. As notations in land registers and rent receipts—curt phrases such as "holding abandoned" or "waste, cultivator fled"—from throughout the medieval era affirm, the vagaries of the medieval economy continually replenished the stock of uprooted peasants. Famine, war, and other factors could also swell the ranks of the displaced. The wars that ushered in the Kamakura Bakufu, we are told in *Azuma kagami*, "nearly emptied the northern and eastern provinces of people," and Yoritomo beseeched the court to succor these "wanderers."[51] A famine in the Jōei era (1232–1233) likewise urged Kamakura to the aid of dislocated hyakushō: in a policy that also conveys Kamakura's normative expectations about peasants and peasant life, the bakufu ordered that wanderers passing a post station in Mino Province be offered sufficient grain to enable them to return to "where they belonged"; those that would stay were to be settled with the hyakushō of nearby Ōgure Estate.[52]

Far from acknowledging any sharp distinction between peasant and wanderer, then, the record establishes a rough equivalence between the two. The notations on land registers indicate a continuous movement of hyakushō from their estate communities. And the references in other materials to the use of wanderers in reclamation projects or to their being settled on vacated hyakushō fields reveal an opposite movement of wanderers onto the estates. We can link peasant and wanderer together, therefore, in a cycle of reproduction by which hyakushō constantly replenished the ranks of the displaced, and wanderers slipped just as easily into the place of hyakushō. Ostensibly archetypes of difference, peasant and wanderer are revealed as points on the same continuum, part of a complexly interwoven movement that belies the rhetorical and ideological linkage of hyakushō with the stability of a bounded community.

It is not my aim, however, to acclaim this "reality" of social flux as somehow more objective or "truer" than the rhetorical and imagistic figures by which the system represented itself. The hyakushō community may often have possessed such permeable boundaries that we can question its solidity or the attachment attributed to its constituents, but we are drawn no nearer to comprehension if we discount the rhetoric of the system simply because it does not seem to jibe with "reality." The goal should not be to resolve the tensions between daily practice and the system's structures, to reveal the contradictions as only "apparent" and to reduce them to harmony on some other plane. The task, rather, is to comprehend a situation in which both these antithetical, contradictory planes of meaning could be true, to understand the effects that created a system which, despite what everyday practice implied to the contrary, represented itself as a concatenation of physical and social boundaries and that identified its subject in terms of that subject's difference from marginalized others.

By insisting that equal weight be accorded both to the system's rhetoric and to fact—to both medieval Japan's self-representations and its broader social and economic realities—I am, in effect, demanding that we investigate the institutional effects inherent in the system's makeup of its hyakushō/subject. To accomplish this task that subject must be given a history. It is to this that I would now like to turn.

Inventing the Hyakushō

In the 1170s, culminating a struggle with provincial authorities that had raged through much of the century, Tōdaiji undertook a major reorganization of Kuroda Estate. Gaining full immunity—from state and provincial taxes and from entry by provincial officials—for the estate in 1174, the temple moved rapidly thereafter to shore up its gains, and over the next few years the estate was surveyed, its lands were apportioned into new units, and a new system of taxes and rents was instituted.[53] By the end of this period of restructuring, the estate had assumed the shape it would retain for the ensuing century and more. Significantly, the earliest extant petition in which the residents of Kuroda refer to themselves as hyakushō comes not long thereafter.[54]

The changes taking place on Kuroda were by no means unique. They are part of a general movement sweeping Japan during the late-eleventh and twelfth centuries, a movement that transformed the land and tax base of the central elite and ushered in the forms that scholars now regard as characteristic of the estate system. Over the first half of the twelfth century, for example, Tōdaiji molded a group of longtime temple fields (jiden) and other lands into Kohigashi Estate, establishing exclusive jurisdiction over the holding and restructuring its fields into new rent-paying units.[55] And at the close of the century, Kōyasan would do the same to Ōta Estate. Between 1186, when the temple acquired the estate, and 1190, when Banna, the monk dispatched to reorganize the estate, issued a detailed report of his accomplishments, Ōta was made into what many regard as a paradigm of the shōen form.[56] This process meant establishing standard rates for rents and other dues, and, most notably, reclassifying the fields of the estate. Thus in his report Banna sorted the estate into fields which had to pay an annual land rent (*kanmostu den*), fields which owed both the land rent and an assortment of labor services (*kuji myōden*), and fields which were assessed no rents or dues at all (*joden*).

As the estate system came into being in the twelfth century it inaugurated a new rent structure, consisting on the one hand of an annual land tax known as *nengu* and on the other of a wide assortment of dues—often corvées or other labor services—known collectively as kuji, or, highlighting the levy's variety, as *zōyaku* (miscellaneous) *kuji*. The former tax was usually collected in rice (at a rate that amounted to about 30 to 50 percent of total yield), although an estate's nengu could also include a variety of other commodities and manufactured goods, including silk, iron, oil, lumber, and salt.[57] Kuji encompassed a staggering range of goods and services. On Ōta Estate these dues consisted largely of labor services, but could include, as on Ōyama Estate, chestnuts, oil, buckets, lacquerware, and a number of other items. A hint of the possible diversity can be gained from an account of the kuji due from Sukekuni myō of Tara Estate: comprising twenty-nine items in all, they included four different types of corvée, rice earmarked to provide food for visiting officials and at festivals, as well as a torch, a bucket, two straw mats, a fish, some salt, and some bean paste (miso).[58]

By most measures the annual land tax, which supplied the bulk of an estate holder's income, was the more important impost, while the kuji have been accorded a definitely secondary status. The great variety, the very miscellany of these "miscellaneous levies," has made them seem decidedly less substantial than their companion, which is glossed in rather more weighty terms as "the basic annual tax" or the "basic rice tax" and the like. But that is to read the importance of these levies on a purely economic register.[59] The "new regime" on Ōta Estate had social as well as economic significance: in Banna's reorganization of the estate's fields we can read signs of a social realignment as well. His classification of fields, in short, encapsulated a certain classification of persons. The distinction, for instance, between rent-bearing and exempt fields can be shown to effect a kind of social engineering. Fields subject to the annual rent comprised the bulk of the estate and consisted of ordinary peasant holdings (which were also subject to kuji), fields managed for the proprietor by estate officials, and a small number of fields administered directly by the proprietor and leased to cultivators on an annual basis. By contrast, lands exempted from taxation primarily included fields set aside for temples and shrines, stipendiary fields for shōen officials, and fields that because of flooding or for other reasons could not be cultivated; significantly lands provided for artisans also fell under this heading. It may be, as many commentators point out, that these exemptions were granted in return for the (tangible and intangible) services performed by temples, officials, and artisans, and that these services stood, in effect, in lieu of taxes; flooded fields, of course, could not really be expected to yield rents.

However, a functional, economic explanation can be pushed only so far; it is difficult, for example, to say why a peasant (such as the cultivator of Sukekuni myō) was required to supply a specified number of straw mats, while a mat maker was not. A more general explanation requires us to view the field classifications and the rent system underlying them in a different light. Encompassing areas allocated to the providers of nonagricultural goods and services, as well as sites not amenable to cultivation, exempt fields offer a sort of symbol of the nonagrarian. Field classifications stake out a space for the nonagrarian, and—by coding it "exempt"—emphasize its abnormality. Establishing, conversely, that the "normal" is agricultural and rent-paying, exempt fields outline another of the divides (like that between hyakushō and rōnin) by which the estate system marked off its social space.

Banna's reorganization of Ōta Estate, like the restructuring occurring on many estates over the same period, can therefore be seen as part of a general redrawing of social boundaries. Kuji played a special part in this process. Examined in association with the reformation of status in the eleventh and twelfth centuries, these seemingly incidental, miscellaneous levies assume added importance. A compound of characters meaning "public" and "thing," kuji referred originally to public observances at court—to the rites and rituals of the imperial state, which were the spectacle that gave the power structure a visible form and legitimated its authority.[60] Translated into the domain of peasant life as the new rent structure of the developing estate system was instituted, the levy retained its public air; as we have seen, common duties imposed under this levy included attendance upon visiting officials (feasting and entertaining them), the provision of oil or incense for religious rites, and labor on the lord's fields.[61] The tax retained, specifically, its close connection with the annual cycles of observances—the calendars of rites that for each temple and each noble house fixed the round of public life.[62] A late twelfth-century

register of the vast holdings of retired emperor Go-Shirakawa underscores this affiliation, revealing that kuji from various estates provided supplies for ceremonies throughout the year, including New
Year's observances and annual lectures on the Lotus Sutra.[63] Performance of kuji, in other words, brought with it participation in the
rites and observances that defined and displayed public affairs; at the
same time, it served as the certificate of eligibility for the "public"
stature that that participation implied. Thus in the cycle of court observances, courtiers both proclaimed and confirmed their place; in
the duties expected of warriors by the shogunate, warriors found
proof of their position.

The same state of affairs held true for hyakushō. For among commoners, kuji were imposed only upon hyakushō. In the scheme inaugurated by Banna on Ōta Estate, for example, only regular hyakushō
holdings were called upon to provide kuji. Whereas nengu fell generally on all the "agricultural" land of an estate, kuji fell uniquely on the
person of the hyakushō, and not on bondsmen, servants, or persons
of other statuses. Direct proof of this can be culled from rent rolls and
other documents, and we have interesting, if somewhat perverse,
confirmation in a late-fourteenth-century petition from a group of
peasants who styled themselves "subordinate cultivators" (gesaku no
hyakushō). Their petition protested the "unspeakable effrontery" of
exacting kuji from non-hyakushō.[64] The performance of the levies
confirmed and conferred status; it was the act that linked the
hyakushō to a wider realm of observances, and that, in return, guaranteed his "public" stature. Not without reason, then, did disputants
in contests over hyakushō preferments emphasize their performance
of these duties, for to claim the status was also to claim recognition as
a political/legal being within the system; it accorded the holder the
rights of a subject, which, in the case of the estate system, included
such privileges as access to the proprietor's courts, the right to demand aid and succor from the proprietor, and the prerogative of re-
monstrating against alleged abuses. By performing kuji the hyakushō
gained the public voice and public stature, without which he would
remain a mute cipher.

If, then, the most obvious changes were economic in nature—the
reorganization of production or the introduction of new taxes and
rents—their most profound effects, I contend, were social and ideological. The economic refashioning of the estate not only altered rent
books and land registers, but also redefined the relationship between
ruler and ruled and proclaimed a new ideology of identity. Perhaps
the key effect of these changes was to constitute the hyakushō group
as the central identity of the system by marking the hyakushō as the

standard subject of the shōen power structure and ensnaring that figure within a system of rights and duties designated by the estate context. In this light, we can see that nengu and kuji served crucially to code agriculture as the norm and to specify the hyakushō as the system's "publicly" authorized subject, even as it made that status dependent on the payment of rents and dues. And we can also recognize, as a broader telltale of this reconfiguring of identity, the system's restatement of the term hyakushō. In documents from the ninth, tenth, and into the eleventh centuries, hyakushō is used in the sense of commoner; for example, a directive from the Minbushō comments on a previous distribution of public lands to hyakushō, and a petition from the monks of Mandaraji refers to hyakushō as "kōmin" (literally, "public subjects").[65] But from the twelfth century, with the establishment of the shōen system, hyakushō comes more and more to be attached to the estate context. Thus, it was during this period that petitions from self-designated "hyakushō of such-and-such an estate" began to assail the temples and noble houses that made up the estate-holding elite. The fact that this development coincided with the economic restructuring mentioned above suggests that the advent of the estate system involved a fundamental reworking of the identity of the subject of its power structures; entrusted with the burden of reproducing the order of the system, peasants were transformed into hyakushō, the residents of estates.

This has led to some very important conclusions about the nature and development of hyakushō status. As it is most often, though not necessarily accurately, told, the history of the hyakushō is one of recruitment. Facing a general financial crisis in the eleventh and twelfth centuries, estate proprietors sought to buttress their rule by recruiting the elite of the peasant community to act as something like lower-echelon estate officials; peasants, for their part, acquiesced in this arrangement in order to maintain their position in the community.[66] Proprietor and peasant were drawn together by a convergence of interest, the former offering protection in return for stability, the latter demanding aid in return for compliance. The genesis of the status is located therefore in a compact between estate proprietors and the upper peasantry. In this conception, proprietor and peasant remain essentially independent entities (neither is changed by the interaction), and the peasant community, antedating the estate, emerges as the nucleus of hyakushō identity.

However, I have sought to offer a slightly different reading of the status and its genesis. Instead of a process of recruitment, I see a series of changes worked out on the level of identity. The system did not simply induct its central subject from a preexisting community. It simultaneously produced that subject and the estate community, establishing them within the system not by means of a compact, but by defining the figures and specifying the features that fixed identity. This, I believe, is the importance of the system of rents we have just considered and also of the rhetorical motifs introduced earlier. Against a social background of unsettling fluidity, the system sought to conjure up a subject constituted within a world of rents, residence, and boundaries—a subject, in other words, entirely of the system, one that could not exist outside it. With the hyakushō the system sought to achieve ideological closure by populating the estates with subjects who were fully determined by and fully compatible with the interests of the estate-holding elite.

And yet, such closure could never be attained. Seen from above, the hyakushō may have appeared as a source of rents, as a device that neatly circumscribed the social realm of the estate within its economic function. But the meanings of the term and the possibilities of the status could not be so easily restricted or controlled. It is notable, for instance, that the formation of the hyakushō/subject directly stimulated a seemingly unending flow of petitions, uprisings, etc., challenging proprietary authority (see Chapter 4). And these challenges were not based in rights conferred by ancient village custom (which is what one would expect if the hyakushō had been recruited unchanged out of the peasant community), but arose out of resources conferred by the system itself. As authorized subjects of the power structure, hyakushō enjoyed certain privileges (remonstrance among them) which could not be denied. For, if in one sense the term signified rents, in another it signified the body of the governed upon whom estate proprietors staked their own claims to "public" authority. One consequence of the breakdown of the imperial state in the tenth and eleventh centuries was the loss of the ideological infrastructure of elite power. The general, public stature that had been guaranteed elites by the imperium had to be secured in other ways. Constituting the hyakushō and figuring it, by means of kuji, according to the same device which confirmed (by displaying for all to see) the status of courtiers, warriors, and other classes, proprietors provided themselves with the audience they needed to proclaim their power. As a consequence, though, they added to the repertoire of meanings inherent in the hyakushō. Beyond this, the history of the term could not be erased: older meanings of hyakushō—"commoner," "public subject"—never quite died out. Not only did the court and the Kamakura and Muromachi bakufu continue to use the term in its older sense, but—given the importance of kuji ("public things") in constructing the hyakushō—the estate system itself served to perpetuate this broader meaning. Composed of materials which proffered multiple meanings, this artifact of the system could never be wholly subject to it. And in another context, these repressed meanings could provide the basis for a very different articulation of society—as in the fifteenth and sixteenth centuries, when peasants and the new warrior elite alike (re)turned to the language of hyakushō as public subject to elaborate a new discourse of authority and identity.

Split Subjects

The fifteenth-century picture book *Sanjūniban shokunin utaawase e* provides, among its illustrations of priests, coopers, carpenters, fortune tellers, gamblers, warriors, merchants, and courtesans, a sketch of a peasant.[67] Clad in a short, striped robe, arms and legs bare, and resting a large hoe against his right shoulder, the figure serves as an icon of the agriculturalist. The peasant shouldering a hoe or guiding a plow, in fact, is a recurrent image in the iconography of medieval Japan. From an eleventh-century collection of Buddhist folktales to thirteenth- and fourteenth-century picture scrolls, to the fifteenth-century picture book just mentioned, hoes, rakes, and plows unfailingly appear as the signs that proclaim the peasant.[68] Devoid of any marks of idiosyncrasy, these figures serve as the de-individuated emblems of a class, culturally inscribed stockpiles of signs that announce identity: the tools mark the man. In these representations, we encounter the reality that identity, at least to some degree, "lies in the eye of the observer," that it is shaped by social and cultural norms and constituted within larger systems of meaning supplied by a culture and its institutions.

The hyakushō I have attempted to sketch in this chapter seem similarly mediated. The figures which at once differentiated and circumscribed hyakushō identity suggest to me that the status must ultimately be comprehended as an artifact of the system, the keystone of the social architectonics of the shōen. The hyakushō was not naturally, transparently, the peasant-cultivator, but a complexly constructed subject (in the dual sense of ego and object, self and subject, of a system of authority). In the lineaments of hyakushō identity, one can discern the lineaments of a discursive realm, a domain within which power operated not solely in the mode of repression, but also by structuring action and identity according to models figured by a restricted set of rhetorical devices. Rent and residence, then, are not simply the appurtenances of an identity established on other ground, or adjuncts of a subjectivity located at a transcendent position outside the shōen: they are the central figures of the language of identity. To suggest that this identity was generated by the discourses of the estate system by no means implies that it was the wholly determined product of a fully constituted totality. If anything, analysis of the hyakushō leads to the opposite conclusion: not only, as we have seen, did the circulation in status between rōnin and hyakushō confound the boundaries established by authority, but the materials out of which the status was fashioned also gave the hyakushō a split personality, linking it both to the estate and to a broader discourse of the public. We must acknowledge, moreover, that this ambivalence can be traced to the system itself. The antithetical impulses discernable in the hyakushō do not record a split between peasant life and discursive constructs (between material existence and ideology), but register the antithetical impulses of a discursive formation. The system stimulated contradictory possibilities. Try as they might to define hyakushō in terms of rents and residence, proprietors necessarily supplied that subject with other, unintended resources. And hyakushō, though they participated in social and economic networks exterior to the estate, could only address proprietors in the name conferred upon them by the shōen power structure. The term hyakushō and the identity it names, therefore, define not a stable, closed structure, but the very complex interplay of possibilities and determinations. And this suggests that we view the estate system not as a secure ordering of meanings, but as an unstable and ongoing process involving the proliferation and policing of significations.

THREE

OFFICIAL TRANSCRIPTS

MYŌ, MAPS, SURVEYS, AND

THE ENTITLEMENT OF THE ESTATE

IN THE ELEVENTH month of 1298, surveyors began the laborious process of registering the fields of Yano Estate; one year later, their task was complete: 1,650 plots of land totaling perhaps 200 hectares had been converted into a scroll 26 meters long.[1] Further transformations were required, though, before these fields could be rendered productive—that is, rent-producing. Individual plots, recorded in an order dictated by the vagaries of geography and the path of the survey, had to be grouped by the cultivator or other person responsible for paying rents; allotments for temples, shrines, and other groups had to be determined; and rates had to be fixed.[2] Captured in marks on a field register, then organized into units for taxation, and translated ultimately onto a rent roll, the fields of the estate had to be reclaimed from the disorder of the natural landscape and mapped onto a new, characteristically ordered, space. The surveyors, scribes, and others who created these registers and rolls produced, in effect, a fiction; they did not record the land, pure and simple, but a version of the land. The neutrality typically ascribed to the survey which aspires to transcribe reality without altering it, to realize a one-to-one correspondence between the object and its transcription, does not hold. Not merely reproductions of reality, the registers also preserve the traces of a process of invention by which fields were fitted to a grid imposed upon them by the shōen apparatus.

Anchoring this grid was an institution known as the myō. Although parcels of land known as *myōden* (meaning, literally, "name fields") appear in the record as early as the ninth and tenth centuries, the reorganization of the estates in the eleventh and twelfth centuries invested the term, which formerly signified reclaimed land to which private title had been granted, with a new meaning.[3] Linked to the hyakushō, the new subject of the emergent system, myō came to denote hyakushō myō, the basis of the extractive machinery of the estates, the unit by which rents were assessed and exacted. Myō, in other words, came to mediate the interaction of proprietors and the estates from which they drew their wealth, to negotiate between the system and its fields.

Myō: Points of Contention

The precise nature of the myō has been the object of intense historiographical dispute. The debate has focused on two issues in particular: whether myō were "artificial" administrative units, fabricated to facilitate the collection of taxes and other levies, or whether they also had a separate existence as "natural" units of possession and cultivation, as parcels of land that were farmed and privately possessed. Closely related is the issue of what authority the possessors of myō (myōshu) exercised over them. Was theirs merely a usufructuary right, held at the sufferance of the proprietor, or were myōshu free to buy and sell or otherwise dispose of myō at will? Were they, in short, first and foremost holders of appointed positions, minor estate officers, or did they enjoy some sort of private authority over the myō?

At odds in these disputes are contrasting conceptions of Japan's medieval era and of the estate system's place within it. Scholars who discern in myō the shape of actual landholdings have been keen to read field registers as revealing of land possession patterns and other economic relationships. These scholars herald, in particular, evidence from some mid-thirteenth-century and later registers of smaller and more numerous myō as signs of a change in the economic base upon which the shōen apparatus rested. The breakup of the myō grid signals that the superstructure imposed by the system was losing its hold. Perceiving in this apparent fragmentation of the myō the development of smaller, more secure tenures, these scholars see it as nothing less than a social revolution, the rise of an independent small-peasant class and the decline of the old estate-based order as a result of the feudalistic economic and social patterns of the medieval era. Thus described, the breakup of the myō marks the farming classes' rise from landless cultivators to independent peasants, and it signifies both the birth of new property rights and of a new stratum of smallholders within the peasantry. The distinctive trait of this line of reasoning, then, is that it locates the defining features of the medieval era not in the structuring principles provided by the estate system, but in (what it regards as more fundamental) developments in landholding, structures considered to have existed prior to those of the shōen.

Scholars who understand myō to be an institutional convention accord much more weight to the framework supplied by the shōen

system. They regard the conclusions drawn from the tale of fragmentation as overstated, the outcome of a failure to appreciate the
constructedness of myō. Myō in this view reveal how proprietors organized their estates for production, but offer few clues to the actual
disposition of landholdings. A fundamental discontinuity separates
the myō, the system's apparatus for ordering production, from the
fields they encompassed. Constructed as a means of facilitating rent
collection, myō cannot be given the same dimension as landownership. Failure to recognize this fact, these scholars argue, falsely
attributes the qualities of the institution to real landholding patterns, concocting seemingly unitary holdings out of what were in fact
"artificial" aggregates of many small, private plots. Conversely, this
failure exaggerates the vulnerability of smaller tenures: the small-
peasant class said to arise out of the breakup of the myō is seen as
a feature of the system from its outset.[4] The estate system is held
in this view to have rested from the start upon a base of independent
smallholdings similar to that proclaimed as a symptom of the system's decline.

At one pole, then, are scholars, typified by Nagahara Keiji and Watanabe Sumio, who maintain that the myō appearing on land registers reflect the extent of peasant cultivation and landownership
(albeit imprecisely, given the capabilities of medieval technology).
In his massive study of estates in the region of the capital, Watanabe portrays myō as the product of a "bargain" struck between
upper peasants and the proprietor.[5] The relative strength of the parties involved determined the form that the bargain (i.e., the myō
structure) would take. Near the capital, where proprietors' power
was greatest, myō appeared in their most "crafted" guise, with many
estates organized into equal- or nearly equal-sized myō (kintōmyō);
proximity enhanced proprietors' power, enabling them to dictate
the size and shape of peasant holdings. In outlying areas, though, the
size and shape of myō more directly reflected local hierarchies of
power and wealth; where the estate holder's grasp was looser, myō
might vary considerably in size, reflecting differences in peasant
holdings. In Watanabe's analysis myō possessed two facets: They
represented, on the one hand, an institution framing the extraction of
rents and kuji; this lent them an undeniably official, even artificial,
air. At core, however, they remained a unit of peasant production
and ownership, a unit cultivated by a single myōshu, his family, and
unfree and semifree laborers under his patriarchal authority. On estates near Kyoto or far removed, the myō structure reveals not just an
official fiction, but a pattern of cultivation; it registers, in a largely
unmediated form, peasant land possession.

Nagahara likewise ascribes a dual character to myō.[6] As an institution they were, strictly speaking, official inventions, units of taxation that had nothing to do with peasant landownership or cultivation. This, he asserts, is why records of land sales do not provide a single instance of the sale of myōden (land being sold was invariably termed *shiryō*, or "private holding") until late in the Kamakura period. Yet, despite their legal classification, Nagahara contends that myō were more than just units of taxation. The size of equal myō in the Kinai, he notes, was perfectly suited to cultivation by a single family, and he points to a parallel between the size and shape of the holder's residence compound (yashiki) and the size and shape of the myō. Thus, although myō served as the basis of the tax apparatus of the estates, they were not merely administrative fictions, but were also plots of land that their holders cultivated and over which they exercised some right of possession. According to Nagahara the formation of myō involved a trade-off: partial recognition of the myōshu's private authority over a parcel of land in return for a more streamlined system for the collection of rents.[7] In any case, as Watanabe also maintains, to read a register of myō is to read something akin to a chart of peasant holdings.

Arguing against this profile of the institution, a growing number of scholars have come in recent years to view the myō solely as an instrument for tax collection. Denying any congruence between the myō and the landholdings, they characterize the institution as an artifice, a created mechanism designed to organize the productive capacity of the estate. Among the foremost proponents of this view, and one of the first to take issue with the Nagahara paradigm, was Kuroda Toshio.[8] Working with mid-thirteenth-century land registers from Tara Estate, he demonstrates how the welter of fields recorded in the earlier survey was reduced to the order of perfectly equal myō in the later register. This change between the field survey of 1254 and the register of 1256, he contends, was not a chance outcome.[9] Tara's equal myō did not arise simply from regrouping actual landholdings under the name of their cultivator, but from a deliberate act of fabrication. They were constructed, with little regard for patterns of ownership or cultivation, in order to create identical units, each with precisely the same mixture of types of fields, and evenly divided rent and labor obligations. The grid that emerged bore scant resemblance to the actual disposition of the estate's lands: individual myō were composites of many private holdings, while individual myōshu possessed fields that were contained in other myō and likewise presided over lands that were the holdings of other myōshu. Kuroda concludes from this that myō were "artificial" units of taxation; myōshu, he asserts, were not simply peasant landowners/cultivators but low-level estate officials.

The work of Inagaki Yasuhiko reinforces this line of reasoning. His studies of estates in Yamato Province, for example, point to the suspiciously even distribution of different types of fields among the myō of an estate as an indication of the "artificial" nature of myō.[10] But in his investigations of land possession, he outlines a more advanced position that carries Kuroda's analysis one step further to radically distinguish the issue of myō from questions of landholding and cultivation. Contesting Nagahara's thesis, Inagaki argues that myō were nothing more than units of taxation, that they expressed a prerogative completely distinct from rights of possession or of ownership, rights which, he contends, were expressed in another form and had long been held by cultivators.[11] A myō thus emerges in Inagaki's inquiries not as a mirror of cultivation, but rather as an impediment blocking the historian's view of social and economic realities, as, in Inagaki's phrase, an "outer covering" that must be peeled away to reveal the (actual) pattern of cultivation and ownership beneath.[12]

Enormously influential, this thesis underwrites most current opinion on the nature of myō or of peasant landholding. If scholars since have sought to expand and refine elements of Inagaki's or Kuroda's argument, few now would contest the basic characterization they proposed.[13] In contrast to the consolidated units under a single holder's patriarchal authority described by Nagahara, myō now appear as composite units, compounds of multiple private holdings, grouped together to facilitate the collection of rents and other levies.

Yet, if it is now generally accepted that myō were constructed things, how they were constructed—what assumptions and negotiations ordered their fabrication—has yet to be adequately addressed. If Kuroda, Inagaki, and others have convincingly demonstrated the incongruities between myō and cultivation or between myō and peasant landholdings, they have not taken the argument beyond the sorts of questions (i.e., those posed at the beginning of this section) which have dogged scholarship on this issue for decades. Yet the issue, surely, is not whether myō were "artificial" or "natural" (or whether myōshu owned private rights in the fields of their myō), but why the institution took the shape it did and what this reveals about the system which formed it. The argument needs to be refocused; instead of attempting to look through the myō to catch sight of the supposedly more "real" patterns of cultivation and land possession, the institution itself, the notions of space which it presumed, and the processes which shaped it must be situated at the center of our gaze. Surveying—translating an estate's paddy, dry fields, forests, and other areas into notations on a scroll—then marshalling these notations into rent-producing units was an act of power, a proclamation of authority over the estate and its production. In what was registered and what was not, in the adjustments wrought as fields were fashioned into myō, and in the broader social claims that these registers served to uphold, we can trace the nature of the intervention that substituted for the variety, confusion, and particularity of individual plots an invented landscape of homologous rent-producing units.

Borders

To comprehend this intervention, however, we must begin where it began: at the borders, with the acts that first partitioned space into estates. For creating an estate meant demarcating a realm, stating its boundaries and driving the four posts that marked its extent.[14] The edict establishing Ota Estate in Echizen, for example, ordered agents to stake out the estate's four borders, while a similar directive for Hine Estate instructed provincial officials to drive boundary stakes and to settle the estate with rōnin.[15] Such edicts, of course, do more than physically demarcate the site of an estate. They also convey a particular conception of what an estate is (or ought to be), and therefore offer insights into the system's engagement with the land it sought to control. As depicted in title deeds, commendation documents, or grants of immunity, the shōen is coterminous with the rectangle established by its four boundary points; it is a single unit, a contained and containable territory:

Communiqué of the Retired Emperor's chancery: To the provincial office of Kii.

That, forthwith, Yamazaki Estate be established as a holding of Daidenpōin of Mt. Kōya . . .

Bounded: On the east, by Ishide Estate
On the west, by paddy
On the south, by the Kii River
On the north, by the south border of Inatei

The aforementioned estate is a possession [shoryō] of the monk Kakua. He has commended it to Daidenpōin. The paddy, dry field, waste, mountain, and other areas within its four boundaries are all to be the possession of the temple; public taxes and provincial levies are hereby rescinded. . . .

Chōshō 1 (1132).12 Ōe *ason*[16]

The impression that such documents give is of unity; they describe an integral territory, a closed and self-evident domain that could easily and naturally be contained within borders—or pictured on a map. A twelfth-century "picture-map" (*ezu*) of Kaseda Estate, therefore, rings its subject with a band of river and road and centers it between mountain ranges; the boundary markers are clearly indicated as prominent black dots.[17] Decorated with crosshatches (tokens of rice paddy) and rough sketches of houses and shrines (tokens of human settlement) the estate is seen in this iconic portrait to be a complete, self-contained property. The ezu, in short, pictures the estate as an all-encompassing domain; everything within its borders—the mountains, fields, dwellings, shrines, even the river—falls equally within the estate. At question here is not how well the features shown on the map correspond to the geography of the estate, or whether Kaseda really looked like its picture. Of importance, rather, is the sort of knowledge about the shōen such maps reproduce. Ezu served not just as images of the land, but as means of constructing a space for authority. Ringed with boundaries that mark the limits of the inclusive realm of the estate, and not the dividing lines of different domains, Kaseda Estate becomes in this map a single, coherent unit.[18]

Heightening the isolated integrity of the property and reinforcing the sense of closure, the Kaseda ezu is notably vague about what lies beyond the estate's borders. Apart from the encompassing mountains and a note in the left-hand margin which records the names of two neighboring estates, nothing outside of the estate is depicted—this despite the "extra," fifth, boundary marker erected on the estate's southern limit to clarify a problematic boundary with Shibuta Estate (which is, however, not mentioned on the map).[19] A picture-map of Tōgō Estate even more strikingly illustrates this isolationist imperative.[20] Beyond the domain of the estate—inscribed with the same stylized representations of fields, dwellings, and mountains that mark Kaseda Estate—there is emptiness. There is, literally, nothing outside of the estate. It stands alone, a self-contained, self-sufficient territory that can be conceived of in isolation. And by decorating this portrait of the estate with a line of ships just offshore, or with a boat of fishermen on the bay at the center of the estate, Tōgō becomes even more: the shōen is seen as a microcosm, a unit encompassing all.

Ezu, in other words, record a particular way of seeing (and hence of conceiving) the estate, and in this they reveal an ideological charge. Depicted as a territory and population that can be withdrawn from its surroundings without losing anything (because it is complete in itself), the estate becomes the indissoluble atom of substance; it is a package, neatly bound up, and therefore possessable.[21] Shōen ezu are portraits of a property, records that along with title deeds, survey registers, and imperial grants of immunity substantiated a proprietor's claim to and possession of the land. Like all maps, ezu exist fundamentally as "texts of possession," as images which mirror the ways a culture appropriates the land.[22] And if ezu seem more in the nature of landscape paintings than of maps intended to situate an estate with respect to other holdings, or (as modern maps do) to place a property within a system of towns, provinces, or nations, ezu share with these other representations a basic cultural function. They fix space, arranging its diversity within an order of representation that opens it up to our inquiries and our knowledge but simultaneously closes it within conventions that order how the land must look.[23] In an ezu, a proprietor could "see" an estate and know it to be his property; he could identify its special features and limits and know it to be different and distinguishable from others of its ilk, yet still recognize it as belonging to that order, still discern in it the traits that identified it generally as an "ownable" property. It will not do, however, to stop now; any mapping will allow this. The specific sort of conversion of space into property occuring here must also be looked upon as a historical product, as testimony to the notions of space ordered by the shōen system.

The advent of ezu, the earliest extant examples of which date from the mid-twelfth century, points to an important shift in how estates were constituted.[24] These picture-maps stand, therefore, as another symbol of the reordering that underwrote and produced the shōen system. Earlier shōen, hodgepodges of fields or sometimes just the income from a specified area of otherwise unspecified fields, often could *not* be mapped in this way—represented, that is, as single, confined properties. Such holdings required a very different sort of mapping, and, consequently, their maps reveal a very different sense of the construction of a holding. Conceived within a land system that had ruled the land's surface into a vast orthogonal grid, estates and other holdings of the eighth, ninth, and tenth centuries appear as aggregates of individual fields set within the rectangles formed by this grid. Tōdaiji's holdings in Kuso-oki mura in Echizen, for example, are built up field by field, by notations within each rectangle that detail the extent of paddy, waste, and other types of field.[25] The shape and extent of the holding are suggested, in short, not by mountains, roads, boundary markers, or other enclosing devices, but by the black ink of the notations that count its fields. And closer inspection can

explode the seeming coherence at any point: in few sections does
Tōdaiji's claim comprise all or even the bulk of the land. The territorial integrity achieved in later representations is here atomized.
Tōdaiji's claim is to certain fields, not to an entire area; the holding is
fragmentary, interspersed with private holders' lands and public
fields; its unity is supplied by the grid within which it is constituted.
Compounded of discrete fields linked together by their placement
within an abstract grid, the holding becomes something quite distinct
from the self-contained property proclaimed in twelfth-century ezu.

The shift outlined here in maps can also be traced in other documentary forms. In the deed, for example, which first (in 845) incorporated Ōyama Estate as a tax-immune holding, the property is outfit-
ted both with boundaries (to the east, west, south, and north) and,
importantly, with a lengthy roster of the fields belonging to the estate.[26] As the subsequent history of the estate makes clear, it was this
roster, not the more general boundaries, that defined the extent of
the estate for the next two centuries and more. For much of the ninth,
tenth, and eleventh centuries, Tōji and provincial officials battled
over which fields were to be considered part of the public domain and
which part of the estate, with the estate for the most part the loser.[27]
Near the close of the eleventh century, however, Ōyama's immunities began to be reaffirmed. And this time, the estate was no longer
specified as consisting of certain fields, but was defined as the entire
area within its four boundaries:

Governor's edict: to the absentee governor's office.

That the four boundaries of Ōyama Estate be established as indicated by
decree of the Council of State [kan senji].

Bounded: On the east by public lands (kōden)
           On the west by Mt. Sayama
           On the south by a river
           On the north by Mt. Ōyama.[28]

Fujiwara Sanetō, the provincial magnate whose holdings provided
part of the region later incorporated as Kuroda Estate, offers another
excellent example of the shift. As Ishimoda Shō noted long ago,
Sanetō's bequest to his son, Nobuyoshi, contains two distinct types
of property.[29] Of the twenty-eight holdings named, some three-fifths
are identified by reference to the province's jōri grid. With area and
location meticulously noted (or provided by reference to standard jōri
maps), these plots belong to a system of landholding that commanded specificity and that could do so because it supplied a context
within which to place individual plots. The remaining eleven of the

twenty-eight parcels, however, are identified only by their four borders. They stake out the sort of claim pictured in the maps of Kaseda or Tōgō estates, a claim to a broad area defined not by reference to an exterior grid, but (seemingly) wholly internally by a description of the property as a naturally unified domain. Dated 1056, a therefore pivotal era in the advent of the estate system, Sanetō's bequest documents the beginnings of the shift from a field-by-field to a territorial understanding of property.

A similar movement can be traced on several estates belonging to Mt. Kōya. In 1049, the temple exchanged a number of fields scattered through four districts for a smaller but contiguous bloc of fields located nearer the temple. It was a move toward territorial integrity, but as on Ōyama the deed specified which fields were to comprise the holding.[30] A series of edicts from the next century establishing several temple properties as shōen, however, are not constrained by such specificity. In each case, the holding is delimited only by the four boundary posts driven to mark its extent.[31]

Yet the estate, which could be staked out and described thus as an integral realm or imaged in ezu as a compact whole, existed in tension with another construction of the domain. Seen from the ground, from, as it were, the other side of the map, an estate could easily lose its coherence. As one complainant on Tara Estate declared (in response to a charge that he had usurped some lands belonging to the estate): "It is normal for a shōen's fields to be mixed in with others' holdings. Such instances are extremely common."[32] Asserting further that "there is no need to look elsewhere for examples," he proceeded to list the several other properties in which fields belonging to Tara Estate were to be found: Imatomi myō (property of the shugo), Koremitsu myō (belonging to the provincial office), Kokubunji (site of the provincial temple), and so on through ten separate holdings. By asserting that Tara was so interpenetrated with and within other holdings that it was impossible to determine precisely where the estate began and other holdings ended, the claimant intended to deflect the charge of having violated Tara's boundaries. His is a self-interested argument, to be sure, but nonetheless it merits closer attention.

In the eyes of this complainant, estates commonly appear as fragmented entities, dispersed among numerous holdings; the ostensibly unitary realm of the estate is presented here not as a single self-evident domain, but as a site of multiple lordships and a conglomerate of private holdings that defies easy description. This complainant's description of the estate meshes surprisingly well with one provided by a modern historian: considering the many and varied interactions of estate residents with other networks of social and economic authority, Irumada Nobuo has concluded that the sort of exclusive, regionwide authority claimed in ezu or set forth in title deeds and other documents was essentially impossible.[33] Estates, in short, existed at the intersection of multiple realms of control. They served not merely as the base for a hierarchy of holders of the sort heralded in Marc Bloch's oft repeated phrase,[34] but, more basically, they described a fragmented realm in which neighboring plots of land might well fall under the jurisdiction of different lords. A look at almost any land register affirms the validity of this assertion: a good portion of any estate was given over to other holders, including temples and shrines, local lords, craftsmen, and the like. Similarly, despite the clearcut boundaries framing the shōen depicted in ezu, large portions of many estates were shared: residents of Namazue Estate in Ōmi, for example, took wood and grass from the mountain areas of four nearby estates, and we may suppose that the same held for the residents of the other shōen.[35] Likewise, part of Ōyama Estate depended on its neighbor, Miyata Estate, for water; Miyata residents, for their part, used the mountains of Ōyama for timber and fertilizer.[36] In each of these instances, the boundaries of estates, in theory clear, fixed, and impermeable, are shown to be fluid, elusive, and complex. And estates themselves are shown to be sites of relations that cannot readily be contained within the system's normative bounds.

Yet (again) these boundaries, elusive though they may seem, figured importantly in the daily lives of estate residents. Visiting officials, for example, often had to be met at the borders of the estate and feasted there in a ceremony of greeting. Criminals, as we have seen, were typically driven from the estate, and a hyakushō who led agents of the shugo onto Tara Estate could have his holdings confiscated.[37] More generally, estate boundaries again and again in the records of medieval Japan prove to be sources of serious conflict. In the thirteenth and fourteenth centuries, residents of Ikadachi and Katsuragawa estates in Ōmi, for instance, were embroiled for decades in a dispute over which estate could claim the mountain area that provided both with wood to make charcoal and boats. From at least the mid-thirteenth century, residents of both estates were accusing their counterparts of illicitly felling trees, opening up fields, erecting charcoal kilns, and otherwise trespassing on the other estate's domain. Similarly, at the close of the twelfth century, residents of Kuroda and Nagase estates clashed over claims to mountain areas.[38] Here, in contrast to the sense of boundaries adduced in the previous paragraphs, estate borders seem to have meaning: they are objects of real significance, worthy, as in the settlement of a boundary dispute between

Ryūmon and Ōishi estates in Ōmi Province, of being established with solemn oaths.[39]

What then are we to make of these boundaries, elusive yet fixed, scrupulously staked out and regularly violated or ignored? I stated above that declarations of boundaries (in ezu or in other documents) carried an ideological charge; in boundary disputes, estate residents enacted the sort of ideology of space proclaimed in establishing an estate. That it was a conflict-ridden and problematic ideology of space, however, is demonstrated by the existence of such disputes. For their presence presupposes both a recognition of the estate as a bounded realm and its contradiction—that estate boundaries were of little or no account in everyday experience (how else could there be such regular traffic across estate lines?). From this tension, though, we can begin to construct a notion of the space of the estate system— not as a statement that, once declaimed by proprietors, would hold for all time, but as a process continually produced and reproduced in the tension between the uniform and bounded site proclaimed by shōen proprietors and the open-ended, variegated space in which residents lived. Shōen proprietors were able to partition space into properties, but into properties that had continually to be remade.

Taking the Measure of the Land

The complete survey, or *shō kenchū*, was the most powerful means by which proprietors sought to remake the land they had staked out as their property. A laborious and expensive exercise, such a survey could involve teams of outside surveyors (dispatched by the proprietor) numbering dozens of men who might require months to complete their task.[40] Estate residents, moreover, might be expected to take part in the effort—to guide the surveyors, to instruct them in precedent, to draw up maps showing the location of fields—and all participants might be required to swear to the veracity of what they reported.[41] A survey, in short, was a complicated procedure, and since it led to the field registers that might remain the basic record of landholding on an estate throughout a proprietor's tenure, it was a serious, and complexly negotiated, business as well.[42] The process— from measuring the fields to producing a field register and the myō and rent rolls that proceeded from it—was attended by a series of interventions which ordered the space of the estate.

The first product of a survey was a field register (*torichō*). Standard in format and content, these registers followed the path of the

survey, noting the location, size, and holder of each plot, and sometimes indicating as well whether a holding lay fallow, had been newly reclaimed, or was perennial waste. *Zappitsu yōsho*, a thirteenth-
century sampler of documentary forms, provides a template for a
typical field register (with the information in brackets to be supplied
as appropriate):

Reported: Survey register for ‹name of estate, year›

    . . .
    1st *ri*
        1st *tsubo*   ‹area›   ‹name› *myō* . . .

The aforementioned is reported, per precedent.

        ‹Date›   kumon ‹seal›[43]

This model, intended, we may suppose, as a guide for scribes
charged with preparing such documents, serves also to identify the
essential features of the genre: a register was required, first to situate
a field (here by reference to its place in the jōri grid), second to specify
its area, and last to append to the field a name—that of the myō unit
to which it was attached or of its holder.

Actual registers conform closely to this style, although they often
adorn the basic framework of the model with additional details. Consider, for example, the following entries from registers for Niimi Estate (1271) and Tara Estate (1254):

Bitchū-no-kuni Niimi-no-shō

    Field survey report for Bun'ei 8 [1271] . . .

Narahara

    site [a]   2 *tan*, 15 *shiro*   Narimatsu Sadahiro
    site [b]   1 *tan*, 15 *shiro*   Muneyasu

    . . .

    site [n]   20 [*shiro*] new   [Narizawa] Shinsei[44]

Wakasa-no-kuni Tara-no-shō

    Reported: Survey register for Kenchō 6 [1254]

    site [a]   2 *tan*   Sanetoshi

    . . .

    site [n]   30 *bu* Sugimoto   Sadakuni[45]

The initial fruit of a survey was, then, a scroll which fixed the size
and location of each field and attached to it a name. As the abbot of
Tōji indicated in a directive to officers of Nata Estate, "in the great

survey (*dai kenchū* = *shōken*) the names of the holders should be listed, and the location [of their fields] specified; these are to be reported to the temple."[46] Conforming to this dictate, the Niimi register describes three fields in a region identified as Narahara. The areas of these fields are noted, along with information about their possession. As shown above, two of the fields are designated part of Narimatsu myō, but are held by different people (the names in smaller type at the end of each line), while the third, designated as newly reclaimed, is attached to another myō. The register for Tara, perhaps because it was a much smaller estate, does not provide explicit indications of place (although "Sugimoto" would seem to be a place name), but in all other respects it fits the standard mold.

That field registers tend to resemble one another should not, however, go without saying. The seeming self-evidence or conventionality of the form conceals the statement contained in the registers. As they moved across an estate, measuring fields, recording holders' names, and jotting down other information, and as they reduced that data to the standardized form of a field register, surveyors and their hyakushō assistants conformed to conventions that guided what they were to record and how they were to proceed. And in these very conventions we can observe the processes which systematized and institutionalized the land.

Although the record has left few details about the actual business of surveying in the medieval era, what does survive suggests a process circumscribed by custom. Surveyors, we know, were expected to rely on earlier records as they carried out their work, but this privileging of precedent created difficulties. As the peasants of Sone Estate in Ise Province complained to their proprietor, who had attempted to resurvey the estate after a hiatus of some eighty years, "Though we sought to follow your wishes, no local officials versed in precedent survive and the elder hyakushō [who remember the earlier survey] are all dead; it was impossible to find anyone who could draw a map of the land or guide [the surveyors]."[47] In addition, the route of a survey may often have been prescribed by tradition. A note on the back of a register from Kyushu, for example, describes the traditional order to be followed and advises that an "auspicious day" be chosen to start the survey.[48]

The process concluded in a similarly ritualized context with a reading of the register. Traces of this ceremony, known as *yomiai*, can be read in the vermilion marks placed next to each entry as the entire register was read aloud and verified. Staged at a dwelling borrowed or constructed for the purpose, or at a local shrine or temple, the yomiai was the culminating act of the surveying process.[49]

Estate officials, probably in the presence of hyakushō, read through the register, placing a vermilion dash next to each entry, both to certify its accuracy and to guard against later changes or additions; after the reading was completed, the register was signed and dated, and copies forwarded to the proprietor. The significance of this act should not be underestimated. As the *kumon* of Akanabe Estate, rebuked by the proprietor for "not listening to the yomiai," discovered, this reading of the register was an important rite of governance.[50] It served at once to certify the register's contents and to authenticate publicly the record established by the register: the yomiai validated the endeavor.

The very nature of what gets recorded also comments on the motives that fueled the project. Cultivated paddy, of course, found its way into the registers, but so, too, did fallow and flooded fields, waste, and some (though not necessarily all) fields earmarked for local shrines and temples or for other special beneficiaries.[51] As the examples above suggest, the evident intent of surveying was to establish the (actual and potential) productive base of the estate—to locate, measure, and determine title to all fields that were presently cultivated or might be cultivatable. Their field-by-field tallies present, in other words, not so much a catalog of an estate's contents as a portrait of its potential for producing rents.

The manner in which the registers inscribe this potential, moreover, reveals some of the underlying notions that informed the system's organization of production. The monotonous litany of "site [a], site [b]" marks the "field" as the basic unit of these registers, figuring it as a sort of universal equivalent by which all production, whether specifically agricultural or not, might be measured. A register of Ōi Estate, which delivered the bulk of its rents in silk, thus offers a painstaking inventory of the paddy and other fields of the estate, but makes no mention of mulberry trees, silkworms, or other materials that figure in sericulture.[52] Likewise, a survey of Mizuno mura, an Itsukushima Shrine holding in Aki Province, divulges no hint that it paid its rents in iron.[53] And on Niimi Estate, otherwise very complete registers from 1271 and 1325 give no indication that the nengu for one area of the estate was assessed in iron.[54] When surveyors set about registering the productive base of a region, they obeyed an institutional imperative which specified production in terms of land and viewed the land as a congeries of distinct fields. Amino Yoshihiko speaks of the profound "institutional and political role" assigned to rice paddy that privileged it above other types of land, that rendered it, for example in the institutions of the Ritsuryō state, the sole object and measure of authority.[55] In the medieval era, in contrast to this earlier epoch, proprietors made an effort to register dry fields or to count lacquer trees, salt pots, and other non-paddy; but the surveys they produced of their holdings commemorate notions of production still bounded by an inheritance which identified productivity with paddy.[56]

The measurements recorded in registers highlight another facet of the convention which shaped the process. Almost invariably, the field areas they report are stated in even, and fairly large, units. Of the 262 fields noted in the Tara register mentioned above, for instance, only 3 have recorded areas that do not fall into multiples of 10 *bu* (about 32 square meters). And thousands of entries in the Niimi registers for 1271 and 1325 provide only a handful of exceptions in which the areas are worked out to a unit smaller than 2.5 *shiro* (about 58 square meters). Indeed, as Yamamoto Takashi observes, the system of notation used indicates that the normative unit may have been much larger: registers frequently give areas in reference to the *tan* (360 bu or 50 shiro, about 1200 square meters).[57] Even allowing for the crudeness of medieval measuring practices, these results cannot be explained away as the fault of inadequate technique. For what is striking about medieval field registers is not their roughness, but the regularity with which they produce fields of even, orderly dimensions.

In part, this feature of field registers can be explained as an act of largesse toward the peasantry. It is this sentiment, for example, that seems to inform a surveyor's oath, in which he vows not to leave a "single bu undiscovered," but immediately qualifies the scope of his commission: small, newly opened plots may be disregarded if contiguous to existing fields, and the same treatment may be accorded fields in "poor land (*usuchi*) which the hyakushō rightfully claim may not support cultivation from one year to the next."[58] The practice of discarding the odd unit may well reflect just such a concern for the peasant's welfare. But it also articulates something about the system's attitudes toward the land. Surveys did not respond to what we might think of as "economic rationality."[59] Despite their often impressive length, field registers display little of that combination of exhaustiveness and exactitude which are the hallmarks of the drive to maximize returns. Their loose measurements, conventionalized content, and custom-laden process speak, rather, of a mode of authority that seems primarily normalizing, not maximizing. In this scheme, the odd unit, vital if one's interest is to produce the greatest possible return, could be cast off because it was insignificant to the larger project of surveying and registering—the project, that is, of routinizing space. Field registers inscribed a version of the land that rendered it amenable to authority; they mapped space into discrete, homogeneous units, which could be combined and adjusted as necessary.

Gathering

As alluded to at the outset, however, the field register marked only the initial step in the process that ordered the land; from the field register issued two other types of records, which completed the transformation begun with the survey. The *nayosechō*, or *myō* register, adding information about rents and clarifying the disposition of prebendary and other exempt fields, produced a grid of rent-producing units. The *mokuroku*, or catalog, recasts the details about cultivation and rents contained in the first two into a summary form that recounted for proprietors the gist of their holdings. Together, the records describe a succession of mediations which refashioned the character of the land; the estate summarized in a mokuroku differs from that inscribed in a myō register, which is in turn distinct from that recorded in a field register. To remark only that each stage encoded a different version of the same land, however, does not probe very deeply into the mechanisms that bestowed order. Each successive stage in the process from survey to catalog represented a distillation and refraction of the previous stage. As Kuroda Toshio and others have shown, certain discrepancies (in reported field areas, etc.) between field registers and nayosechō, or between both these and mokuroku, underscore the constructed nature of each documentary mode.[60] But their argument should be taken farther, for each successive phase, by imposing a new form on that information, bent it to a new purpose. The different modes of representation describe different modes of power over space and conditioned the social uses to which these documents were put. Field registers, for example, addressed the particular and local. Their rosters of fields and names served as an indispensable local referent, a baseline that in suits could establish title to disputed fields or that could function in bills of sale and other land transfers to specify a field's location.[61] Significantly, the originals of torichō, unlike those of other registers, seem frequently to have been kept on the estate; they remained, in a real sense, tied to the land they sought to transcribe.[62]

In contrast to the specificity of field registers, mokuroku articulated an authority stripped of particulars. Taking the process of abstraction initiated in the survey one step further, mokuroku delimited the compass of the proprietor's wealth not by enumerating fields, but by generating a train of figures that summed up an estate's area, its rent-bearing and exempt fields, and the rents it owed. These numbers established the benchmarks against which proprietors could measure at a glance the extent of cultivation and the amount and disposition of rents. In effect, mokuroku ceased to speak of the land; their referents were not the realities of cultivation, but the organizational categories of a system of production. In short, they specified the value of an estate to its holder and certified the holder's expected return.[63] Affidavits of ownership, they thus figured prominently among the documents that established a proprietor's possession of an estate. Indeed, Tomisawa Kiyoto speculates that the transfer of mokuroku denoted the transfer of proprietary authority; and Tōji's archives include a number of mokuroku apparently ceded to it at the same time the estates came into its possession.[64]

Negotiating the passage between the forms at either end of the surveying process, culling information about landholdings from the field register and reproducing it in a form amenable to summary in the mokuroku, was the myō register. The following entry, from a myō register for Yano Estate, is paradigmatic. It first enumerates the fields (noting their area and quality) which comprise the myō, then calculates its taxable area, and finally specifies the rents due from the unit:

Sadatsugu *myō*

site [a], 1 *tan* medium   site [b], 30 [*shiro*] inferior

site [c], 25 medium 15 inferior 10   site [d], 25 flooded

[Area], as above: 2 *tan*, 30 [*shiro*] 25 flooded

Taxable paddy (*jōden*): 2 *tan*, 5 [*shiro*]

medium, 15 [*shiro*]   Rent: 4 *to*, 2 *shō*, 9 *gō*

inferior, 40 [*shiro*]   Rent: 1 *to*, 8 *shō*, 4 *gō*

Rents, as above: 6 to, 1 shō, 3 gō[65]

Comparing this register to the field registers cited earlier, we note several important differences. First and most obvious, myō registers introduce a new organizational principle: where torichō follow geography, locating fields in space, myō registers beat a different track, situating fields within an institutional framework. In nayosechō, fields strewn across the landscape are "gathered together" (*yose* derives from the verb *yoseru*, to draw together) into myō (an alternative reading for *na*, name). Shigenobu myō on Niimi Estate, for instance, is shown in a fourteenth-century register to comprise twenty-eight fields from widely separated parts of the estate.[66] Similarly, the myō of Tara Estate drew together fields dispersed throughout the estate, while a nayosechō from Ōyama Estate reveals each myō to be composed of from five or six to a dozen or more fields.[67] The effect of myō registers is to create unity out of these scattered plots. Laid out next to a single name (often that of a resident of the estate at the time the myō grid was first instituted), the disparate fields seem to "belong" to the person whose name the myō bears. Reversing the form of field registers—fields are attached to a name, not the other way round—myō registers adopt a language of possession to underwrite their institutionalization of space.

Second, while the basic unit of the field register is the field, that of the myō register is the taxable field (jōden), an object produced by adjusting the cumulative area of fields within the myō to account for noncultivated regions and tax-exempt lands. In the example just cited, for instance, the taxable area of Sadatsugu myō corresponds to its total area minus the area of the flooded field; that of Yoshizane myō, also of Yano Estate, was produced in a similar fashion, by deducting the area of one fallow and two inundated fields, as well as that of plots earmarked for two local temples, one shrine, and for well fees. In the process, the area of the myō was cut almost in half.[68]

Often, too, nayosechō provide information not contained in field registers. Certain prebendary fields (kyūden) seem to have been allocated only at this stage. For instance, plots assigned to two local officials—not mentioned in the field register—are noted in the myō register for Mizuno mura.[69] Tōji's records note a similar example from a temple holding in Aki Province, where fields for two estate officials and a local shrine were added in only as the nayosechō was drawn up.[70] Another conspicuous departure concerns rents, an element on which field registers are notably silent. Appended to a myō register for Niimi Estate is a summary of rents due from the estate; and some, though not all, entries for individual myō furnish details about rents.[71] A nayosechō for Ōi Estate is more systematic, specifying the rents due from each myō,[72] and a roster of myō for Tara Estate apportions fields among five different rent levels.[73] In none of these instances does the field register from which the nayosechō derives mention rents, grade fields, or otherwise indicate the land's productive capacity.

This addition of information about rents and exempt fields signals an important rupture. The process that created myō contained space within a framework focused around rents, and in doing so effected a disengagement from the natural landscape and replaced it with an institutionalized topography. A number of scholars have described

the sorts of slippage this act entailed. Tracing variations in the reported areas of the myō of Tara Estate, Kuroda Toshio notes a gap
between actual peasant holdings (recorded, he contends, in field registers) and the officially constructed holdings—the myō—that comprised the basis for calculating rents.[74] Hashimoto Hiroshi, in a study
of Niimi Estate, points to the substantial allowances incorporated
when calculating the taxable area of myō; these allowances, he concludes, provided a margin that made it possible to adjust myō areas
to appropriate levels.[75] And Yasuda Tsuguo, analyzing the myō structure of estates in the Kinai region, emphasizes how myō areas were
manipulated to equalize the rent burden.[76] All of these studies aim to
show how myō were "artificial," crafted units, more institutional fictions than the natural outcome of landholding patterns. They also
demonstrate how the very "ground" upon which myō rested differed
from that detailed in field registers.

The landscape depicted in myō registers, in short, has been aligned
to meet the requirements of rent production. Resolving the jumble of
fields into discrete units, and condensing each unit further into a single, "taxable field," the process of gathering that produced these registers systematized space, recomposing it within an explicitly institutional framework. Nayosechō record an act of ordering; they attest to
an intervention that further distanced the estate from the land. All
that remained to complete the conversion of land from a site where
people lived and worked into an institution supplying rents was to
extract the totals from myō registers and sum them up in a mokuroku. If field registers, as we have seen, stand at some remove
from the realities of cultivation, they nonetheless refer back to the
land. Myō registers, by contrast, take as their organizing principle the
extractive mechanism of the system; they contain space within a series of categories all of which refer to production. Mokuroku, going a
step beyond, seem entirely self-referential. The system speaks to itself through such documents; mokuroku construct the estate not out
of cultivated plots, but entirely in terms of the categories which
framed the system's rent-producing apparatus. Ultimately, then, the
surveying process culminated in a landscape dissociated from its spa-
tial/geographical context and reconstituted within the categories of
the system. It produced a space over which proprietors could claim
authority because they supplied the categories which ordered it, rendered it known and hence controllable.[77] Seen in this light surveying
takes on a political significance that may have overshadowed the economic benefits to be gained from discovering new fields or reassessing rent rates. Surveying reclaimed space for production, but also for
the reproduction of proprietors' authority.

Myō and Hyakushō

At the end of a twelfth-century mokuroku he had just finished copying, Jinson, a fifteenth-century abbot of Kōfukuji, added the following comment:

> These are the thirteen original myōshu [of Izumo Estate]. In recent years the name of the cultivator has been used as the name of the myō. This must not be! The names of cultivators change from time to time; they are not fixed. The original myō names should be used.[78]

Jinson's admonition represents the names of the thirteen original myō of the estate as bulwarks against chaos: in the face of the turmoil that would result from the adoption of actual, living cultivators' names, the use of the original myō names guarantees stability. His warning sets the value of institutional continuity above that of accuracy in depicting the state of cultivation or the actual pattern of landownership on the estate.

Thus far, I have depicted myō as the mechanism through which space was marshalled into a rent-producing regime. They marked, as well, another sort of nexus: that joining the system with its subject. And as was the case with myō and the land, here too we can note a discontinuity between the cultivator/landholder, whose labor produced the surplus upon which the system depended, and his institutional double, the myōshu, whose name identified the unit which framed the extraction of that surplus. Implicit in Jinson's coda, this break is also evident in some petitions and oaths from the peasants of Yano Estate. In each, the petitioners use not their personal names but the names of myō—signing the documents "Sadatsugu" or, more explicitly, "Sadatsugu myō," and not Michiie or whoever actually held the myō—as if the petitions were being submitted by land units rather than by people.[79] These, admittedly, are rare examples (most petitioners used their own names), but they only make manifest a more widespread problem. By assuming the names of myō, the petitioners profess an identity delimited by the system; as we will see in the following chapter, this was a general condition of meaningful communication between peasants and proprietors.

Myō registers assert a set of congruences between fields and the myō unit and between the name of the myō and its holder. But, in fact, they describe discontinuities. In myō, the system provided itself with a fictive landscape by which to organize its extraction of rents and with a subject to charge with these rents. The use of myō names instead of personal names in the Yano petitions and oaths, or Jinson's criticism of the use of cultivators' names, indicates a substitution on the level of the subject that parallels the topographic displacement discussed in the preceding section. The double entendre—myō literally means "name"—inherent in naming a myō with the name of a hyakushō masks the gulf that separates the institution and the person. It elides the subject and his possessions with the myō and its fields. Yet, the professed agreement takes place only within the reified categories of the system.

The questions remain: What aims guided the formation of myō? Why did the system create this unit, which (despite its pretense) could not be mapped onto a particular holder's possessions?

Some clues may lie in the uses myō fulfilled. As has been noted, they served as the vehicle through which rents were assessed and collected. Appointments to myōshu posts thus commonly enjoined the holder to satisfy the unit's nengu and kuji obligations, and notices for arrears in rent cited myō holders rather than the cultivator directly responsible for the delinquency.[80] Some bills of sale from Settsu Province make the connection explicit: they specify that rents be paid through the myō.[81] Myō also played a role in supervising cultivation. They often, for instance, contained some demesne, which, at least one source indicates, it was the myōshu's responsibility to portion out to cultivators.[82] Such evidence of the unit's utility upholds the pivotal place we adduced for it from nayosechō, yet it does not adequately explain why the institution took the form it did. Arguments based on function—an emphasis on the supposed administrative and economic efficiency of the myō system—cannot explain why this system, out of a thousand possible administrative schema, found such widespread application.

A closer examination of the responsibilities of myō, however, suggests that more was at stake than efficiency. In this respect, the connection with diverse labor and other levies known collectively as kuji seems critical. With regard to rents, specialists generally distinguish two major classes of peasant lands within the shōen: myōden, which were subject to both nengu and kuji; and the proprietor's demesne (known commonly as *isshikiden*), parcels of which were rented out to cultivators on (probably) an annual basis and exempt from kuji.[83] Although this distinction is typically phrased in terms that emphasize the latter's difference from the norm (payment of both imposts), we might well turn this phrasing on its head and speak, instead, of the myō's distinctive liability for kuji. In rent rolls from Niimi Estate, for example, only myō have kuji levies assessed against them.[84] Likewise, a late-twelfth-century account of the kuji due from Ōta Estate establishes a clear connection between the two. Identifying the units from which these levies are to be collected as "kuji myōden," the document specifies that the hyakushō myō of the estate are to bear the burden.[85] And Watanabe Sumio has shown, more generally, that the "equal myō" (*kintōmyō*) of numerous estates in the Kinai area formed the basis for a system of equalized kuji levies.[86] Ultimately, then, the myō is identified by that same marker which distinguished the hyakushō. The myō system therefore effects an identification—between the subject, rents, and fields—that had normative as well as utilitarian value; and this, not the supposed efficiency of the system, seems to me the force behind its adoption.

In part, too, the choice of myō was conditioned by received practice. The myō of the shōen perpetuate a terminology that first appeared in the ninth and tenth centuries. Several sources from that period refer to myō, often in association with reclamation. In a ninth-century bill of sale, for instance, a parcel is described as "reclaimed land, a myō of [the seller's] father," while a tenth-century monk complains about the purchase of some reclaimed lands called "Saneyuki no myō."[87] Deeds referring to myō centered about dwellings or residence plots also survive.[88] These documents suggest that many early myō were formed around a nucleus of reclaimed fields or household plots—types of land which, in contrast to public lands, were officially recognized as "private" and alienable (i.e., exempt from the periodic redistribution public lands underwent)—and establish a seemingly straightforward connection between such holdings and myō: the institution would seem to derive from the practice of naming private holdings after the person who opened them up.

Yet, the evidence also indicates an institution in flux. Alongside the sorts of myō just outlined appear such entities as a "Tōji myō" or a "Tōdaiji myō"—even one named after an imperial prince—as well as myō that in later sources are called shōen.[89] These references to manifestly nonpeasant myō, or to myō that straddle supposedly exclusive categories, muddy the picture. Such usages highlight the flexibility with which the term was applied. They reveal that it contained a broader range of phenomena than can be encompassed by a direct identification of myō with reclaimed lands or peasant household plots. What distinguished these myō, then, was not so much the type of land they incorporated or the character of their holder, as the relationship their creation engendered between the holder and the provincial authorities. Much of the information about the early myō comes in connection with the process of official registry (*rikken*) by which holdings, including estates, were legally constituted. Whether or not their core consisted of household plots or newly opened fields,

myō therefore represented something distinct from "ownership"—
they expressed a publicly authorized right of possession that in turn
engaged the holder to pay the taxes and other levies due from the
unit.

The hyakushō myō of the shōen inherited this feature of their
ninth- and tenth-century forerunners. Tara's myō contained fields
which Kanshin, Tokizawa, Sanetoshi, and the other hyakushō who
"named" these units could claim as their own, perhaps even by virtue
of having opened them up. But the gist of the myō remained the relationship it forged between hyakushō and proprietors. In myō, the estate system found a ready-made terminology describing a particular
confluence of land and person within a rent-producing apparatus.
Within the shōen the institution was redrawn—its scope restricted
and application regularized—with the hyakushō at its core. But it retained its basic function of expressing an officially sanctioned relationship. We saw in the last chapter how peasant identity was refigured in the term hyakushō according to a set of tropes which had no
meaning outside the shōen. We have traced in this chapter an analogous process which installed fields in a new site, the myō, structured
by the categories of the system. Joining the two, as proprietors did
when they appointed hyakushō to myōshu posts, bound the constructed subject of the system to its redrawn landscape. The myō thus
served as another means by which the system cemented ties with the
peasant-producers from which it derived its wealth.

Orderly Places, Contested Spaces

In *The Practice of Everyday Life*, Michel de Certeau distinguishes between the "space" of daily life and the "place" defined by a system of
authority:

> At the outset, I shall make a distinction between space (*espace*) and place
> (*lieu*) that delimits a field. A place is the order (of whatever kind) in ac-
> cord with which elements are distributed in relationships of coexis-
> tence. . . . The law of the "proper" rules in the place: the elements taken
> into consideration are beside one another, each situated in its own
> "proper" and distinct location, a location it defines. . . . [A place] im-
> plies an indication of stability.[90]

A space, by contrast, describes a site permeated with the contingencies of daily life. It is defined by practice, by use—people walking
along a road, cultivators working in a field—not by the order of a sys-

tem. Space is fluid, temporal, multivalent, "like the word when it is spoken, . . . situated as an act of a present (or of a time), and modified by the transformations caused by successive contexts. In contradistinction to the place, it has thus none of the univocity or stability of a 'proper.' "[91]

The "space" of an estate—including not only its cultivated fields, but also its mountains and forests, its irrigation channels, the roads that joined it to networks of communication—contrasts sharply with the "place" defined in field registers or nayosechō. Where the former is the scene of movement, fields being opened (or falling out of cultivation), people traveling to markets or simply "wandering," the latter is static, fixed, stabilized. Myō and field registers substitute for the space of everyday life a place with its own valences and temporality. Reconstituting space within the categories of the system, these registers nullify the historical and productive processes that conceived particular patterns of landownership or of cultivation and construct instead an unchanging place upon which proprietors could ground their rule.

Surveying, in sum, demonstrates a need to stabilize, to still the ever-changing human and natural landscape. Much as the rhetoric of hyakushō identity sought to locate the subject within a bounded realm, the dislocations induced at each stage of the surveying process, from the initial measurements through the "naming" of myō and the mokuroku that tied it all up, speak of a desire to fix the estate, its fields, and its production by relocating them, by withdrawing them from space and situating them within an ordered place. Simultaneously, by marking this place with a name—the myō—proprietors "populated" it. The effect of the process, then, was to assign each subject a proper location (the place of its name), to draw together peasants and cultivated fields as hyakushō and myō, and thereby to achieve the sort of stability that Jinson, for example, extolled when he recommended the use of original myō names. An orderly place, a place stabilized in script on a register and within categories defined as the system's own, is the survey's goal. For it is in this place that proprietors could read without ambiguity the extent of their authority.

Yet this orderly place, the site of proprietors' authority, continually jostled with the space of daily life. If myō or the fields and assessments reported in torichō and rent rolls rarely changed, cultivators and the lands they cultivated frequently did. The estate as it was experienced by the people who lived within its boundaries differed, sometimes quite sharply, from the estate as written in the proprietor's books. The tension between these two sites outlines an important dynamic for the system, defining a realm of possibility for the interaction of peasants and proprietors. The space of everyday experience took shape within a terrain structured by the system; conversely, the place delineated in land registers had to be reconciled to the space which it purported to represent. These negotiations between place and space could be converted into the exchanges of rebellion.

FOUR

THE THEATER OF PROTEST

W HEN THE PEASANT INHABITANTS of medieval Japan's estates rose in protest against the actions of their proprietors, they did not (by and large) run riot, attacking local officials or laying waste to buildings and fields. Instead, to borrow the contemporary idiom, they "melted into the mountains and the forests." Invariably, their flight was preceded by a petition expressing the peasants' grievances, and that petition was often backed by a solemn oath that affirmed the righteousness of the complaint. These gestures—petitions, oaths, and flight—were the tropes of peasant rebellion; they comprised the repertoire of tactics that defined the theater of protest in medieval Japan.

To cite the theatricality of its protests as the mark of Japan's difference, however, is to imply an opposition between the brute struggle of interests and symbolic play, between societies marked by violent protest and societies in which rebellion is figured according to certain codes, which must immediately be qualified. I use the phrase "theater of protest" advisedly. I do not mean by it to suggest that peasant rebellion in medieval Japan was any less real than elsewhere or at other times, or that the antagonisms between ruler and ruled were less acute than in other societies. It would be a mistake to suppose that, because protest followed a script, the seigneurial regime of medieval Japan was somehow more harmonious than that which produced the Jacqueries or the English Peasants' Revolt of 1381. The evidence of numerous war tales and picture scrolls, as well as documents describing the torture of peasants at the hands of local lords, warns against any overly idyllic view of premodern Japan.[1] By the same token, however, the violence of an uprising is surely no guarantee that the protesters' grievances are more genuine or their actions less culturally scripted than complaints that find expression through more overtly ritualized forms.[2] Rather, in stressing the theatrical, I wish to call attention to the fact that the social meaning of protest depends, at least in part, on its being "staged." For in medieval Japan, absconding as an act of rebellion had somehow to be distinguished from merely running away, an action more suggestive of resignation than of defiance. To make that difference clear, absconding peasants enacted a complex of coded behaviors; they called upon a store of actions with symbolic or ritual overtones, which rendered protest and rebellion—acts historians tend to construe as spontaneous and impulsive[3]—an overdetermined theater of signs.

No less than their counterparts in Europe and elsewhere, protesting peasants in medieval Japan drew upon a script of characteristic processes to proclaim the significance of their uprisings and to make their meaning known:

> If we have spoken falsely, may the vengeance of all the deities, great and small, of the sixty-six provinces of Japan, especially that of the temple's Daishi and Hachiman and of Myōjin and the related deities of the five shrines of the estate, be visited upon us.[4]

This oath, which concludes a petition of grievances against the overseer of Yano Estate, is a sample of the script of protest. Its language confirms the virtue of the peasants' actions in terms that, because they conform to a certain code, compel. According to Marc Bloch, incessant struggle was the hallmark of the manorial economy of medieval Europe, while agrarian revolt provided the reaction that served to characterize the system.[5] In the Japanese case, too, a reading of the script of protest may not only serve to decipher the actions of medieval peasants, but may also lead to a new understanding of the system within which they lived. As Michel Foucault has suggested, rebellion can offer a revealing glimpse into the nature of a social system, affording access to its (normally unseen) plays of power and structures of practice:

> Another way to go further towards a new economy of power relations . . . consists of taking the forms of resistance against different forms of power as a starting point. . . . Rather than analyzing power from the point of view of its internal rationality, it consists of analyzing power relations through the antagonism of strategies. . . . In order to understand what power relations are about, perhaps we should investigate the forms of resistance and attempts made to dissociate these relations.[6]

The moment of crisis, in sum, presses the system to its limits, exposing the operation of its power structures not merely in the forces that contest or suppress the rebellion, but in the very forms rebellion takes and in the cultural conditions that govern how its meanings are made known. The interplay between rebellious peasants and estate proprietor reveals not only the opposition of two classes, but, more generally, the framework of their relations, the aims and assumptions that define and confine the system of the estates.

Rebellion

In the last decades of the fourteenth century, Yano Estate was twice rent by protracted and violent struggles.[7] In 1377 and again in 1393–94 residents led concerted campaigns against the temple-appointed overseers (*daikan*) who managed the estate. The revolt in each instance reached beyond the boundaries of the estate: the peasants of Yano were in communication with residents of nearby estates, and provincial authorities (the *shugo* and his men) provided the force that ultimately quashed each rebellion. To many modern commentators, the uprisings on Yano epitomize the shocks that attended the estate system in its declining years; attenuated, moribund, the bonds that joined proprietor, peasant, and others in the shōen hierarchy were giving way to new linkages based on region and class.[8] Especially to those scholars who view the shōen as self-sufficient, self-contained realms, the way the disorders spilled over the borders of the estate into neighboring domains and jurisdictions can only lend support to a narrative of decline. However, a closer reading, I believe, recommends a different view.

If we suspend our surprise at boundaries breached (estate boundaries were never unbreachable), the uprisings become less portents of the breakdown of the system than revealing commentaries on its operation. In the pages that follow I will restrict my analysis to the earlier outbreak, for the simple reason that it comes to us via an exceptional, even unique source: the annals of the Gakushū-gata, one of the two assemblies within Tōji responsible for Yano Estate.[9] With these annals we can trace the almost daily course of the interplay that characterized the governance of this prominent estate.

The Gakushū-gata annals for 1377 (third year of the Eiwa period, from which the uprising takes its name) open with little premonition of the troubles that were soon to engulf Yano Estate. The epigraph that ritually commences the annals of that year affirms with assurance that "our scholarship flourishes and our holdings prosper" (1/5). The first mention of Yano comes in a pair of documents that treat overdue rents from the previous year (1/16). The arrival two days later of Kurō Shirō, styled in the annals as "representative of the hyakushō," alerted the monks to troubles of a different sort. Bearing a petition and a collective oath, Kurō Shirō informed the monks that Yano's residents had sworn a complaint against Yūson, the estate's overseer, and had fled en masse on 1/14.[10] Close on Kurō Shirō's heels were two more messengers, sent by Yūson and Hon'iden Iehisa (the estate's *tadokoro*, a lower officer concerned with tax collecting) to report on the incident. Convening on the 20th, the monks held their first deliberations about the crisis on Yano, deliberations that would continue, almost uninterrupted, for the remainder of the year.

The monks' first response was to condemn the hyakushō for their "unspeakable outrage" and to issue directives ordering them to return to their fields (1/20, 1/22). Refusing even to consider the peasants' petition and oath, the monks returned these unanswered. The language of the monks' decisions, however, did not amount to a blanket condemnation of the revolt. Not the flight itself, but its procedure and timing provoked their ire; outrage at a subverted chain of command informed the monks' response. "If the hyakushō have any complaints, they should address them to the temple," reads the record for 1/22. "Instead, they have fled without warning. This is the height of insubordination." The hyakushō were denounced for having absconded without first airing their grievances to the temple, for having failed to clear outstanding arrears in rents, and for leaving the estate at the beginning of the year, which was also the beginning of the agricultural cycle. As we shall see, petitions, oaths, and flight, whether merely threatened or actually carried out, constituted a process of negotiation between proprietors and peasants; such confrontations amounted, in effect, to a form of privileged communication and provided one of the tensions upon which the estate system was founded.

Since the monks had neither acknowledged the peasants' grievances nor authorized estate officials to force the rebels to capitulate, there was little likelihood that the peasants would concede. And, indeed, the peasants' response to the temple's order was to dispatch a second messenger with another petition, threatening this time that if the temple did not respond to their demands they would "leave the estate for good and take up residence on other estates" (2/13). A few days earlier, Yūson and Iehisa confirmed that they too had failed to persuade the peasants to return, and they recommended forceful suppression of the uprising. Asking to be empowered to jail the ringleaders and confiscate their holdings, Yūson and Iehisa further suggested that the temple contact the shugo and other proprietors of estates in the area, that they might lend their force to the repression.[11] The monks, though, balked at countenancing such a plan, fearing that it might invite further disorder on the estate and the erosion of the temple's authority. Instead, they asked for a roster of the ringleaders and ordered Yūson and Iehisa to place new cultivators on the fields vacated by fleeing hyakushō.

By the beginning of the third month, the monks were beginning to believe that their overtures were having some effect. They had heard nothing from either the peasants or Yūson for three weeks, and were inclined to interpret this absence of news in a favorable light. A report from Iehisa shocked them from these reveries. Revealed to the council on 3/5, this report (substantiated by a sworn oath) stated that not a single plot was being cultivated and that what little crop there was (some wheat or barley had evidently been planted) had become "food for deer." The peasants obstructed the temple's attempts to settle new cultivators on the vacated fields and intimidated would-be cultivators with oaths of "disobedience to the overseer down to the seventh generation." A somewhat more hopeful account from Yūson (arr. 3/7) notwithstanding, the monks realized that tensions were unrelieved, and they resolved to dispatch an agent to ascertain the true state of affairs.

Returning a week later, the agent upheld Iehisa's report, but he also brought word of a possible compromise. Discussions with the hyakushō revealed them to be adamant in their opposition to Yūson; however, they also appeared willing to accept a compromise whereby the temple would appoint a special agent (jōshi) to assume charge of the estate while the monks considered appointing a new overseer. Seizing this opportunity to salvage some of their rents, the monks eagerly grasped at the proffered straw. Within a few days they had selected a representative, who proceeded to Yano on 3/18. The peasants' acquiescence is somewhat more difficult to comprehend: the deal guaranteed them nothing, especially as the temple still had not acknowledged their grievances. Behind their acceptance of the settlement, however, we can detect one of the invariant conditions of agrarian unrest in medieval Japan: to an even greater extent than the proprietor, the peasants depended upon the product of the fields. Where the proprietor faced a loss of income, the peasants faced the loss of livelihood. At any rate, by the middle of the fourth month, nearly three months since they had fled the estate, the peasants were back, working their fields.

During the summer months—the high agricultural season—the conflict entered a cease-fire. But beneath the calm, two fundamental problems lingered: what to do about Yūson, and whether to punish the rebels. The monks displayed extreme reluctance to deal with either issue. To the peasants' entreaties that Yūson be dismissed, they voiced doubts that someone could be found to take his place (4/22, 4/27). But, by the same token, they ruled out punishment of the rebels (as demanded by Yūson), fearing that this would lead to further trouble and loss of rents (4/27, 6/19).

An appeal by Yūson, considered by the Gakushū on 8/6, underscores the unallayed tensions on the estate. To halt the stream of petitions ("false suits" according to Yūson) from the peasants, Yūson asked the monks for a deed confirming his tenure as overseer and for authority to arrest the leading peasants and confiscate their fields and crops. His connections with the shugo, he claimed, would allow him to deal easily with hyakushō who persisted in disobeying. Understandably, in view of their reticence to upset the status quo, the monks rejected Yūson's request. Not only would it be folly to arrest hyakushō during the growing season, they felt, but to bring the shugo in would be courting even greater disaster. Nevertheless, Yūson's petition signals the beginning of an alteration in the monks' mood. Though still hopeful of a peaceful resolution, Tōji in the ensuing months shifted increasingly toward the hard line recommended by Yūson.

Thus, on 9/8, the monks dispatched an agent to the estate with instructions to the hyakushō to repair relations with Yūson or have their fields seized. And when, on 11/2, a messenger from the hyakushō presented a new petition and oath from the united peasants and notices from several hyakushō that they were giving up their fields, the temple was prepared to move toward open repression. In the middle of the month, a directive was issued authorizing Yūson to punish the hyakushō if they persisted in their disobedience (11/15). In the twelfth month, the confrontation on the estate flared into open violence. Leading several dozen armed men, including housemen of the shugo, Yūson attacked the peasants as they gathered to plot their next move. According to the report that reached the monks on 12/8, Yūson rounded up and imprisoned thirty-five leading hyakushō and "countless" small peasants and attempted to force them, under threat of torture, to acknowledge (in writing) his authority. His followers, we are told, raided the peasants' dwellings, smashing jars, pots, and pans, and robbing the inhabitants of their possessions. All this proved too much for the monks, especially as no rents were forthcoming, and they denounced Yūson's action as "unthinkable savagery."

The peasants themselves offered the temple a way out of the crisis. Before the last skirmish they had hidden away the rents for the year on neighboring estates. These they promised to pay in full if the temple appointed a new overseer. Although the monks did not dismiss Yūson, they moved swiftly to remove him from any involvement in collecting rents. Directives to the estate instructed the hyakushō to forward rents directly to the capital (12/12), while Yūson was ordered not to interfere with any aspect of the rent-collecting process. Yūson, however, would not capitulate so readily; he attempted to retain control by force, going so far as to torture hyakushō to find out where they had hidden the rents. Despite this interference, by the end of the year rents began to trickle in to the capital (12/23, 12/27). The year-long struggle thus resulted in de facto recognition of what the peasants' had demanded from the outset: removal of Yūson from involvement in managing the estate (he would finally be dismissed the following spring, 3/23/1378).

Some aspects of this story require comment. First, one cannot but be impressed by the solidarity and determination of the peasants. They absconded en masse to open the rebellion, and Yūson's attack, which brought it to an end, caught them in general assembly; reports of collective oaths, of petitions and messengers from the estate, stud the monks' records. The peasants' refusal to submit to Yūson even under torture attests dramatically to the steadfastness with which they held to their demands.

Second, we must note the extensive role played by groups exterior to the estate proper. To press home their case, the peasants threatened to take up residence on neighboring estates (3/5), and before rekindling the protest in the winter months they secreted rents on nearby domains. Yūson, for his part, was constantly in contact with the shugo's men and other powers in the region. Throughout the uprising he urged Tōji to allow him to tap these connections; as we have seen, followers of the shugo were instrumental in suppressing the rebellion. Clearly, Yano's inhabitants (including Yūson) took part in networks that carried beyond the boundaries of the estate and that tied them to parties other than the proprietor.

Yūson's role in the uprising also calls for explanation. Overseer of the estate since 1359, Yūson occupied an ambiguous middle ground between Yano's peasants and Tōji, and between Tōji and the shugo of the province. He was both agent of the temple and a local power, whose extensive holdings (many amassed as a consequence of his official position) and connections with provincial authorities allowed him a certain independence of action. In these respects Yūson seems typical of a class of local lords who played on their various connections to further their own ends.[12] And like other members of this class, Yūson has been heralded as an agent of the estate system's decline; his ties with the province's shugo, in particular, seem representative of the dwindling of proprietary authority, wrested away from the temples and noble houses which constituted the old elite and replaced by new networks of power centered on the shugo and local lords.

These aspects of the revolt have attracted much notice and supplied two related explanations for the decline of the estate system. On the one hand, the uprising has been viewed as one of the culminating forms of a tradition of peasant resistance against the estate order. On the other, Yūson's part in the incident has helped historians to plot a parallel "invasion" (*shinryaku*) of the estate by local lords. Satō Kazuhiko's work on peasant resistance illustrates the first tendency by establishing a hierarchy of protest that charts a progression from isolated petitioning campaigns, through petition and flight, to estatewide uprisings (into which category the 1377 experience falls), and eventually to revolts embracing entire provinces.[13] Each stage in this progression marks a strengthening and broadening of peasant solidarity—a further development of peasant self-consciousness away from the ideological bounds of the system—and demonstrates the increasing inability of the estate framework to contain and control peasant actions. The case of Yano is important for it indicates that regional communications existed among the peasantry and demonstrates the existence of an extensive basis for unified action. The uprising of 1377 involved not just a few well-placed hyakushō, but all the inhabitants of the estate.

Matching this taxonomy of peasant action to a narrative of the rise of local lordship, Satō may also stand in for the second tendency.[14] He outlines for local lords the same sort of developmental path he described for peasants: isolated lordships in the twelfth and thirteenth centuries, constrained by the power of the estate-holding elites and the Kamakura Bakufu, from which emerge local and familial bands (often connected with shugo), then, from the closing years of the fourteenth century, regional confederations of local lords (*kokujin ikki*). Here, too, development is characterized by growing self-consciousness and multiplying regional bonds that cut across and negate the hierarchical divisions of the estate system. Yūson's maneuvers during the uprising serve in this scheme as examples of how new systems of regional ties were linking local powers with networks of authority that did not owe to the "traditional" estate-based order.

Such a construction has appeal, for it creates a smoothly escalating movement that merges neatly into the truly cataclysmic upheavals— the province-wide revolts (*kuni ikki*) of Yamashiro and Harima, the seemingly ceaseless overthrow of one lord by another—that mark the fifteenth and sixteenth centuries. It posits a steadily widening orbit of activity by both peasants and local lords that constituted a mounting challenge from below to the dominant structures of authority. But let us explore the narrative a little further to see if it does not also tell us something about the estate system itself, distinct from its disintegration. We must note, for example, despite the involvement of the shugo and others, the centrality of the proprietor. In part this stems from the nature of our source; the annals of the proprietor naturally give primacy of place to the proprietor. Still, it was to the monks that the peasants repeatedly directed their petitions; to the same body Yūson addressed his appeals to be allowed to call on outside force. The force of the shugo, though decisive, appeared in an adjunct role, activated by the proprietor.[15] There was, in short, no suggestion from any party that the monks' council was not the proper forum in which to pursue the dispute; Tōji was acknowledged on all sides as the proper court of appeal. The uprising, although it plunged the estate into crisis, in no way challenged the system. Mediated throughout by the monks, the conflict pitted the peasants against the overseer, not the temple; the uprising worked itself out entirely within the context of the estate. The pervasiveness of the shōen context requires some explanation if this rebellion is to stand as a sign of an enervated and powerless system.

The Eiwa uprising on Yano is usually portrayed as a straightforward contest between peasants and authority. The lessons drawn concern chiefly the tenacity of the peasantry, the inability of the temple to resolve the matter on its own, and the growing power of the shugo. But the events also lend themselves to a different reading. A concern with tracing the manner in which the rebellion unfolded, instead of with forcing it into an overarching teleological progression, draws us to an appreciation of the extraordinary forms invoked throughout the episode—flight, collective oaths involving elaborate communal rituals, petitions signed by the entire body of myōshu. Viewed in this light, the uprising takes shape not simply as an act of rebellion against a system of rule, but also as a richly orchestrated play of signals that required the mediation of the system to reveal their specific meaning. And this raises a further possibility: that one might read in this play of signs something of the system that imbued them with meaning.

We are concerned, then, with the conditions of possibility for shōen revolt. And this calls for a shift in emphasis. Instead of asking, as many writing about this incident have, "Why did the Yano uprising happen, and what did it mean (for the institution of proprietorship, for the fate of the estate system)?" we must ask, "*How* did the uprising mean?" How did the peasants of Yano make their discontents known? How did the gestures they employed come by the cultural authority that sanctioned their use? And how were the power relations that underlay the system implicated in the contest? The shift in focus I am suggesting entails, therefore, a move away from the concern for causes and consequences that drives much of the scholarship on rebellion in the estates. The developmental paths described by Satō and others represent an attempt to link rebellion to larger cycles and shifts in Japanese history, but they do so at a cost. First, there is a tendency to celebrate all protests as intrinsically subversive of the estate order, and, second, to conceive of protest only in terms of opposition and subversion. In Satō's teleology, for instance, every uprising contains within it the germ of the overthrow of the estate order (hence the germ of historical progress); rebellion is restricted to this single significance, and the history of rebellion is essentialized as the long, slow destruction of the estate system. This produces a particularly monolithic vision of peasant protests, one that denies, specifically, the complexity of their construction. I do not wish to deny the radical possibilities of rebellion, much less to endorse the opposite extreme, which holds that rebellion, particularly when marked by ritual, serves only to reinforce the status quo; but consideration of how the Eiwa uprising worked demands a much more nuanced understanding of the relationship between protest and order than is offered by this paradigm.[16] Without understanding how shōen uprisings work both with and against the rules and structures of the estate order, it seems premature to declare them either the revolutionary antithesis of that order or mere steam-valves serving to consolidate the system.

A second shortcoming of the standard portrayal of peasant uprising follows from the first. More concerned with charting the system's progress through time, this scholarship tends to deflect attention away from consideration of the processes that constituted the system in practice. In refusing to allow rebellion the possibility of conveying multiple, even contradictory, meanings, it performs a similar operation on the estate system as a whole. Peasant struggle (or the actions of local lords) is assigned the main responsibility for effecting historical change, and the system is set in place as the unchanging order against which this struggle takes place and by means of which any changes may be measured as "development," "decline," or, simply, "progress." By this operation, the system is divorced from the contingencies and contradictions of practice and furnished instead with the coherence and direction proper to a category that might order the march of Japanese history.[17] Concord and stability are valorized as norms, and instabilities and conflicts are viewed as failures of some sort, signs of dysfunction, decline, or (at the opposite end of the timeline) immaturity. Protest and system, and by extension peasants and proprietors, may therefore be treated as if they were self-contained opposites rather than mutually implicated entities.

This, however, is to ignore the complex ways such contestations and interactions produced and defined the system; it is to overlook the fact that rebellious peasants and recalcitrant local lords were co-eval with the estates, that the system constituted not a static order but an arena of competing and contradictory practices—a field of struggle. To investigate the conditions of possibility for the sort of resistance the Yano uprising exemplified is to highlight precisely these problems. By asking how petitions and oaths could command attention, or how an act like absconding could proclaim a specific significance, I aim to elucidate processes, to draw attention to the ways meaning and significance are constructed, regulated, and contested. I am arguing, in short, that the form resistance takes is as meaningful as its supposed rationale (that the ways people rebel are as telling as why they do so), and that by interrogating such processes we can produce an understanding of the estate system that is more dynamic and more closely tied to practice than that available in much of current scholarship. Finally, I aim by this method to raise, much more directly, the question of power—how it was exercised and how it operated—within the system of the estates.[18]

The codes of rebellion marked the insurgents as the owners of a recognized status; in their petitions and in their flight, peasants stepped into a privileged role that obliged the proprietor to respond. The ability to tap such resources was a source of strength to the peasants, but it could only be mobilized within the context of the estate. The rebellious peasant thus appears as a strangely equivocal figure, at once defiant of authority and subservient to its broader structures; the rebellion itself, both antagonistic and acquiescent, an expression of opposition to existing relations of power (serious enough for people to risk their lives) but also dependent on the structures that underlay those relations. Both the organic unity of the community (which is usually what is signified by mention of peasant solidarity) and the political unity of the estate conferred strength. In this moment of rebellion we see the former activated in support of goals proper to the latter and pursued through forms—petition, oath, flight—sanctioned and imbued with meaning by the system. In the language of oaths and the rituals of flight, the peasants tapped undercurrents that ran throughout medieval society, and thus equally throughout those structures within which, and by means of which, the shōen system operated.

The Rituals of Rebellion

When the inhabitants of Tara Estate, a Tōji holding in Wakasa Province, protested the outrages committed by the jitō's deputy, they, like their counterparts on Yano, presented an oath along with their petition of grievance.[19] The closing line of the petition notes how the oath was enacted:

> We ask that the jitō's deputy be dismissed and that we be allowed to deliver rents under the supervision of an impartial steward. In order to be granted this request, the hyakushō and others, together partaking of the sacred water (*ichimi shinsui*), respectfully submit this petition.

The phrase "ichimi shinsui" hints at the ritual within which the oath and petition were fixed.[20] *Ichimi*, literally "of one disposition," signals, first, that this was a collective event; the fifty-nine signers of the oath represented perhaps the entire adult male population of the estate. Social divisions and antagonisms that normally ruled the life of the domain were suspended. Among the signers we can identify leading myōshu and small peasants, some whose names suggest that they were artisans and moneylenders, others who appear elsewhere as opponents in bitter wrangles over property and inheritances.[21] The ritual context that informed acts of resistance thus began by conceiving a collectivity, by posing against the divisions of everyday life a vision of communitas. In this "blurring and merging of distinctions," Victor Turner's phrase, we can detect what he terms *liminality*, the distinctive space-time of ritual.[22] By calling into being this special space, the community emphasized the serious intent of the oath and increased its power to bind. Originating from a space exterior to daily life, the oath laid claim to a transcendent authority.

Ichimi, as an avowal of solidarity, regularly accompanied acts of resistance by the peasants of Tara. On Yano, too, as we have seen in the narrative recounted above and at other junctures in that estate's history, petitions to the proprietor were similarly impressed with the seal of solidarity: *ichimi dōshin*, "of one disposition and like mind." Elsewhere, as on Niimi Estate in the fifteenth century, we observe an overseer complaining that he was unable to gather rents because the peasants had collectively (*ichimi ni*) sworn to refuse payment, while a hundred and fifty years earlier we witness the peasants of Okunoshima Estate adopting rules that threaten expulsion to any residents who violate the will of the collectivity.[23] An insistence on solidarity characterizes peasant action during the entirety of Japan's medieval epoch. Ichimi stands out as the common denominator of challenges to authority; as we learn from a mid-Kamakura source, it was "the custom of hyakushō."[24]

Significantly, though, ichimi also echoed calls to collectivity that are dispersed throughout the language of the elites. The term appears, for example, in the basic law of the Kamakura Bakufu, in a declaration that judicial decisions must be based in unanimity.[25] But ichimi alludes especially to the stress on solidarity and unified action found within religious institutions. Mongaku's rules for Jingoji, drawn up at the beginning of the medieval epoch, refer repeatedly to the need for unity.[26] The rules of deliberation for Tōji's Gakushū-gata likewise enjoined the monks not to persevere in idiosyncratic individual views, but, "like fish," to merge with the predominant flow; the guidelines for other assemblies reiterate this theme.[27] Banna's injunctions, as he surrendered the governance of Ōta Estate to the monks of Mt. Kōya, also instructed them to act in concert should difficulties arise.[28]

The assertion of solidarity appears as a general need; ichimi in its various guises emerges as a precondition of political action, the claim of corporate identity necessary to act in a world articulated through corporate bodies. The hyakushō of Tara, Yano, and other estates prefaced their contests with proprietors with proclamations of their "corporateness" not merely because such claims would strengthen their cause (there being strength in numbers), but because, more basically, such claims linked their concerns to the broader networks of meaning and significance to be found within the culture at large.

With *shinsui*, the second half of ichimi shinsui, we move into the ritual context that informed the rites of oath swearing and union. The Tara source unfortunately reveals only that the oath swearers drank the shinsui; it provides nothing further about the ceremony itself. Fortunately, we know from other sources that the ceremony typically involved writing out an oath (and probably declaring it orally as well), then burning it, mixing the ashes with water or some other consecrated liquid, and swallowing the potion.[29] Bells, too, may have been rung to mark the rite.[30] Frequently the ceremony took place at a local shrine or temple, as the timing of the Yano rebellion suggests (the peasants absconded on the 14th of the first month, the day after a convocation at a local shrine [the *jū-san nichi kō* or "13th-day assembly," held on the 13th of each month] attended by all the myōshu).[31] Although we cannot know for certain what effects these gestures produced in the mind of a medieval peasant, the sanctifying intent of the act stands out. The lifted voices and the rising smoke called on the gods to descend (*kami oroshi*), to witness, and to lend their sanction to the issue or action at hand. Through the ritual of oath swearing the peasants created a moment of communion with the divine; in the act, though, the sacred was bent to a dual purpose—to bind the swearers under threat of divine retribution and to lend weight to a more profane communication. Diplomatic forms suggest this duality between the sacred and the worldly: on the one hand, the oath, sworn aloud, written then burned, its immaterial message intended for the gods; on the other, its material trace, the duplicate, with names and seals duly affixed, sent to the proprietor.[32] In this latter guise, oath swearing appears as a stratagem of rebellion, and it takes its force from the universality of its claim.[33]

Oaths of this sort were a general feature of peasant uprisings. As we have seen, the Yano peasants invariably buttressed their complaints with oaths, while the residents of Tara anchored their opposition to the deputy jitō in the ritual ground of shinsui. That the Yano peasants' oaths, too, arose from this same sacral context is affirmed at one point in the narrative: shinsui is explicitly referred to in connection with the peasants' vows of disobedience to the overseer (3/5). It is not difficult to imagine that the same might have been true on other occasions. A threat from 1324 by the peasants of Yugeshima Estate to abandon the estate also alluded to shinsui, as did a complaint lodged in 1275 by the peasants of Ategawa Estate against the jitō.[34]

But, like the notion of solidarity, oath swearing and the shinsui ritual were hardly the property of seditious peasants alone; ubiquitous forms, they breached class and status boundaries. In a celebrated instance, recounted in *Genpei seisuiki*, the monks of Hakusan, one thousand strong, gathered "before the image of the deity of Hakusan, . . . wrote out oaths (*kishō*), burned them to ashes, mixed the ashes with water, and drank the mixture."[35] In a more prosaic mode, oaths featured commonly among the instruments of authority. A Kamakura-era jitō, for example, seeking to amplify his prestige, forced the peasants of his holding to swear subservience.[36]

Likewise, Tōji could compel the residents of its estates to swear their acquiescence to temple mandates or to attest to the truth of complaints with oaths.[37] The overseers of Tōji's domains also had to swear fealty to the temple upon appointment to office, while rent collectors were often called upon to swear to the correctness of their accounts.[38] But oath swearing was not merely a form of coercion exercised downward through the ranks of society. Both Tōji and Tōdaiji used oaths to detect criminals in their midst, while the monks of Tōdaiji might swear an oath to renounce gambling in the temple precincts.[39]

In the last few paragraphs, I have attempted to show that the language of authority and the language of rebellion, ostensibly opposites, in fact turned upon identical forms. Rebellious peasants obeyed the same mandates for communal solidarity as did temple monks, warriors, and other ranks of the elite. This urges us toward a somewhat paradoxical result: the shōen rebellion derived its power and its threat not from any unique capacity for unified action on the part of the peasantry, but rather from its appropriation of the same forms that underlay the language of authority.[40] This conception contrasts with much of current scholarship in that it locates the force driving agrarian revolt not in some vaguely defined, quasi-mystical potency derived from the solidarity of the primitive peasant community, but instead in the sophisticated manner in which shōen inhabitants manipulated the symbols that underwrote the identity of *all* groups in medieval Japan.

The language of oaths reinforces this conclusion. Consider, for instance, the following samples:

> If we have uttered untruths or falsehoods, may the vengeance of Bonten on high and the stern deities below, especially of the Great Buddha, Hachiman and the guardian deities of the estate, and of all the deities, great and small, of Greater Japan, be visited upon each of the pores of us who affixed our seals to the estate-wide pledge (*isshō ichimi*).[41]

> If this account errs by even a thousandth or ten-thousandth part, may the punishment of all the gods, great and small, of the sixty-odd provinces of Greater Japan, beginning with Bonten and the Four Heavenly Guardians, and especially of Daishi and Hachiman of Tōji, of the guardian deities of this province and of the Myōjin of the three shrines of this estate, be visited upon the bodies of the hyakushō.[42]

> Should we, now or in the future, transgress these stipulations, may the divine vengeance of Bonten and the Four Heavenly Guardians, . . . of Amaterasu, and of all the deities, great and small, of Japan, especially of Hachiman, guardian of Tōji, and of Inari and Daishi, be visited upon each of the pores of our bodies.[43]

Strikingly similar in terminology, these oaths, from three different estates and spanning more than a century, possess another more arresting quality for our purposes. Each invokes the proprietor's particular deities in support of petitions that challenge aspects of the proprietor's rule. To some commentators, the cosmological order expressed in these oaths indicates the subjugation of estate residents to the ideological systems of authority.[44] Use of the proprietary deities, suggesting an inability to counter the proprietary ideology with an indigenous one, marks in this view but another aspect of their thralldom. I believe that it is a mistake to view these oaths only as a symptom betraying the subjection of the masses. To be sure, the appellation of deities in descending order from national to local indicates the peasants' adherence in an ideological order to which temples and others in authority also subscribed. But it is precisely this that gives force to the oath as an instrument of defiance. And this, too, that explains why the peasants should specifically name Tōji's own deities in support of their complaints. Naming these deities was an appropriation of the guardians of authority to sanction an act of rebellion. Or rather—since "appropriation" hints too much at the seizure by peasants of something properly belonging to the temples, when what I wish to emphasize are the structures shared by the two—the naming of deities resonates upon the common ground linking proprietors and peasants, emerging as one of the recurrent motifs rendering the one intelligible to the other. Oaths, petitions, and flight were part of the general language of the estate system.

That it was a general language, one in which both peasants and proprietors phrased their claims and counterclaims, should not imply the absence of real conflict; indeed, the context in which this common ground is revealed—i.e., rebellion—warns against that interpretation. "Shared" does not mean "harmonious": the language itself must be seen as constituted in the struggles to which it gives expression. Structure, that is, must be interrogated as it is put into practice, strategically and tactically, in a field marked by the exercise of power in certain forms and by the range of resistances to that power.

Petitioning

Episodes from Yugeshima and Tara estates offer excellent examples of how this language functioned in the dialogue between proprietor and peasants. In 1313–1314, Yugeshima residents found themselves beset by what they claimed were "novel burdens" imposed by the estate's overseer. Their initial petition, dated the sixth month of 1313, complained, among other things, of excessive corvées, exorbitant rents, slaughtered livestock, and other evils.[45] The temple at first refused to accept the petition because it lacked proper seals, but after the hyakushō resubmitted the document duly signed and backed by an oath, the monks accepted the petition as a formal suit.[46] The meager sources fail to provide us with any more satisfactory denouement to this opening exchange; that the residents' grievances remained unallayed, however, is certain. For in the following year came another petition, this time announcing that the hyakushō had "renounced their generations-old inheritance of *myōshu shiki* and dwellings and left the estate."[47] In the succeeding months Tōji ordered an investigation of the affair, but the hyakushō, unsatisfied with the temple's response, sent three of their members to Kyoto to renew the demand for a new custodian. The hyakushō were allowed to confront the custodian directly before the monks;[48] however, the sources again leave us hanging as to the outcome. Although we do know that a new custodian was appointed two years later, what connection, if any, this had with the current events remains unclear.[49] Still, the record presents us with a nearly complete round of negotiation in which the functions of oaths and flight stand clear. These acts serve as richly symbolic adjuncts to the dialogue between the estate's proprietor and the estate's residents.

A series of protracted struggles for rent relief waged on Tara Estate between 1304 and 1306 allows further opportunity to follow this dialogue in its course. Damages to crops occasioned by flooding, drought, insects, and other natural catastrophes sparked the difficulties on Tara during these years. Considerably more mundane than those incidents we have considered until now, they nonetheless expose a significant element of shōen governance: full-fledged rebellion was only the most sensational form of a general current of communication, laid out in a cycle of petition and response and marked by signifying gestures such as oaths and flight, joining the different strata of the system. In 1304, the round on Tara began with a petition that received no reply.[50] A second followed swiftly thereafter, and like its counterpart on Yugeshima was returned with the instruction that the hyakushō should swear an oath to their complaint.[51] Complying with this directive, the hyakushō appended an oath to their next petition, whereupon the temple ordered some reduction, albeit not as extensive as the residents had wished.[52] Once again, the combination of petition and oath evoked a response.

The round commencing in the autumn of 1305, however, should warn us against an excessively programmatic reading of the communication between Tōji and its estates. Instead of oaths, we have in this instance a remarkable series of petitions.[53] During the eighth and ninth months of that year, the Tara hyakushō drafted a total of five petitions that pressed for rent exemptions. Insects and high winds, they claimed, had severely damaged the crops, and they pleaded for considerable reductions in rent. When Tōji granted them only a small exemption, they played on proprietary pride to criticize the relative meagerness of the relief offered: "The damage has been province-wide. Yet of all the domains in the province, only Tara has received such an insubstantial reduction."[54] Apparently, this ploy met with some success, for a rent record from the following spring reveals that Tōji initially offered a six koku exemption, but then allowed an additional three koku "because of complaints from the entire body of hyakushō."[55] Among the many points of interest in this episode, one is of special note for our present purpose. We learn here that negotiations with the proprietor did not necessarily proceed in a lockstep fashion, with the progression from petition to oath to flight replicated in every instance. We must conclude, then, that it was not the oath (or flight) per se that privileged the interchange and commanded the temple's response; the petition itself was a privileged instrument.

This carries us to an issue of critical importance for comprehension of the nature of the estate system. The forms and rituals I have discussed thus far constituted the spectacular gestures of the theater of protest. Yet, it must be acknowledged, their functioning presupposed a more prosaic communication, one that cast the proprietor as the proper court of appeal and set peasants in the role of subjects. It is impossible to consider the petition campaign on Tara (or anywhere else) without asking by what claim on authority the petitioners could so steadfastly challenge the temple's management of the estate. The relationship that joined ruler and ruled within Tōji's estates was clearly complex: a relationship of power, but also one that empowered. It conferred upon peasants rights of remonstrance, and, conversely, above all in these very moments of crisis, commanded the proprietor to respond to their (suitably formulated) pleas. Power within the estate system cannot therefore be conceived as a commodity that belonged to proprietors in order to be applied to the peasantry. Nor can power be thought of as an essence adhering to peasants from the solidarity of their community. Rather, the system revolved about a decentralized power that belonged to no one group, but was everywhere implicit in their interactions; power, in short, was an effect of their exchanges, an effect, indeed, nowhere perhaps more evident than in the exchanges of rebellion, which as their basic result confirmed proprietors as the seat of authority and estate residents as their subjects.[56] Our pursuit, then, must be to investigate exactly how the system gave rise to this power. And the peasant petition, or *hyakushō mōshijō*, was the vehicle by which shōen inhabitants activated the play of power. An examination of the evolution of this instrument may lead us to a better understanding of the system's central bond and, I believe, draw us very near to the core of the shōen system.

Hyakushō mōshijō

A search for the beginnings of the hyakushō mōshijō takes us back to the mid-twelfth century, when a change took place in the documents expressing agrarian unrest. Prior to that point the normal vehicle of protest was the *ge*, a form originally devised (in eighth-century law codes) for transmissions from inferior to superior within the ranks of the government but extended in the ensuing centuries to cover a variety of other communications, including bills of sale and appeals from residents of estates to their proprietors.[57] By the eleventh century *jūnin ra no ge*, or "ge from residents and others," comprised the bulk of appeals to proprietors.[58] From the middle years of the twelfth century, however, the instrument of protest began to change: hyakushō mōshijō replaced jūnin ra no ge. In place of residents, one now had a new subject of power, the hyakushō; in place of the quasi-official ge, with its provenance in the judicial codes, one had the mōshijō, an extra-codal innovation.[59] Of course, the changeover did not occur instantaneously; a period of perhaps fifty years, during which the term of identity, "*jūnin*," gave way to "hyakushō," then the ge itself succumbed to the mōshijō, was required to effect the change. Thus for a period one finds hybrid forms of the documents, such as a petition from Yugeshima Estate in which the petitioners identify themselves as hyakushō but retain the ge format, as well as a certain fluidity—two months later the residents of the same estate issued an appeal that adopted the full jūnin ra no ge format.[60] By the early years of the thirteenth century, however, the hyakushō mōshijō was firmly established as the regular document of protest.

Much has been written about the crises that beset and eventually transformed the shōen during the eleventh and (especially) twelfth centuries.[61] The emergence of this new form of petition just as the estate system was reaching maturity is emblematic of the profound changes being worked within the system, and the hyakushō mōshijō stands witness to a new bond being fashioned between proprietors and the estates. But what precisely had changed with this shift in forms?

To answer this question we need to know more about the two types of appeal. The following examples from Ōyama Estate afford us a clue to the complexion of the earlier form: Twice in the 1130s the residents of Ōyama petitioned Tōji to wield its influence to stop provincial officials from assessing corvées and other levies against the estate.[62] Among the signers of these appeals were the estate manager (*geshi*) and another resident official. This inclusion of shōen officials in the resident group is a general feature of petitions from the eleventh and early twelfth centuries; from Yugeshima Estate we have petitions that bear the seal of the resident manager, as well as a petition in which the manager stands in for the estate community.[63] Kuroda Estate and elsewhere afford additional examples.[64]

The subject matter of these petitions is also of interest. Most often they decry violations of the estate's immunities by provincial authorities (confiscated fields, sequestered crops, and the like) and seek the intercession of the proprietor to bring an end to the violations. For example, the two ge from Ōyama sought Tōji's intervention—in the first case to halt provincial officials from entering the estate to cut timber, and in the second to enforce the estate's exemption from provincial corvées. Likewise, the ge from Yugeshima all concerned attempts by provincial officials to exact what the residents claimed were illegal levies, as in a complaint from 1167 in which the residents maintained that the provincial authorities had exacted a timber levy despite the estate's history of exemption from such imposts.[65] In an earlier example, from a Tōdaiji domain, the residents (estate officials among them) of Akanabe Estate in 1053 asked the temple to persuade the court to rescind orders altering the boundaries of the estate.[66]

Other instances could be produced, but the examples cited should suffice to allow us to draw some more general inferences. Both the collectivity behind these complaints and the nature of the stated grievances suit an estate structure still set within the frame of the Heian imperial state. Though the petitioners declare themselves to be estate residents, the rhetoric of their pleas consistently point beyond the estate—to state and provincial authorities, and to the networks established by the imperial state and its bureaucracy.[67] Befitting an era in which the immunities of estates were still fluid and subject to repeated attack by provincial officials, these petitions posit and require mediating agents: shōen officers in the resident group, the proprietor with the state apparatus, and other members of the central elite. Jūnin petitions describe a bond between proprietors and estates that was indirect and riven by exterior agencies. The estate proprietor figures here not as the primary locus of authority, but as a mediator in an older and yet more basic relationship—that between the state and its public.

Hyakushō mōshijō describe a different sort of tie. One notable change is the withdrawal of estate officials from the resident group. No longer do peasant demands require the support (or mediating influence) of resident officers. With few exceptions, the petitions are exclusively hyakushō affairs; in none of the petitions from Tara and Yano cited in preceding sections, for instance, do we find local magnates among the petitioning group. In this, mōshijō give evidence to the new cast of characters the estate system brought into play. The community of officials and peasants posited as the norm in jūnin ra no ge has been split; no longer lumped together, the two groups will in the new paradigm be divided into shōkan (estate officials) and shōmin (estate inhabitants).[68] On the one hand, as many commentators have noted, local notables were incorporated within the estate order as officeholders. Thus, in the classic transaction that founded an estate, a local magnate surrenders title to his lands in return for investiture as overseer of the newly formed estate. Described repeatedly in scholarship on the shōen, this pattern has been heralded as creating a new hierarchy of interests in the land; and the disappearance of estate officials from residents' petitions is a token of this change that constituted local lords as a distinct group within the system. On the other hand, though this is less widely heralded, the new form of petition also indicates that the peasant portion of the community was set upon a new basis: invested with the right to demand relief in their own name, peasant residents were similarly being established as a distinct group within the system. The changes indicate a new technique of governance, for frequently the two groups were posed one against the other,[69] but they also point to a more far-reaching process—a redefinition of the categories by which groups within the system would be recognized. These petitions, with their recognition of an independent peasant voice, herald a crucial realignment of the relationship between proprietors and their estates.

Hyakushō mōshijō also address a different set of grievances. Certainly some complain about violations by provincial officials, but most commonly petitioners aim their protests squarely at the proprietor, demanding relief from burdensome rents or the dismissal of rapacious managers. Instead of a document designed to operate through the proprietor upon some other agency, we have a text that more often than not quarrels directly with the proprietor himself. Peasants, rather than seeing in proprietors spokesmen who would speak for their interests on another stage, now saw them as the sole audience for (and object of) their protests. And proprietors, for their part, recognized the peasant community (without officials in attendance) as a legitimate subject, empowered with rights of remonstrance. In this the hyakushō mōshijō proclaims its distinctive character as the peasantry's principal instrument in the ongoing struggle to gain concessions from proprietors. This does not mean that their predecessors of the jūnin ra no ge stage did not engage in that same struggle, for surely they did; rather, it suggests that the context within which the struggle took place had altered dramatically.

We must again pose the question: what had changed with the shift in forms? One guide is found in an early mōshijō from Arakawa Estate, which draws a distinction between hyakushō and jūnin: describing raids by armed bands which had forced the hyakushō to abandon the estate, the petitioners relate how the raiders burned and looted, "killing both hyakushō and jūnin."[70] This document suggests the reorganization occurring on estates; an undifferentiated body of "residents" was being restructured into a community of hyakushō. Working with the rich materials of Yugeshima Estate, Shimada Jirō, too, posits a change in the shōen community. Citing the congruence of the styles adopted by the signers of the estate's first hyakushō mōshijō in the 1270s with myō names appearing on a register of the estate drawn up a century earlier, he asserts that the hyakushō community on Yugeshima emerged with the reformation of the estate into myō fields in the late twelfth century.[71] Generalized, the argument proposes that upper peasants enlisted in governing the estate with appointments to myōshu *shiki* or *hyakushō shiki* were offered in return security in their possessions and the right to demand redress from the proprietor. Concurrent with this reorganization came the demise of jūnin appeals and the advent of hyakushō petitions.

This pattern, culled from the sources for Yugeshima Estate, is replicated elsewhere. On Kuroda Estate, for example, the last ge and the first mōshijō neatly bracket Tōdaiji's achievement of full immunity for the estate and the estate's consolidation into sixty-six myō.[72] The transformation of Tara Estate after Tōji gained control provides another example. Tōji's proprietorship began in 1239, but was not securely established for some time. A dispute between some leading peasants and a local warrior (a jitō), pursued before the Bakufu at the temple's urging, spurred the initial advance of its authority over the estate. A judgment in favor of the peasants, delivered by the Bakufu in 1242, earned Tōji a pledge of loyalty "down to the seventh generation" from the peasants, while a subsequent Bakufu ruling, in 1247, distinguished the respective extents of the temple and the jitō jurisdiction.[73] From this base, Tōji in the next decade carried out a thorough reformation of the estate: the fields were painstakingly surveyed, bundled together into myō fields, and apportioned out to hyakushō; and types and quantities of rents were fixed.[74] With these acts, Tōji settled its governance of the estate squarely on a compact with the hyakushō. And, as if in echo of the change, the first petitions from the self-proclaimed hyakushō of Tara followed not too long thereafter, in 1270.[75]

In each of these examples, the advent of hyakushō mōshijō succeeded a fundamental change in the body comprising the subject of

governance. Shimada explains this change in community in terms of the
increasing solidarity, strength, and organization of the peasantry. Already in the eleventh and twelfth centuries, however, the inhabitants of estates could display formidable solidarity, as the long-running campaign of peasants of Yugeshima against attempts by the provincial office to rescind the estate's immunities proves. We should therefore be wary of overly emphasizing this factor. More fundamentally, what had changed, it would seem, was not so much the cohesiveness of the community, but the manner in which it was constituted within the system.

The challenges of the twelfth century worked a revolution within the estates, reconceiving the subject of governance as a status conferred by (and ultimately dependent upon) the proprietor, and at the same time engaging the proprietor as the final guarantor of this status (and its privileges) and as court of redress. The peasant petition thus bespeaks a new type of affiliation on the estates: an interaction that cast each group as the other's audience, implicating peasants in the exercise of authority, but also involving proprietors in creating and sustaining the very subjects whom they governed.

The assertion of status and identity that heads every petition—"the hyakushō of such-and-such an estate respectfully submit"—is a marker of this new relationship, one sign that the unmediated discourse between peasants and proprietors rested on a fundamental change in the manner in which the two parties were constituted. In identifying themselves as peasants of a given estate, petitioners fulfilled a necessary condition for meaningful dialogue and affirmed that their identity was vested in the larger system. They simultaneously identified themselves as subjects of the system and named the proprietor as guarantor of their status. It is in this sense that petitions occupied a privileged place in the communication between estate and proprietor. Lodged in the instrument of protest was a discourse of mutual dependence or, what amounts to the same thing, of mutual empowerment. At the heart of their interaction, in the cycle of petition and response, one can catch a trace of the dual act of creation implicit in the new peasant-proprietor tie.

Closing in on the Subject

The task remains to characterize this tie. It is tempting to apply the language of contracts and speak, as I did above, of a compact uniting hyakushō and proprietor, in which the former was awarded various prerogatives in return for service to the latter.[76] Yet the sources do not permit such an interpretation. In all their contests with the temple, the peasants of Yano, Tara, and Yugeshima never once staked their claims on a notion of contractual rights, nor did Tōji ever consider itself as responding to the peasants out of any reciprocal "contractual" obligation—Tōji, in its own judgment, acted by fiat. To be sure, both parties acknowledged a general and abstract right of the powerless to expect succor from the powerful, and an attendant obligation on the elite to extend aid to their inferiors, but this hardly amounts to a contract.[77] In no way can a relationship expressed on the one hand through incessant pleas and threats of rebellion and on the other by summary orders be likened to a contract. But even as a purely conceptual tool through which to comprehend the underlying pattern of the relationship, a contractual view is flawed. It overlooks the cardinal feature of the peasant-proprietor tie, which is that the two parties did not enter into the interaction as equal and independent entities, but rather were ineluctably joined to a common, constituting discourse.

A theory adequate to comprehend the estate system might begin by attending to the codes that underwrote behavior. Such a theory must be capable of explaining the handful of gestures, seemingly endlessly rehearsed, that marked peasant revolt in medieval Japan. Why the insistence in both camps on duly signed petitions backed by oaths? Why the iteration of status terms like hyakushō at the opening and close of every petition? Why the stream of appeals to the proprietor? The theory must, in short, encompass the totality that made certain motions imperative while disallowing others.

It might be argued that these gestures were merely cultural givens, tropes of society at large, not of the estate system in particular. Unquestionably, as we have seen, oath swearing was commonplace, and fleeing peasants certainly antedate the arrival of the shōen. The events that mark the system's rebellions and protests followed culturally preordained modes of interaction precisely because that was how the events could be instilled with meaning and opened to interpretation.[78] But therefore to dismiss oaths and the like as so much dross enlivening but ultimately irrelevant to more substantive historical inquiry is surely premature. The estate system of medieval Japan, like any social edifice, rested on more than just rents and boundary lines. At root it posited an association between producing peasants and the central elite. Brute force, although it played a role—the climax to the Eiwa uprising on Yano Estate confirms this—did not, indeed could not, set the leading tone for the association; instead, various devices, laden with significance by the culture and the system, were marshalled in support of the intercourse. This is the message, and the import, of oaths, absconding, and petitions.

Viewing the shōen system in terms of the symbolic utterances it motivated draws attention to the formations implicit within the relations between estate residents and estate holders. Their interactions did not comprise a random aggregation of expressions/acts; again and again in the charged exchanges of rebellion and protest, an ordering mechanism can be seen at work, demanding that the actors rehearse certain forms, that they produce certain types of statements. This mechanism must be understood not as something imposed upon the intercourse, channeling and delimiting it from some exterior point, but rather as an integral part, a condition, of the dialogue: the declarations of corporate identity found in the rituals of oath swearing, the claims of status made in hyakushō mōshijō, are not just ornaments, they are the preconditions of meaningful communication.

The idea of discursive formations affords a potent means by which to venture an analysis of this communication. As explicated by Michel Foucault, a discursive formation describes the (often unarticulated) rules that make knowledge possible.[79] Repeatedly in his treatments of linguistics, clinical medicine, criminology, and sexuality, Foucault studied the rules that called disparate domains of objects, statements, and concepts into being, ordered them, and rendered them knowable. Simultaneously, he described how power operates within discourse, rejecting the notion of it as something that only represses and emphasizing instead the creativity of power, the ways it has stimulated discourse.[80] In attempting to uncover the "social grammar"—the patterns of petitioning and rebellion and oath swearing—governing the interaction of peasants and proprietors, we have been engaged in a similar task. We have been attempting, that is, to read the actions and social formations associated with the estate system in a way that is sensitive to the power relations inherent in them, to discern in the enunciations of the estate regime the forms of power and possibilities for resistance inscribed within it.

The key creative act for Tōji's estates and, I would argue, for the system as a whole was the reorganization of cultivators into the hyakushō group. We find in this act the same sort of self-reflexivity, the same dual, and conflicting, meaning of "subject" (subject as both ego and as an object of study or target of authority) that lies at the core of the discourses analyzed by Foucault. Within the shōen system, hyakushō were at once the object upon which proprietors grounded their rule and the subjects who affirmed proprietors' authority; proprietors were simultaneously guarantors of hyakushō status and oppressors who demanded taxes and tribute. Our analysis of the processes of petitioning and rebellion highlights another feature of the system: power functioned not in the single dimension of repression, but more generally, by inciting a dialogue coded in such a way that it served repeatedly to reaffirm its own validity. Peasant protest, with its stylized gestures and conventionalized script, seems to describe such a dialogue.

A characterization of the shōen, then, is not to be found in a catalog of the entities with which the system was populated. Instead of attempting to define the system as the total experience of all estates, all proprietors, and of all peasants and anyone else whose life ever touched an estate—a positivist nightmare—it seems far more fruitful to search for the system in the strands of connection running between these entities. The curious blend of defiance and pleading that characterizes hyakushō mōshijō, and the paradoxical stance of the shōen rebel, testify to a general feature of the system. In the well-rehearsed forms of the theater of protest, one can detect a relationship between cultivators and proprietors that was mutually constitutive and confirmed again and again in a flow of communication that presupposed the very categories it had created.

It is important, however, to remember that this process of mutual constitution takes place within a context of discord. Protest may require a kind of theater to reveal itself as such, the identity of peasants and proprietors both may be founded in a common system of discourse, but this does not suggest that system marks the end of conflict. Indeed, the contradictory nature of each of these relationships highlights the basically conflictual nature of discourses. It suggests that we regard discourse (or system or structure) not as specifying one unequivocal and acknowledged meaning for every action, but rather as supplying a stock of gestures that may take on different meanings in different hands. It obliges us to recognize in social actions and social formations a broader confrontation over meanings, and to acknowledge the plays of power and resistance inherent in the manner in which social groups and their interactions are conceived.

FIVE

CONCLUSION

THE DEBATE ABOUT DECLINE

S OMEWHERE we cross a line, step over a threshold," write Philip Corrigan and Derek Sayer in *The Great Arch*, an analysis of the cultural transformations (embodied in rituals and routines, in what they term "persisting practices") that made the modern nation-state something all recognize and acknowledge. But, as they concede, "it is extraordinarily difficult to say when."[1] Like Corrigan and Sayer's, my essay has been an attempt to define an institution in terms of the "persisting practices" that lent it structure, that made it cohere, that, in short, rendered it palpable to the people whose lives it informed. Corrigan and Sayer's central contention that the state is a cultural construct and that state formation must be grasped as an intricate and wide-ranging cultural revolution—and not simply as the development of a political, legal, and bureaucratic apparatus—resonates with the argument I have put forth regarding the estate system of medieval Japan. The register upon which to tally the effects of estates or states, in other words, is cultural, not institutional; a state's fundamental mode of operation, moreover, is discursive:

> States [and estate systems, I would add] . . . state; the arcane rituals of a court of law, the formulae of royal assent to an Act of Parliament, visits of school inspectors, are all statements. They define, in great detail, acceptable forms and images of social activity and individual and collective activity; they regulate, in empirically specifiable ways, much . . . of social life. Indeed, in this sense "the State" never stops talking. . . . Out of the vast range of human social capacities—possible ways in which social life could be lived—state activities more or less forcibly "encourage" some whilst suppressing, marginalizing, eroding, undermining others. . . . This has cumulative, and enormous, cultural consequences; consequences for how people identify (in many cases *have to* identify) themselves and their 'place' in the world.[2]

Rents, maps, land registers, procedures for surveying estates, guidelines governing the acceptance or rejection of petitions—these commonplace enunciations of the estate regime functioned on a very broad scale. They enshrined basic social classifications, established preferred and excluded identities, specified a vocabulary and grammar by which estate residents were to articulate their existence. But, as Corrigan and Sayer also note, state authorities or estate proprietors are hardly the only ones possessed of a voice. Cultural forms are not set forth in monologues. Like all discourses, the enunciations of (e)states inscribe oppositions; they record the exercise of power, but of a power that is itself marked by the resistances it gives rise to: the hyakushō by the figure of the rōnin; the estate by social networks that ignored it; a rhetoric of identity that sought to neutralize its subject by mapping it to a fixed and unchanging site engendering instead petitions, oaths, and flight. Like Corrigan and Sayer's State, then, the shōen system does not so much name a closed order as an open-ended process of ordering. And I have tried to highlight the contradictions underlying its attempts to prescribe order, to describe both the system's orchestration of meanings (identities, etc.) and the inevitable and uncontainable excesses produced in the process, precisely because the impossibility of achieving a structure in which everything fell into its place specifed the conditions under which the system reproduced itself, the conditions that demanded that it begin to "state" its order and never stop talking.

But, like Corrigan and Sayer's State, the shōen somewhere crossed a line, stepped over a threshold. In the opening chapter I outlined one of these thresholds: a period in the eleventh and twelfth centuries during which the context of landholding was rapidly and profoundly altered, ushering in the forms, practices, and patterned interactions characteristic of the estate system. I would here like to consider another threshold: the point at which the system of estates ceased to enunciate a social ordering. The difficulty, of course, is to determine when and how this happened. For it is not a straightforward, nor even a single, problem. Determining when the estate system ceased requires a series of prior determinations—about the nature of the system, about mechanisms of change, about the standards by which to gauge change—that necessarily affect the judgments made. Depending on one's stance on these issues, on what one chooses to emphasize, the reign of the shōen can be seen as brief or long, its formations fundamental to Japan's medieval world or peripheral to the main course of Japanese development.

The choice of an endpoint, then, can signal a particular judgment about the essential characteristics of the system. Accordingly, the debate about decline is also (and perhaps fundamentally) a debate about the system's nature. Conversely, by advocating another way of comprehending the shōen, I am calling implicitly for a different history.

Viewing the estate system as a discursive, cultural formation demands an intrinsically different approach to basic questions about historical change and causality and the relationship between order (or system) and disorder. In part the need is for a history that can reconcile synchronic analysis of the deployment and operation of a cultural formation with the diachronic question of change through time. More specifically, the challenge is to recognize the myriad ways social and cultural systems exert a powerfully determining influence on much of social existence (delimiting the boundaries of identity, governing the meaning even of resistance) without at the same time portraying them as static, fully closed structures endlessly and changelessly reproducing themselves. If, in other words, conventional harbingers of the decline of the shōen (such as rebellion) can be seen instead as "persisting practices" embodying the system (i.e., if contradiction can be enabling, not only disabling), then a new mode of explanation must be sought to account for the disappearance of estates. My aim, in bringing up the system's demise, is to address this problem. I am not interested in finding another endpoint for the system or in uncovering some hitherto overlooked mechanism that might neatly explain its decline. Instead, I hope to outline some of the considerations that need to be addressed in an analysis that seeks to engage the systemic, structural level without producing a "history that stands still."[3] And I would like to set the stage for that discussion by first considering other perspectives on the system's decline.

Encompassing two conflicting appraisals of the system's nature, existing historiography is of two minds about when to date and how to account for the system's end, with one influential group of scholars arguing that the system died out in the fourteenth century and the other holding out for the sixteenth century.[4] The former thesis, first advanced in the 1950s by Matsumoto Shinpachirō, but identified chiefly with Nagahara Keiji, who has been its most forceful advocate, contends that in the wars of the Northern and Southern courts (*Nanbokuchō*, 1336–1392) the estate system crumbled.[5] Pressed from without by the incursions of warriors, but also from within by economic advances that undermined the entire estate-based economic order, the system faltered. The tumults of the Nanbokuchō era wrote an end to the political privilege of the traditional estate-holding elite, displacing their hegemony with one in which warriors predominated; at the same time, longer running economic trends jeopardized the economic basis of the system. Increased use of money, the spread of new rice strains and new agricultural techniques, and greater regional specialization and the growth of markets from the mid-thirteenth century onward spelled the end of the landholding patterns and economic linkages that defined the estate system.[6] This version relies,

then, on a belief that shōen were an economic and political construct belonging to Japan's antiquity; it understands estate holding and the authority structure of estate proprietorship as the antithesis of the warrior lordship (reaching maturity in the fourteenth century under the Ashikaga shoguns) and of trade and commercialization. The shōen system is thereby aligned with a mode of production characterized by an imperial-aristocratic political apparatus and an autarkic agrarian economy. Politically, the system is seen to rely on the mantle of the imperial court, and therefore to be vulnerable to any diminishing of that authority. Economically, it is portrayed as heeding an imperative for self-sufficiency. By this reasoning, each estate comprised a self-contained and self-sufficient entity providing for itself and its proprietor; while, for their part, proprietors amassed networks of estates to supply their every want without recourse to markets and exchange. The market-oriented, commodified economy developing in the Kamakura and Nanbokuchō eras simultaneously rendered this doctrine untenable and made room for new forms and new holders of wealth. As the economy developed and warriors gained political power, the twin telltales of decay in the system make their appearance: widespread and growing arrears in estate rents and the usurpation of local authority by warriors bespeak the end of the shōen.

The fourteenth century thus emerges as an era of some moment. It marks not only the demise of the shōen, but represents as well the shift from a classical, state-centered system of landholding to a medieval, i.e., feudal, political economy; the estates, archetypes of an earlier mode of production, in effect are done in by the onslaught of the medieval era—understood to signify a regime founded upon independent local lordship. Within the narrative of decline, then, lurks another story—the rise of local lordship. Indeed, the distinctive feature of this approach is not so much its recital of how economic development subverted the estate order as the link it draws between the demise of the shōen and the triumph of feudal lordship; it might be argued, in fact, that the latter narrative is the vital one and that the decline of the estate system really is of only peripheral interest. For a key effect of this line of scholarship is to associate Japan's middle ages with Europe's by emphasizing the growth of military lordship. By plotting the decline of the shōen as the overthrow of a large landholding nobility by a newly emergent military elite, it draws a parallel between the evolution of Japanese society and one of the stock narratives of feudal development in Europe, and corroborates the world historical significance of Japan's past.[7]

The second group of scholars—identified most often with Araki Moriaki, its most outspoken and controversial exponent, but including as well Kuroda Toshio and Amino Yoshihiko—postpones the final fall of the system until the end of the sixteenth century.[8] To these historians the shōen itself is a medieval form, and the sixteenth century, not the fourteenth, describes the end of the estates and the transition to a new economic order. They take issue with the first view both for its characterization of the estate economy and for its emphasis on the rise of lordship. They accuse its advocates, first, of "post-dating" economic advances—of, in effect, posing as developments of the late thirteenth and fourteenth centuries trends that were already present in the twelfth. Markets, regional specialization, etc., though certainly not as prevalent as they would be two centuries later, are a feature of the shōen system from the outset, not a symptom of its decline; up to a point (which arrived in the sixteenth century) the system, they contend, could and did subsume the sorts of economic currents that Nagahara and others present as undermining it. This second group of scholars rejects as well the first group's insistence on the disruptive effects of warrior power. Individual estates may have been subject to warrior assaults from the Kamakura period on, but the basic forms of the estate system persisted for centuries thereafter. The challenge presented by warriors was not to the estate form of landholding; indeed, as estate administrators, land stewards, or provincial constables, warriors depended on the estate for their own livelihood. The Kamakura warrior who usurped elements of a proprietor's authority, or the Muromachi constable who claimed a one-half share of all estate revenues from the province he commanded, did not, proponents of this view claim, fundamentally alter the setup of the system. By the fifteenth century warriors in many instances may have supplanted traditional aristocratic and ecclesiastical proprietors or wrested control of large portions of estates, but this does not mean that they inaugurated new methods of organizing and exploiting the land. The rise of local lordship takes place within, not against, the estate framework and indeed relies upon the imperial power structure that supported the system. Thus, even though individual estates disappeared and certain proprietors failed, the essence of the system remained: the estate persisted as a unit of landholding and as a framework for the extraction of rents. From the twelfth century until the cadastral surveys by Toyotomi Hideyoshi literally drew the map anew in the sixteenth century, the shōen system remained the basis of land possession.

In this view, then, shōen constituted a method of economic exploitation in which all of medieval Japan's elites—warriors as well as absentee proprietors—participated. The defining feature of Japan's medieval era, in fact, is seen to be its commingling of small-scale feudal lordship and large-scale landownership sponsored and supported by

the imperial state. Local lordship was not the antithesis of shōen proprietorship but, rather, its partner, coexisting with it throughout the
medieval era. For this reason the end of the system should not be
understood as the ascendancy of local lords over estate holders, but
as the simultaneous overthrow of both groups and both modes of
rule. Accordingly, the end is sought in peasant struggle against both
local lords and shōen proprietors. The narrative of economic development offered in the first account is here recouped, somewhat de-
layed, to demonstrate how centuries of rising class antagonisms culminated in the uprisings of the sixteenth century (such as the Ikkō
Ikki), sweeping aside the estate system and Japan's medieval order
and clearing a space in which class alignments and mechanisms of
economic exploitation could be reformulated, as they were over the
first few decades of the Tokugawa era. As with the first approach,
therefore, this telling of the tale contains an important subplot. In rejecting the notion that the rise of local lordship was inimical to the
estate order, and arguing instead for the continuing vitality of the imperial state and traditional elites, this approach also seeks to reject the
parallels drawn between Japanese and European experience. To advocates of this view the shōen system, incorporating local lordship
within an imperial state structure, presents a distinctly Asian variant
of a feudal mode of production.

The antithetical conclusions the two groups reach obscure basic
harmonies in the way they approach the system. Despite their evident disagreements, the two share a particular posture and a common problematic. First, they position themselves alongside the proprietors and adopt a distinctly top-down perspective. For example,
by arguing the fate of the estate system in terms of the rise of military
lordship versus the continued strength of civil and ecclesiastical
elites, both approaches indicate that the important question is,
"Which elite dominated?" Since, moreover, the specific argument
about shōen contains a general argument about the course of Japanese history, both approaches lend themselves to a historiography
that locates historical significance in the fate of an era's ruling groups.
In the first instance, this is manifest in the criteria used to judge decline: dwindling rents and increasing difficulties in managing estates
are precisely the sorts of standards by which proprietors might measure the deterioration of their holdings.[9] (Whether residents, for instance, would experience the same situation as decline is another
matter entirely, and one that cannot be engaged in this account.) The
second approach accords the system a more general, abstract existence and therefore avoids any direct connection between falling
rents and the demise of the shōen. Still, the system is identified with

the articulation of managerial interests or with the command structures through which proprietors governed the extraction of wealth from their estates. And though peasant struggle provides the force that in the last instance leads to the overthrow of the shōen, this view has difficulty comprehending the relationship of estate residents to the system unless reified as class struggle or false consciousness. The result in both cases is an emphasis on changes in the administrative superstructure (although these are likely to be read as symptoms of changes in the determining economic base). In the first view, warriors ruptured the administrative fabric; in the second, they wove themselves into its pattern. Both, however, agree that the marker of change, hence, by implication, the system's essence, can be located in its administrative and fiscal patterns: significant changes are those which upset this structure.

If one of the effects of this positioning is to focus attention on administrative patterns, it also works to restrict the range of phenomena deemed critical to comprehending the system. For both schools of thought on the shōen share a common understanding of the problem: they privilege the economic. Their analyses conceive of the estate system as essentially economic in nature; it is the embodiment of a specific, narrowly construed mode of production. Pursued in order to place Japanese history on the world stage, the controversy over which mode (ancient or feudal, European or Asiatic) fits the case results, I believe, in an abstracted and impoverished view of the estate system. Rents, by this standard, are simply rents (or rather, measures of the amount of surplus extracted); maps and land registers are useful only as indices of landownership and class structure; other phenomena, such as oaths and rituals, are scarcely thematized at all, save as examples of the ideological obfuscation of reality. One is left with the impression that the shōen system can be described fully by the class character of its ruling group and by the nature of the method used to organize and extract the fruits of production. Proprietorial interests and relations between peasants and proprietors are thus refracted—and reduced—through an economic lens, to become mere reflections of a basic and determining economic relationship.

This endeavor, pursued in the name of historical materialism, results in a severely restricted understanding of the material life of the system and its inhabitants. To be sure, proprietors' main concern may have been with the revenues their estates could produce, but viewing the system solely as a mechanism for extracting rents simply recapitulates that vantage point and obscures the complex and conflicted processes it subsumes. Such an approach makes the shōen into a seamless edifice, imposing sameness where there is difference and dictating single meanings for actions, like uprisings, that in fact contain multiple possibilities. To privilege the economic is, in fact, to privilege an exceedingly abstract conception of economic causality over analysis of the interactions that informed the everyday experience of shōen residents. And it precludes investigation of precisely those areas that might offer insights into that experience.

More or less explicitly, my study has been a critique of views which attempt to approach the system of the estates on economic grounds. The system's diversity cannot be reduced to variations on a single economic type or confined to a specific pattern of land possession; its structures and its modalities of power defy narrowly economic construction. And there is little to be gained from such an endeavor. My concern with the system's language, with the images it produced, with its mundane artifacts, is prompted by a belief that these are not just reflections of an exterior reality—mirrors that reflect back the mode of production embodied by the system—but are themselves constitutive of the system's realities. Maps and land registers, I have argued, do not just record the lie of the land, they in some sense create it as a socially useful and meaningful object. In the same vein, peasant petitions and oath-swearing rituals are not merely echoes of discontent, but are constitutive of the notions that defined peasant and proprietor and ordered their relationship. Uprisings, too, lose much of their complexity and significance if they are viewed simply as outcries against the exactions of authority or plugged into a transhistorical teleology that prescribes for them a predetermined meaning. I have emphasized the rhetoric of status or the language of rebellion over the supposed socioeconomic realities of class or class conflict in order to show that terms like hyakushō or the forms and patterns of rebellion are themselves important determinants of social reality. These, as much as rent collectors, shaped everyday experience and defined the system within which estate residents lived. The very language of the system, in short, was part of its repertoire of power: the signifying practices by which and in which the system of estates was constituted as a cultural order.

My aim in all of this has been to suggest another paradigm for conceptualizing the shōen, one that puts back some of the complexity other approaches obscure. The basic argument of this study has been that to comprehend the estate system one must shift registers and approach it not on an economic or political level, but more broadly as a cultural system. Of course, culture in this usage does not refer to those bastions of value that are taken to embody the "best" in society—the "highest" art or the most refined creations of thought. The term is to be understood in a wider sense, something akin to Raymond Williams's "whole way of life" of a society, the "meanings and values implicit in a particular way of life . . . not only in art and learning but in institutions and ordinary behaviour,"[10] or in the sense proposed by Clifford Geertz:

> [Culture is the] ordered system of meaning and of symbols, in terms of which social interaction takes place. . . . Culture is the fabric of meaning in terms of which human beings interpret their experience and guide their action . . . .[11]

Cultures in this sense resemble discourses. Both presume "complexes of signs and practices which organize social existence and social reproduction. In their structured, material presence, [they] are what give differential substance to membership in a social group or class or formation, which mediate an internal sense of belonging, an outward sense of otherness."[12] Understanding cultures as systems that organize meaning and significance—further understanding meaning and significance as fundamental vehicles for the interpolation of power relations in everyday life—cultural analysis looks generally to the practices by which meanings are created and communicated, and seeks to determine the conditions under which this communication can take place. Concern with culture thus brings to the fore questions of meaning—not, it must be stressed, with the intent of identifying what things mean or uncovering how ideas and events reflect (or effect) some hidden community of understanding. The aim, that is, is not simply to describe the system of differences, the conceptual grid, that produces a given set of meanings, but to understand how the grid itself is produced, how power relations inflect its workings to arrange that certain meanings will naturally attach themselves to certain terms. The cultural analysis I have in mind seeks in particular to identify the struggles through which certain meanings are produced and deployed (while others are suppressed) and to show how the assumptions that endow actions and institutions with significance are arrived at, structured, and upheld.

Culture (and the estate system) must therefore be seen as a production, not a ground. It takes shape as a contest delimited, on the one hand, by attempts (most prominently by elites, but all social groups engage in the activity) to specify identity, action, and experience so that they communicate an unambiguous significance, and, on the other hand, by the impossibility of absolutely controlling the production of meanings. Not only do different groups put a different spin on things (peasants, as we have seen, used oaths in ways not envisioned by proprietors), but even within a given system the stability of meanings cannot be taken for granted (even if this is what its inhabitants strive for). Meanings are not static or problem free, and efforts to establish a single meaning for an action (so that, for instance, peasant rioting can unerringly be taken as sign of a subsistence crisis) can only proceed by excluding other possibilities (e.g., that rioting might signal an outraged moral economy); in the process, however, the excluded possibility becomes a condition of the authorized meaning. Any of the oppositions that structure the discourse of the estate system—resident/wanderer, estate/not-estate, rice paddy/dry field, rent-bearing/tax-exempt, etc.—can be seen to operate in precisely this manner. In each, the first and dominant term relies on the suppression of the second; and to proclaim the first normal and the second abnormal is simply to reiterate the reliance of the first on the second. Thus estate residents argue their status via the figure of the wanderer (see Chapter 2); maps and boundary markers seek to establish the estate as a fully enclosed, self-contained realm, but can do so only by marking it off from something outside, thereby belying the self-unity those devices claim; and land registers that turn iron or silk into the produce of so much paddy—as if they, like rice, grew out of the ground—record the contradictions of an ideology that equated productivity with rice, even as it relied on a host of nonagrarian products. Critically, this problem arises not only between the terms of a discourse, but within a single term. Creating a hyakushō, for example, who belonged to a particular estate, who, indeed, was "named" by its fields, meant that another sense of the term, one that established the hyakushō as a generic public subject, had to be jettisoned. At the same time, proclaiming the "new" hyakushō to be the authorized subject of the estate system kept alive something of the earlier meaning. Contradictory meanings—a specific one that completes the power circuit, giving proprietors subjects to people their estates and rule over, and a general one that reaches beyond the estate system—confront each other within the same term. What I have been calling the "system" or "structure" or "order" of the estates is, in the broadest sense, the attempt to manage this confrontation so that certain meanings become the norm and the alternative possibilities unthinkable; and the reproduction of the system is intimately tied to the impossibility of ever completing this task.

To observe, therefore, that there is system or order to a culture is not to suggest that it is anchored to an unchanging and undisputed grid of shared understandings, but rather to note how power relations inflect processes of producing and policing meanings. Looking at the estate system in this light means, first, attending to the networks of meaning that organized the use of its political and economic institutions and that interpreted their significance to the people whose lives they informed. Further, it means recognizing these networks as an important field for the expression of political, economic, and other types of power. Interpreting this field demands serious consideration of the conflicts that are patched over in the act of attributing a specific significance to the estate or to residence, to kuji or to myō. This does not, however, imply that the aim of analysis should be to "crack" the cultural code in order to gain access to the economic and social base which produced it and which it obscures. The task of interpretation is instead to detail how and to what ends these networks of meaning functioned, and how their functioning shaped, structured—even produced—social existence. The system's documents and practices must not be taken simply as so much fungible evidence—data, which, suitably manipulated, can be coaxed into revealing socioeconomic realities. Rather, they must be regarded and read as texts whose form must be valued equally with their content.

Throughout this study I have sought to show that the documents of the shōen system must be inspected as much for how they say something as for what they say, and that the discursive strategies embedded in their very language comprise a vital part of the system. Peasant petitions, for example, have much more to say than that peasants objected to proprietors' exactions. The language of petitions and the symbolic practices within which they were embedded—i.e., those features that constitute the form of appeals—also tell of the nature and operation of authority. Indeed, language and ritual do much more than "tell" of the nature of authority. One of the central concerns of this study has been to show that symbolic practices stand in a much more complex relation to the "real" than is generally allowed. They reflect the material conditions of existence, but at the same time construct them. Analysis of the estate system demands that neither be assigned priority, that the system be viewed as the expression not of a determining mode of production, but of a complex interaction between material conditions and the ways estate residents and others experienced, defined, and explained them.

Viewing the estates as a cultural form, then, draws attention to the relational character of the system, to the fact that it does not represent a stable mass, but a "field of struggle," an arena defined by the confrontation of competing practices and constructions.[13] The system I have described cannot be identified solely with the creations of proprietors; nor can its "essence" be seen to reside in a preexisting system of villages onto which proprietors grafted their rule. It was not a set of rules imposed from above nor a group of dispositions welling up from below, but a field negotiated by competing perspectives. The notion of space set forth in proprietors' maps and land registers vied with a rendering of space that contested the boundaries drawn by authority; likewise, the easy circulation in status between hyakushō and rōnin resisted the proprietorial identification of the system's subjects with residence. It is here, in this rivalry, that we may locate the system—not as a structure which expels contradiction and installs harmony, but as a field delimited by sites of conflict. In the shōen, key notions such as boundaries, rents, and hyakushō mark these sites. Terms and concepts that in proprietors' rent books seem to anchor the estates to one particular configuration of the field, they prove capable of supporting radically different constructions. In the end what distinguishes the estate system, what, generally, defines its distinction from other manorial regimes, is the set of figures upon which the competing constructions focus. This is not, I must add, to say that the estate system can be defined simply by the presence (singly or in conjunction) of myō and hyakushō, kuji and nengu, oaths and petitions. These features are not sufficient to define, in any specificity, the shōen system. Rather, what reveals the shape and operation of the system's power structures is the way these terms do multiple duty, describing points of danger, of possible slippage between discourses, and not islands of security. This, too, is what reveals it to be an open-ended structure, not a closed totality.

Just as there was more than one way of understanding an estate border or defining a hyakushō, there was, in effect, more than one "estate system"—as many, potentially, as there were possible meanings for its key terms. Between the constructions promulgated from on high and those developed from below there is invariably a gap, a contested space of possibility. As Peter Stallybrass and Allon White observe,

> It would be wrong to imply that "high" and "low" . . . are equal and symmetrical terms. When we talk of high discourses—literature, philosophy, statecraft, the languages of the Church and the University—and contrast them to the low discourses of a peasantry, the urban poor, subcultures, marginals, the lumpen-proletariat, colonized peoples, we already have two "highs" and two "lows." History seen from above and history seen from below are irreducibly different.[14]

To say that the two perspectives are irreducibly different is not, however, to suggest that they are arbitrarily different or wholly alien to one another. Indeed, the premise of this study is that the dislocations one encounters in passing from "high" to "low" and vice versa—from the account books, maps, and judgments that register the proprietor's perspective to the practices in which we may read something of the concerns of estate residents—are somehow associated, and that the gap can be exploited for analysis. My contention is that these dislocations allow access to the fundamental workings of the cultural field that comprised the system, for the conditions of possibility underwriting the system are found precisely in the contradictory interplay of practices and the constructions which underlie them.

This mode of access demands a very different construction of the estate system from that propounded in most accounts. The system explicated in this study is a construct framed by contradictions. This, it might be objected, is nothing new, for the theme of conflict and contradiction is certainly a familiar one. Yet conflict is always conceived of as occurring between integral entities: between, for example, proprietors and peasants, each constituting an independent, fully realized group; or between two modes of production. And contradiction is typically seen as disabling. By this reasoning, manifest contradictions, as in peasant rebellion, must be taken as signs of dysfunction; they are the antithesis of system, that which checks conflict and resolves contradictions. By contrast I would emphasize that contradiction is the core of the generative process that (re)produces the system—that constitutes peasants and proprietors and defines each in relation to the other. Repeatedly, conceptual categories central to the shōen prove to be founded in contradiction. The idea of the estate itself, for example, partakes both of representations which portray it as a bounded whole and of practices that continually transgress those boundaries. Likewise, the transformation of peasants into estate residents turned upon casting wanderers as the antithesis of the system's subjects, thereby placing transgression at the heart of the definition of its subjects. The system, in short, embraces its own subversion, not as a symptom of its (eventual) inviability, but as its enabling condition.

In a sense, then, this study has described conflicting estate systems, just as, seen from opposite ends, there are two highs and two lows to any hierarchy. Or rather, it has sought to produce a new conception of the estate system as none other than the constellation of discursive practices that attempted to elide the gap between the proprietary gaze and peasant practices in order to effect coherence. At the core of the estate system we have found conflict and contradiction; yet these did not, as teleological models of history would have it, produce synthesis and progress. Rather, and shōen uprisings provide the perfect example, these founding tensions incited a flow of discourse within which the system was constituted and structured.

. . . . .

It is time, then, to return to the question with which I began: How and where does one draw the line? To ask this question is, of course, to pose a series of other problems: How is one to gauge change in the shōen system if not by the disappearance of a certain configuration of institutions or the demise of a particular mode of production—if not, that is, by declining rents, the breakup of myō, the displacement of traditional proprietors? What constitutes change in a discursive formation or cultural system understood as a mechanism that regulates the meaning of institutions and practices? A common critique of discursive analysis (and, by extension, cultural analysis that makes use of the idea of discourse) is that it constructs unchanging, self-referential totalities, and thereby removes itself from history. By insisting on radical discontinuities between discourses, such analysis, critics assert, offers no sense of how one discursive formation might give way to another, or of how social change in general might take place.[15] If all gestures are already scripted, and if all possible statements and thoughts must conform to the conditions that produced prior statements, how can a system ever do other than reproduce itself?

My response to these questions begins with the insistence that discursive formations are not totalizing abstractions or perfect monoliths. Discourse does not name a fully closed circuit in which every gesture, every resistance, serves only to reinscribe the status quo. Discursive formations, rather, are inherently part of social and cultural practice; even as they organize and structure practice, discourses are produced and shaped by that practice. Any society is thus constituted in and through discourses that are continually being negotiated, formed and reformed in the interplay of social groups.[16] To regard them as abstracted from practice, directing everyday life but untouched by it, is to subscribe to the illusion of the powerful, to proclaim as "nature" that which is eminently man-made.

A discursive analysis does not preclude the possibility of change, but it does demand that the process of change be reconceived. Instead of holding to an evolutionary model, in which events such as the demise of the estate system can be attributed to changes quietly and inevitably accumulating over the years, discursive analysis characterizes change as a much more haphazard and radical matter. And instead of latching on to one or two institutions or social groups (that can be identified as, say, harbingers of new classes or precursors of new institutional arrangements), it looks to the general connective tissue that joins institutions and social groups into particular constellations, that underwrites certain configurations of identity, that sanctions certain types of authority.

This is to suggest, first, that one cannot rely on the patient accretion of numerous small adjustments to account for and produce major historical changes. Such adjustments (renegotiations) occur constantly, but it takes a linear narrative, selecting, sorting, and orienting the changes, to guarantee that they will add up to something. But this, as I have argued, is a model of change that removes us from history, that seeks nothing so much as to abolish contingency and disorder and repetition from everyday existence in order to show that things *had* to turn out as, in hindsight, one knows they did. The history of the shōen demonstrates the need for a different model of how cultural formations change. On the one hand, change is not hard to find. Fields, rents, estate boundaries were constantly in flux; local arrangements between estate residents, managers, and proprietors were continually renegotiated; individually and in aggregate, estates were always in motion. On the other hand, it is difficult to claim that all this flux and variety, apparently directionless at the surface of the system, can be reconciled at some deeper level with a basically progressive model. A fundamentally repetitive movement, with certain patterns of interaction, certain configurations of authority, repeated throughout wides spans of time and space, underlies the system (seems, indeed, a condition of its "system-hood"). And such a pattern of repetition, with constant yet chaotic variation, cannot be accommodated to a mode of historical explanation (common to the two schools of thought just discussed) that proceeds by aligning changes in chronological sequence and insisting that they chart a course to the next era.

As a corollary, then, one must recognize that the appearance of the "new" (in the guise, say, of new social groups or new economic and political arrangements) does not necessarily bespeak the advent of a new cultural formation. Nor, conversely, does the persistence of "old" elements necessarily deny that radical structural transformations have taken place. Since a great deal of the work of culture takes place independently of its observable apparatus,[17] changes in the apparatus can be fully encompassed by the culture as constituted, and important changes in the cultural system may occur despite an apparent lack of observable change. Precisely this transpired, I argued earlier, in the shōen of the eleventh and twelfth centuries; the cultural, political, and economic structure changed markedly without similarly refashioning the institutions or terminology of estate-holding; estates, proprietors, hyakushō—none a new element—remained the apparatus of estate-holding, but each took on different significance as it was positioned within a new grid. Such a history, frustrating expectations of a correspondence between institutional change and structural shifts, demonstrates the shortcomings of a simple historical model in which the cumulative weight of events will eventually override cultural reproduction. This model, which relies on repeatedly uncovering new elements to explain change, runs the risk of obscuring transformations that involve the rearticulation of existing components. Neither, however, can a purely structural model in which events are inevitably reinscribed in a determining structure (therefore requiring some sort of outside shock to dislodge the system) do justice to a reality that is both historical and structural—a reality for which both teleological and determinist explanations are unacceptable. A system such as that of the estates forces one to realize, as Marshall Sahlins has put it, that "history is culturally ordered, differently so in different societies, according to meaningful schemes of things. The converse is also true: cultural schemes are historically ordered, since to a greater or lesser extent the meanings are revalued as they are practically enacted."[18] The crucial question, therefore, is not the simple one, "How or why does change occur?" but the rather more complicated one, "Under what circumstances can the renegotiation of meanings (i.e., change, which never ceases) produce a general rearticulation of the cultural scheme?"

Applied to the present case, this reasoning suggests that we look for the end of the shōen not in a process of erosion by which estates and proprietors faded gradually into oblivion, but in a shift in context. Just as the advent of the estate system did not proceed from the slow maturation of the estate form, but from a thoroughgoing reconstruction of the political, social, and cultural networks within which estates were constituted, the system's end came with another reconfiguration of the realm. Like the earlier shift, this one, too, is to be gauged by a displacement of the discourses that structured identity, underwrote landholding, and mediated the relationship between ruler and subject. To account for this shift, therefore, one needs to account for the particular dialectic between structural reproduction and systemic transformation that produced a general rewriting of the sign systems within which the shōen were placed. Since, moreover, we have rejected teleological or deterministic renderings of history, no single cause, no unified story line, can recapitulate this process of change. In contrast to the two views outlined earlier, both of which rely implicitly on a mode-of-production narrative, for example, our analysis can have no recourse to a determining base, no confidence that the economic will spin off appropriate social and cultural formations. Instead, one is left with a history that proceeds along many unpredictable avenues at once, and takes shape, in the end, as the conjunction of myriad disparate elements.

To say that the process of change is unpredictable does not imply that its course is entirely contingent. For instance, a term like hyakushō connotes a number of possible relationships between ruler and ruled, but that range is not infinite, and usage of the term, even in a new discursive/cultural space, will still be conditioned by the range of meanings ascribed to it in the earlier formation. Nengu and kuji, likewise, carried certain economic and political meanings, and any new significances they might assume in a different context are constrained, at least to some extent, by the scope of their previous usage. As Pierre Bourdieu has observed, the social practices in which meanings are produced and enacted must respond to "the past conditions which have produced the principle of their production."[19] The same is true of the structures embodied in practice. They, too, are constrained by the histories incorporated in the principles of their production. Thus, if the shōen system can be seen to impose a structural logic on the practices subsumed in terms like hyakushō, nengu, and kuji so that they would tend to reproduce the conditions of their enactment, in the same manner the system must engage the practices that take place under these names, practices that revaluate the terms, appropriating their meanings, and, within limits, creating for them new possibilities. Any structural transformation, any rewriting of sign systems, must observe a double constraint: it must be consistent with the logic of this process of practical invention, which itself operates within limits (or dispositions) imposed by structure.

Hence the necessity of conceiving of systems as fundamentally unstable. Only because meanings are not fixed and certain, because every element in a discourse encompasses a range of possibilities, can the process of cultural reproduction produce something different from itself. Ultimately, perhaps, the shortcomings of existing descriptions of the decline of the estates can be traced to their treatment of the system as a fully coherent entity, a monolith to be worn away by economic and political currents foreign to it. These descriptions posit something like an "age of the shōen" in which competing practices had been vanquished by the triumphant estate form—otherwise the shōen could not have defined a "system," let alone one central to Japan's medieval era. Such reasoning, I believe, quickly leads to an impasse. Without some notion of the open-ended nature of the estate system, it is impossible to comprehend either the diversity of the shōen economy, which from the outset incorporated many elements held to be symptoms of its demise, or how restless warriors and rebellious peasants could for some three centuries be part of the system, only in the fifteenth and sixteenth centuries to become antithetical to it. It is difficult, as well, to understand where the resources for change are to be found, unless outside of the system (but then how could it be so central to Japan's medieval world?) or in some suprahistorical economic or other cause.[20] On the other hand, by recognizing the system as a field of struggle, a field continually being renegotiated in practice, one realizes that the materials out of which it was constructed can be put to other uses. The system can be seen to harbor within it the possibility of other, different configurations, and practices which assert the latent or suppressed meanings of key terms can be the basis for a radical rearticulation of the social grammar which

links and activates those terms. (Re)affirming alternative understandings of the vocabulary of subjectivity or community, (re)instating
suppressed relations of authority or relationships to production and
to the land, such practices can be the means by which the estate system was written out of existence *in its own terms*. To press the point,
for this is where my analysis departs most significantly from standard
accounts, the system's end is to be found in the conjunction of a number of developments that rearticulated key notions underwriting the
estates. This restatement of a vocabulary consonant with the estate
system secured the reproduction of its structures, but in a transformed form. It produced a new system of discourses about authority, about subjectivity, and about the land, which refashioned the
realm, setting out new possibilities for warrior power and peasant
practice and leaving in it no meaningful place for the shōen.

By the close of the sixteenth century, new discourses were manifestly in place. Oda Nobunaga's rhetoric of *kōgi* (public good)
and *tenka* (lit., "under heaven," i.e., the realm) resurrected a public
and imperial formulation of political authority, but in the mouth of a
warlord it worked to significantly different ends. Similarly, Toyotomi Hideyoshi's nationwide cadastral surveys revived the concept of
a uniform national domain to put a new face on the land.[21] And in
peasants who named themselves "public hyakushō" (*kōgi no onbyakushō*) or were identified as imperial subjects (*hyakushō wa ōson*),
not as the "hyakushō of such-and-such an estate," we may note an
older sense of the term resurfacing to articulate a distinctly different
mode of conceptualizing identity.[22] When, therefore, the house code
of the Rokkaku family (1567) proclaimed that "customs of the estate"
(*shōrei*) would no longer be consulted, we must recognize an emblem
of a larger shift.[23] Within these constructions, the estate is no longer
a referent; the system has been displaced.

It is easier, of course, to remark the presence of a new articulation
of society or a new language of identity than it is to describe its appearance or to divine the process by which it laid claim to authority.
In this respect the era of Nobunaga and Hideyoshi provides a convenient anchor and a sense of ending—their formulations stake out a
discursive space distinctly different from that of the shōen and hence
furnish a sense of ending. Yet the displacement that denotes the end
of the estate system must, I believe, be set in the fifteenth, not the
sixteenth, century. For the elements out of which Nobunaga and others fashioned the discourses and ideologies that would envelope the
operation of power in Tokugawa Japan underwrote as well the warfare that engulfed Japan during and after the Ōnin War (1467–77).
And the common condition of the appearance, both of Nobunaga's

and Hideyoshi's "conceptual cocoon in whose dark center [early modern] power could hide" and of the "naked power" of military might that subtended lordship in the Sengoku age,[24] was the displacement of the discourses that underwrote the estate system and of the power relations they authorized. The century-long conflagration ignited by the Ōnin War laid waste to traditional centers of authority, but the advent of this warfare presupposed a new logic of society and a new "fabric of meaning" by which to interpret the significance of actions.

Already by the middle of the fifteenth century the estate system was being dislodged by a language that substituted the village for the estate, "public good" for the estate proprietor, and a generic peasant-subject for the hyakushō. As this suggests, the shift that marks the system's end must be registered on several levels. In a number of disparate areas a language implicit in the discourses of the shōen but marginalized by its power structures was resuscitated, and in combination this language and the concepts it contained outlined a systemic break. They articulated an altered social grammar and, therefore, a shift in the mechanisms that accorded value to social acts and social formations.

Like the one that inaugurated the system, this second shift entailed a redrawing of spatial and social boundaries. The contiguous domains Miyagawa Mitsuru recognizes as characteristic of fifteenth-century lordship, and the village communities that underlay these areas, presumed a very different sense of boundaries—physical and social—from those that subtended the estate system.[25] Tōji's last survey of Tara Estate (1429) reveals something of this change. Organized about villages (*mura*), the survey anticipates Tara's early-modern metamorphosis (the estate is next surveyed as part of Hideyoshi's nationwide effort in 1588) into Tara-no-shō mura, itself an amalgam of four separate communities, one in each of the valleys over which the estate had extended; and, as Amino notes, this reconception of the estate as distinct mura is implicit in peasant uprisings and disputes from the latter half of the century.[26] The physical rearrangement of Tara into mura thus found echoes in other areas of peasant life, suggesting that these mura constituted not just places on the map, but new social spaces as well. Hints of this new space are present in village codes that proclaimed the village's juridical autonomy or enforced participation in village councils.[27] In an oath from 1458, for example, residents of Kuze Estate adopted a new style for naming themselves,[28] and this change accompanied a break in the composition of the estate's resident group. According to Kurushima Noriko, in the fifteenth century Kuze's myōshu were frequently moneylenders or petty lords who had purchased property in the estate, not the upper peasants and low-level estate functionaries their predecessors had been.[29]

In line with these rearticulations of identity, one of the most telling indications of the social realignment in peasant communities is a change in nomenclature. In the fifteenth century a new kind of hyakushō, *onbyakushō*, meaning literally "honorable peasant," predominated peasant self-descriptions. After 1407, all peasant petitions from Ōyama Estate were issued by self-professed onbyakushō; the same is true of other Tōji holdings, and Fujiki Hisashi indicates that the pattern is a general one.[30] Formed by the addition of the honorific *"on"* to hyakushō, the term suggests an altered valence for hyakushō identity. The honorific prefix carrying the weight of "public" or "state," its addition has the effect, as Miyagawa Mitsuru notes, of attaching an abstract public stature to the hyakushō.[31] Against the particularizing valences of the term hyakushō in the discourses of the estate system (which, as we have seen, always used the term in a link between identity and residence on a particular estate), onbyakushō asserts a status for estate residents that does not rest on that link with an estate or its proprietor. Invoking the sense of the hyakushō present in pre-estate system discourses, onbyakushō repeats, with crucial differences, the terminology of the estate system.

This change in peasant self-designation heralds as well a change in the conceived nature of authority. In the language of fifteenth-century daimyo one finds an understanding and assertion of authority very different from those of the estate system. Asakura Toshikage's *Seventeen Articles* (an exemplary daimyo code, composed between 1471 and 1481), for instance, assert a vision of rule that has none of the self-imposed boundaries of proprietary authority: his vision encompasses all the people within his realm and his claim to rule does not derive, and is not bound by, proprietary rights.[32] His stipulations that no fortresses other than the Asakura family's own be allowed in the domain and that overseers be placed in each village anticipate the Tokugawa order, but proffer as well a conception of the domain very different from the finely parceled spaces of the shōen system. Likewise, Asakura's order that "trustworthy and able" inspectors should be sent throughout the domain three times each year to hear the complaints of the people (*domin hyakushō*) conceives a generic populace to match the lord's broad claims to rule.[33] The Rokkaku, a powerful daimyo family based in Ōmi Province, offer another example of the shifts that these reconceptions of authority spurred. The spread of their influence upset proprietors' authority and peasant practices. In a series of disputes examined by Hitomi Tonomura, the Rokkaku over the latter half of the fifteenth century assumed jurisdictions formerly held by estate proprietors and acted on a different set of premises in adjudication. Significantly, the articulation of Rokkaku authority correlates with a shift in the legitimizing tactics pursued by a merchant community that Tonomura studied. The combination of "ancient prestige and medieval precedent" by which these merchant-residents of an estate held by Enryakuji had pressed their claims no longer counted for much in the new rationales posed by the Rokkaku. This shift in practice I take as further proof of the changing conception of authority and of types of claims this recast authority could countenance.[34]

A thorough consideration of these developments is beyond the purview of this study; indeed, this quick sketch can hope to have accomplished little more than to point out the need for further research. But it should be evident that the concepts of authority developing here, the networks of meaning within which terms like hyakushō or ideas of community were being placed, and the relations through which these notions were brought into substance, entail, indeed require, a displacement of the estate order. And, conversely, I hope that I have been able to show that the displacement of the shōen system is to be sought precisely in this rewriting of the codes of authority and identity, in this invocation (or the reinvocation) of alternate discourses by which to configure practice—in, that is, the language inscribing peasant practices and daimyo authority. Within the rewritten codes promulgated in late-fifteenth and sixteenth century discourse, estates (and their boundaries) held no privileged place, a hyakushō could not claim status by affiliation to an estate and its proprietor, and both ruler and subject would have to find new ways to demarcate their relationship.

NOTES

ABBREVIATIONS

DNK   *Dai Nihon komonjo,* iewake monjo, comp. Tokyo Daigaku Shiryōhensanjo (Tokyo: Tokyo Daigaku Shuppankai, 1901–). In citations, the first number after DNK represents the series, then the volume and page.

DNS   *Dai Nihon shiryō,* comp. Tokyo Daigaku Shiryōhensanjo, ser. 6 and 7 (Tokyo: Tokyo Daigaku Shuppankai, 1901–).

HI   *Heian ibun,* comp. Takeuchi Rizō (Tokyo: Tōkyōdo Shoten, 1963–68).

KI   *Kamakura ibun,* comp. Takeuchi Rizō (Tokyo: Tōkyōdo Shoten, 1971–90).

THM   *Tōji hyakugō monjo.* All citations use the numbering scheme standardized in *Tōji hyakugō monjo mokuroku,* comp. Kyoto Furitsu Sōgō Shiryōkan (Tokyo: Yoshikawa Kōbunkan, 1976–79). References to the *hiragana* series of documents are *italicized* (e.g., *ha* 5); UPPER-CASE indicates the *katakana* series (e.g., HA 5).

.   .   .   .   .

CHAPTER ONE
IN GO-SANJŌ'S ARCHIVE

1. In contrast to Fukuzawa, whose "out-of-Asia" (*datsu-A*) philosophy characterized Japan's Asian heritage as an impediment to national progress, the first professional historians of Japan's medieval era—men like Hara Katsurō or, somewhat later, Nakada Kaoru and Asakawa Kan'ichi—resuscitated the nation's past in studies that celebrated the vitality and fertility of the premodern era. Nagahara Keiji offers a succinct appraisal of the ideological mission of these historians in "Rekishi ishiki to rekishi no shiten," *Shisō* 615 (September 1975): 1–22. Overviews of prewar historiography on medieval Japan can also be found in Nakano Hideo, *Chūsei shōenshi kenkyū no ayumi* (Tokyo: Shinjinbutsu Ōraisha, 1982), 132–53; and Amino Yoshihiko, *Chūsei Tōji to Tōji-ryō shōen* (Tokyo: Tokyo Daigaku Shuppankai, 1978), 1–32.

2. Asakawa Kan'ichi, "Some Aspects of Japanese Feudal Institutions," *Transactions of the Asiatic Society of Japan* 46, no. 1 (1918): 82. Reprinted in *Land and Society in Medieval Japan* (Tokyo: Japan Society for the Promotion of Science, 1965), 193–218. Asakawa's sentiments have been echoed by many. See, for example, Edwin O. Reischauer's "Japanese Feudalism," in *Feudalism in History,* ed. Rushton Coulborn (Princeton: Princeton University Press, 1956).

3. The amount of primary documentation on the shōen is staggering: at times it seems as if most documents from the medieval era somehow pertain to the estates. Shōen, as might be expected, also constitute a major object of

medieval law. Shōen limitation regulations (see pp. 18–20) testify to court concerns with the estates; laws dealing with estates (especially laws regulating warrior activities on estates and vis-à-vis estate proprietors) are prominent in the corpus of Kamakura and Muromachi Bakufu law. The standard compendium of medieval law is Satō Shin'ichi and Ikeuchi Yoshisuke, comps., *Chūsei hōsei shiryōshū*, vol. 1, *Kamakura Bakufu hō*, vol.2, *Muromachi Bakufu hō* (Tokyo: Iwanami Shoten, 1955–57). The first two volumes contain the Kamakura and Muromachi bakufu laws, respectively. For an English translation of the corpus of Muromachi law, see Kenneth Grossberg, ed. and trans., *The Laws of the Muromachi Bakufu* (Tokyo: Monumenta Nipponica, 1981). The estates have a much more limited place in historiography until the modern era. Jien makes passing reference to the shōen in his *Gukanshō* (1219), as does Kitabatake Chikafusa in *Jinnō shōtoki* (1343). Concerned primarily with chronicling imperial reigns, neither, though, displays much interest in the institution per se. What seems to be the first extended analysis of the institution appears in *Dai Nihonshi*, where a section of the volume on food and currency is devoted to the estates. See Delmer Brown and Ichirō Ishida, trans. and ed., *The Future and the Past* (Berkeley and Los Angeles: University of California Press, 1979); H. Paul Varley, trans., *A Chronicle of Gods and Sovereigns: Jinnō Shōtoki Of Kitabake Chikafusa* (New York: Columbia University Press, 1980); and *Dai Nihonshi*, ed. Gikō seitan sanbyakunen kinenkai (Tokyo: Nihon Yūbenkai, 1928–29), 12:319–33.

4. See especially, "Ōchō jidai no shōen ni kansuru kenkyū." First published in 1906–7, this and other important works were reprinted in Nakada Kaoru, *Shōen no kenkyū* (Tokyo: Shōkō Shoin, 1948).

5. See Asakawa, "The Origin of Feudal Land Tenure in Japan" and "The Early *Shō* and the Early Manor: A Comparative Study," both in *Land and Society in Medieval Japan*.

6. The phrase is Nagahara Keiji's, from "The Medieval Peasant," in *The Cambridge History of Medieval Japan*, vol. 3, *Medieval Japan*, ed. Kozo Yamamura (Cambridge: Cambridge University Press, 1990), 301. Similar sentiments are expressed in virtually every study of the estate system; rarely does the analysis make clear what this might mean—beyond that there were a lot of estates and therefore a lot of people dependent in some way on them.

7. Furet, *In the Workshop of History*, trans. Jonathan Mandelbaum (Chicago and London: University of Chicago Press, 1984), 8–9; cited in Hayden White, *The Content of the Form* (Baltimore and London: Johns Hopkins University Press, 1987), 221. Furet goes on to criticize narrative for its tendency to preselect events and to predetermine their significance: "Since history thus defined has a meaning that predates . . . the set of phenomena that it encompasses, historical facts need only be arrayed on the time scale to become meaningful within a process known in advance. . . . [The significance of events] derives from an external source. But as that significance tends to turn events into markers of change, signaling the dips and breaks along the imaginary route of time, they are chosen for their capacity to embody change and the phases of change." I realize that what I have labeled "narrative description" is but one mode of narrative—a storytelling mode that White links to history's disciplinary roots in "late nineteenth-century social science and

mid-nineteenth-century art"—and Furet's notion that a properly "analytic" (i.e., quantitative, social-scientific) history can escape all determinism seems to me naive. The problem is not narrative per se (which may well be, as Roland Barthes notes, a fundamental mode of cognition), but the ways in which much historical story telling unself-consciously takes the story as the "natural" mode of expression and smoothes over discontinuities in the name of getting the story straight. In choosing not to tell a story of the shōen, I do not pretend to have escaped narrativity; in reading against the grain of traditional accounts of the estates, however, I hope to offer an analysis that is aware of its rhetorical structure and that does not gloss over the contradictions and inconsistencies of its subject in order to produce a coherent story line. On narrative and the rhetoric of historical discourse, see Hayden White, *Tropics of Discourse: Essays in Cultural Criticism* (Baltimore: Johns Hopkins University Press, 1978), 43; for narrative as a mode of cognition, see Roland Barthes, "Introduction to the Structural Analysis of Narrative," in *Image, Music, Text*, trans. Stephen Heath (New York: Hill and Wang, 1977); on the "narrative" quality of "non-narrative" historiography, see Hans Kellner, "Narrating the 'Tableau': Questions of Narrativity in Michelet," in *Language and Historical Representation: Getting the Story Crooked* (Madison: University of Wisconsin Press, 1989).

8. Good examples of this tendency can be found in introductory surveys of the estate system, e.g., Kudō Keiichi's article in the Iwanami series or Abe Takeshi's general history. Nagahara's contribution on the demise of the estates in the recent Cambridge history is another example, and my article on the decline of the system also evinces this desire to master the estate system by tying it down to a coherent narrative line. Most articles and monographs on the shōen, however, tend to avoid direct confrontations with broader questions about the trajectory of the institution, preferring instead to cast themselves as detailed case studies. That the historiographical questions these works invoke almost always concern the advent or decline of the system signals, implicitly at least, that they are inspired by a similar desire. See Kudō Keiichi, "Shōensei no tenkai," in *Iwanami kōza Nihon rekishi*, vol. 5, *Chūsei 1* (Tokyo: Iwanami Shoten, 1975); Abe Takeshi, *Nihon shōen shi* (Tokyo: Ōhara Shinseisha, 1972); Nagahara Keiji, "The Decline of the *Shōen* System," in *The Cambridge History of Japan*, vol. 3; Thomas E. Keirstead, "Fragmented Estates: The Breakup of the *Myō* and the Decline of the *Shōen* System," *Monumenta Nipponica* 40 (Autumn 1985): 21–39.

9. Peasant rebellion and relations between the estates and warriors represent the most troublesome examples of "untimely practices." Most narratives of shōen development link peasant rebellion to the decline of the estate system. These treatments must often go to some lengths, however, to explain away the presence of rebellious peasants from origins of the shōen era. Likewise, most renditions of the system's demise make much of a variety of arrangements (common from the thirteenth century on) by which estate proprietors relinquished administrative control of estates to warriors in return for guarantees regarding the delivery of revenues. But warriors had from the outset functioned as estate managers. How different, after all, were such arrangements from the situation created when a local landholder commended

lands to a proprietor and in return managed the estate and turned over a rent? Nagahara Keiji's "The Decline of the *Shōen* System" offers a case in point. His narrative portrays the *jitō* as a leading cause of the decline of the estate system; yet jitō were part of the estate structure from the late twelfth century on—almost, that is, from the beginning of the system. And unless one is willing to entertain the idea that the shōen were in decline from the start, then one has to admit that something has gone awry. Precisely because they insist on forcing the history of the system into a linear narrative mold, accounts such as Nagahara's exhaust themselves in this sort of "before-and-after" game.

10. As Michel Foucault observes "an entire historical tradition (theological or rationalistic) aims at dissolving the singular event into an ideal continuity." It seeks, in other words, to trace, not events, but "the gradual curve of their evolution" as it is managed by some suprahistorical regulatory mechanism (base, superstructure, the Idea, etc.). Its focus, therefore, will always be on supposed origins and ends, and not on the "singularity of events." See Foucault, "Nietzsche, Genealogy, History," in *Language, Counter-Memory, Practice: Selected Essays and Interviews*, ed. Donald F. Bouchard (Ithaca: Cornell University Press, 1977), 139–64.

11. The main effect of such an approach is to remove the possibility of contingency from history, and to make a given course of change seem inevitable when surely that path became inevitable only in hindsight. This, of course, is something like the burden of the charge of "presentism" that historians frequently hurl at each other. But the antidote implied in the "presentism" charge, to try to approach more closely and more rigorously the perspectives of contemporaries, merely skirts the issue. For the problem is not simply that the voices of contemporaries are drowned out by the insistent whine of the present, but that an entire technique of writing history is structurally indisposed to accommodate the "haphazard conflicts" that comprise human existence. (The quotation is from Foucault, "Nietzsche," 154.)

12. Paul Carter makes this point in *The Road to Botany Bay: An Exploration of Landscape and History* (Chicago: University of Chicago Press, 1989), 4. This remarkable "spatial history" demonstrates the consequences of historians' emphasis on cause-and-effect narrative: a devaluation of the "specificity of historical experience" in a desire to impose order on chaos by legislating the flow of events. With respect to the shōen, one sign of this winnowing of evidence can be found in articles treating "daily life" on the estates. They tend to adopt a relentlessly static mode of description in their discussions of social stratification in villages, cultivation patterns, etc. See, for instance, Nagahara Keiji, "The Medieval Peasant," or Ōyama Kyōhei, "Medieval *Shōen*," in *The Cambridge History of Japan*, vol. 3, *Medieval Japan*.

13. Giddens, *A Contemporary Critique of Historical Materialism* (Berkeley and Los Angeles: University of California Press, 1981), 1:45–47. Giddens, I should note, speaks only of the "social." In adding the term "cultural" to his description and in speaking of "social and cultural systems," I am grafting the terminology made famous by Clifford Geertz to Giddens' definition. Their respective definitions of "cultural" and "social" do not differ substantially, and,

though I have grave reservations about Geertz's understanding of cultural systems, I prefer the broader connotations carried by the term. See Geertz, *The Interpretation of Cultures* (New York: Basic Books, 1973) and Chapter 5.

14. This, as Giddens is at pains to point out, does *not* imply consensus. While the existence of a social system presupposes some level of common recognition as to the meaning of an action or the role of a given institution, this does not mean that the members of that system necessarily agree about the importance or priority assigned to any particular item.

15. An analogy drawn from the contemporary U.S. justice system may help clarify the distinction I am attempting to draw between institution and order. This system is composed of a number of layers of courts, various levels of police or prisons, etc. These I regard as the *institutions*—i.e., the positive manifestations of the system of justice. But the system also embodies certain assumptions about crime and criminal behavior, about punishment, about the role of law, etc. These are the *orders* within which, and according to which, the positive institutions/instruments of the justice system are conceived and arrayed.

16. A map in Kishi Toshio et al., eds., *Asahi hyakka Nihon no rekishi* 4, no. 2 (Tokyo: Asahi Shinbunsha, 1986): 58–59, graphically details the range of products extracted from estates as rents. Among the estates which figure prominently in this study, Niimi and Yugeshima were known as major producers of iron and salt, respectively. Hiranodono Estate's annual rents included several *matsutake*, a particularly esteemed delicacy.

17. To note just a few of the more common terms for landholdings and tenures: *myōden* in many places constituted the basic unit of peasant tenure (see Chapter 3); *sanden* and *isshikiden* represent types of conditional tenure (renewed on a periodic basis); *ukiden*, literally "floating fields," which may mark a tenure not tied to any specific plot. There are taxable and tax-exempt fields (*jōden* and *joden*), and numerous categories of grant fields (e.g., *kyūden*, *shinden*, *jiden*, *menden*). *Gensaku* and *tokuden* suggest fields under cultivation; *jōkō*, permanent waste; *sonden*, damaged fields (hence exempt from taxes for the year). Residence plots are accorded special treatment in the system and have special names, most commonly *yashikichi* or *kaito*. In addition, there are special fields/tenures peculiar to individual estates: the records of Tara Estate, for example, speak of *jōyōbata*, which were assessed a tax (the meaning of the term, though, is unclear).

18. Good general treatments of the early shōen can be found in Abe Takeshi, *Nihon shōen seiritsushi no kenkyū* (Tokyo: Yūzankaku, 1960) and *Nihon shōen shi* (Tokyo: Ōhara Shinseisha, 1972). Also useful are Miyamoto Tasuku, "Ritsuryōseiteki tochi seido," and Inagaki Yasuhiko, "Ritsuryōseiteki tochi seido no kaitai," both in *Tochi seidoshi I*, ed. Takeuchi Rizō (Tokyo: Yamakawa Shuppansha, 1973), 49–138; 139–172. In English see, in addition to the works of Asakawa mentioned above (n. 5), Elizabeth Sato, "The Early Development of the Shōen," in *Medieval Japan: Essays in Institutional History*, ed. John W. Hall and Jeffrey P. Mass (New Haven: Yale University Press, 1974), 91–108.

19. Early (pre-eleventh-century) estates typically possessed an exemption from state taxes, and this was extended only to fields which had been specif-

ically recognized as possessing this immunity. The lands remained, moreover, within the general jurisdiction of the provincial apparatus (hence subject to surveying, etc.). Tax exemption was thus only secondarily an effect of "estate-hood." It did not accrue automatically to all lands recognized as shōen, but rather stemmed from the estate's belonging to a temple or other specially favored group. See Sakamoto Shōzō, *Nihon ōchō kokka taisei ron* (Tokyo: Tokyo Daigaku Shuppankai, 1972), 18–125.

20. For Tōji, see Amino Yoshihiko's comprehensive account in *Chūsei Tōji to Tōji–ryō shōen*, 79–160, 215–53. Joan Piggott offers a detailed portrait of Tōdaiji's estate management: "Hierarchy and Economics in Early Medieval Tōdaiji" in *Court and Bakufu in Japan*, ed. Jeffrey P. Mass (Stanford: Stanford University Press, 1982), 45–91.

21. On this, see Koyama Yasunori, "Shōenseiteki ryōiki shihai to chūsei sonraku," *Nihonshi kenkyū* 139/140 (March 1974): 103–19, and Mizuno Shōji, "Chūsei sonraku to ryōiki kōsei," *Nihonshi kenkyū* 271 (April 1985): 54–81. Estate maps make the difference readily apparent: early shōen are marked as aggregates of fields, each carefully noted within a space defined by the rectangles of the *jōri* grid. Later maps refer only to the estate itself; the estate, not the field, is the basic unit. See Chapter 3.

22. The earliest usage of shōmin would appear to be in a directive to the provincial office of Yamashiro. The order exempts Tōdaiji's Tamai Estate from a state levy: Tengi 2 (1054).2.23 Kan senji (HI, no. 709). The term finds widespread usage from the closing decade of the eleventh century (see, e.g., HI, nos. 1353, 1422, 1441, 1444, 1530, 1546).

23. See, for example, Elizabeth Sato's discussion of Kuwabara Estate in "Early Development of the Shōen," 97–101.

24. Some estates, like Ōyama, managed to hold on, in much straitened circumstances, to become the nuclei around which estates would later be resurrected. For a detailed history of Ōyama Estate, see Miyagawa Mitsuru, comp., *Ōyama sonshi*, vol. 1, tsūshi hen (Tokyo: Hanawa Shobō, 1964).

25. Foucault, *The Archaeology of Knowledge*, trans. A. M. Sheridan Smith (New York: Harper Colophon, 1972), 104.

26. Sato, "Early Development of the Shōen," and "Ōyama Estate and Insei Land Policies," *Monumenta Nipponica* 34 (Spring 1979): 73–99. By this time, in fact, Ōyama Estate, its tax privileges revoked by the state and its administration assumed by provincial authorities, existed in name alone. Only in 1086 would the estate regain its fiscal and administrative exemptions.

27. A number of theories have been advanced to account for the decline of the Ritsuryō state. One set of explanations proposes that a greedy nobility, exercising its privileges to exempt its possessions from taxation, essentially bled the state dry. See, e.g., Kozo Yamamura, "The Decline of the Ritsuryō System: Hypotheses on Economic and Institutional Change," *Journal of Japanese Studies* 1 (Autumn 1974): 3–37. Another school emphasizes the inability of the Ritsuryō apparatus to cope with economic change; Toda Yoshimi's *Nihon ryōshusei seiritsushi no kenkyū* (Tokyo: Iwanami Shoten, 1967) remains perhaps the exemplary exposition of this view. A third strain, exemplified by William Wayne Farris, *Population, Disease, and Land in Early Japan, 645–900*

(Cambridge: Harvard University Press, 1985), cites the "economic backwardness" of eighth- and ninth-century Japan: the Ritsuryō system collapsed in the face of insurmountable natural obstacles (given the state of its technologies, agricultural and otherwise).

28. This is the substance of Kuroda Toshio's *kenmon seika* theory. The phrase, which might be translated as "powerful institutions and flourishing houses," refers to the emperor and imperial line, the aristocracy, the military elite, and religious establishments. According to Kuroda, the medieval polity was characterized by the coexistence of these clusters of authority, each with overlapping responsibilities and powers. The political framework of medieval Japan thus made structurally possible a good deal of room for maneuver, something less conceivable in a more unitary state. See Kuroda, *Shōensei shakai* (Tokyo: Tokyo Daigaku Shuppankai, 1967).

29. This information is discussed in Ishii Susumu, "Insei jidai," in *Kōza Nihonshi*, ed. Rekishigaku Kenkyūkai and Nihonshi Kenkyūkai (Tokyo: Tokyo Daigaku Shuppankai, 1970), 2:208–9; and Kudō, "Shōensei no tenkai," 254–55.

30. Amino Yoshihiko provides figures which suggest that the number of Fujiwara estates may have quadrupled during this period. See Amino, "Shōen kōryōsei no keisei to kōzō," in *Tochi seidoshi I*, ed. Takeuchi Rizō, 229–30. Wakita Haruko also discusses the formation of Fujiwara family landholdings in *Nihon chūsei shōgyō hattatsushi no kenkyū* (Tokyo: Ochanomizu Shobō, 1969), 156–68. Information about imperial-family holdings can be found in Peter Arnesen, "The Struggle for Lordship in Late Heian Japan: The Case of Aki," *Journal of Japanese Studies* 10 (Winter 1984): 105.

31. On this, see Jeffrey P. Mass, *Warrior Government in Early Medieval Japan: A Study of the Kamakura Bakufu, Shugo, and Jitō* (New Haven and London: Yale University Press, 1974), 3–5; Nagahara Keiji, "Land Ownership Under the Shōen-Kokugaryō System," *Journal of Japanese Studies* 1 (Spring 1975): 269–96; and John W. Hall, *Government and Local Power in Japan, 500–1700: A Study Based on Bizen Province* (Princeton: Princeton University Press, 1966), 124, 220–24. Peter Arnesen's case study: "Suō Province in the Age of Kamakura," in *Court and Bakufu in Japan*, 92–120 is also of interest.

32. Ōishi Naomasa, "Shōen kōryōsei no tenkai," in *Kōza Nihonshi*, vol. 3, *Chūsei 1*, ed. Rekishigaku Kenkyūkai and Nihonshi Kenkyūkai (Tokyo: Tokyo Daigaku Shuppankai, 1984), 139. For more on the function of kokugaryō, see Inoue Toshio, *Yama no tami, kawa no tami* (Tokyo: Heibonsha, 1981); Nakagomi Ritsuko, "Ōchō kokka ki ni okeru kokuga kokunai shihai no kōzō to tokushitsu," *Gakushūin shigaku* 23 (April 1985): 45–63; and Takada Minoru, "Jūni-jūsan seiki ni okeru kokka kenryoku to kokuga shihai," *Shichō* 99 (June 1967): 6–25. Amino Yoshihiko's wide-ranging reappraisal of public authority offers stimulating and important insights into the place of the public in medieval Japan: Amino, *Nihon chūsei no hinōgyōmin to tennō* (Tokyo: Iwanami Shoten, 1984).

33. G. Cameron Hurst, "The Reign of Go-Sanjō and the Revival of Imperial Power," *Monumenta Nipponica* 27 (Spring 1972): 65–83, discusses Go-Sanjō's rule in some detail.

34. Exactly how many estates were confiscated is not known; Hurst, *Insei*, 110–19, cites several examples. For insight into the operation of the kirokujo, see Enkyū 3 (1071).6.24 Daijō kanpu (HI, bui, no. 11).

35. Foucault, *Archaeology of Knowledge*, 129–30. Emphasis Foucault's.

36. Thus, for example, John Hall's evaluation of Go-Sanjō's shōen regulation ordinances: "As a consequence [of the records office] a number of minor irregularities were discovered and some shōen were confiscated. Yet no fundamental attack was made upon the shōen system itself." Hall, *Government and Local Power in Japan*, 120.

37. Kuroda, *Nihon chūsei hōkensei ron* (Tokyo: Tokyo Daigaku Shuppankai, 1974), 41–45.

38. Several of these local magnates have prominent places in the historiography of medieval Japan. The Fujiwara family of Aki Province, for example, has received extended analysis in Jeffrey Mass, "Patterns of Provincial Inheritance in Late Heian Japan," *Journal of Japanese Studies* 9 (Winter 1983): 67–95; Peter Arnesen, "The Struggle for Lordship"; and Sakaue Yasutoshi, "Aki-no-kuni Takada gunji Fujiwara shi no shoryō shūseki to denryō," *Shigaku zasshi* 91 (September 1982): 1375–412. Ishimoda Shō devotes a large portion of his seminal *Chūseiteki sekai no keisei*, rev. ed. (Tokyo: Iwanami Shoten, 1985) to Fujiwara Sanetō of Iga Province. Hata Tamekane, founder of Hisatomi ho (which formed the nucleus of Yano Estate) is discussed in Miyagawa Mitsuru, "Harima-no-kuni Yano-no-shō no seiritsu jijō ni tsuite," *Hyōgoken no rekishi* 18 (September 1981): 1–9, and Kimura Shigemitsu, "Harima-no-kuni Akaho gun Hisatomi ho no kaihatsu ni tsuite," *Chihōshi kenkyū* 178 (August 1982): 69–82.

39. Details of Sanetō's holdings are given in a bequest to his nephew: *Tōdaiji monjo*, Tengi 4 (1056).2.23 Fujiwara Sanetō shoryō yuzurijō an, in *Iga-no-kuni Kuroda-no-shō shiryō*, comp. Takeuchi Rizō (Tokyo: Yoshikawa Kōbunkan, 1975), 1:55–59.

40. See, e.g., Mass, "Patterns of Provincial Inheritance," for a description of the precarious position of several prominent provincial families.

41. Chōkyū 2 (1041).3.5 Fujiwara Sanetō kugen funshitsujō an, in *Iga-no-kuni Kuroda-no-shō shiryō*, comp. Takeuchi, 1:32–3.

42. *Itsukushima jinja monjo*, Hōen 6 (1139).6 Fujiwara Naritaka kishinjō, in Hiroshima ken, comp. *Hiroshima kenshi, kodai-chūsei shiryō* (Hiroshima: Hiroshima ken, 1974–80), 3:1467–71.

43. Shōtoku 2 (1098).10.15 Nanaebe mura rikkenmon an (HI, no. 1398). Cited in Kawane Yoshiyasu, *Chūsei hōkensei seiritsushi ron* (Tokyo: Tokyo Daigaku Shuppankai, 1971), 162.

44. *Aki-no-kuni Chōko zasshō*, Eiho 3 (1083).3.16 Uekatsu Nagatomo no ge, in *Hiroshima kenshi, kodai-chūsei shiryō*, 5:1367–68, cited in Ōishi, "Shōen kōryōsei no tenkai," 131.

45. For an example of this, see *Kujō ke monjo*, Kōji 2 (1143).10.4 Minamoto Takakane kishinjō. A photograph of this document, with commentary, can be found in Nihon rekishi gakkai, ed., *Enshū komonjo sen*, shōen hen (Tokyo: Yoshikawa Kōbunkan, 1980), 1:108.

46. The hierarchies created by commendation also supply the one widely recognized structural characteristic of the shōen system—*shiki*. A term that

once indicated an official post or position, shiki in the medieval period connoted an income right—specifically a share in the income from an estate. As most studies of the estate system note, all administrative and economic rights in an estate found expression in terms of shiki: proprietors held *ryōke* or *honke shiki*, local administrators *azukari dokoro* or *zasshō shiki*; upper peasants (*myōshu*) were appointed to *myōshu shiki*, and jitō to *jitō shiki*, etc. This has lead some historians to equate the shōen system with the network of shiki rights. While shiki were certainly central to the articulation of administrative and economic authority within the shōen, an overconcentration on this feature leads, I believe, to a limited view of the system. First, it constructs the system in overwhelmingly economic terms: the estate system becomes in effect a structure for the administration and extraction of land rents. Such a construction clearly will have difficulty accommodating noneconomic aspects of the shōen. Second, by positing that the shiki framework can stand in for the entirety of the system, this line of reasoning commits what Pierre Bourdieu calls "fallacies of the rule." The same fallacy proposes that kinship structures can stand in for the practice of the people who live those structures, so that it becomes enough to say that someone occupies the position of "father" to describe his practice—or that the practice of proprietors or jitō is immanent in the shiki they hold. This leads to a basically static understanding of the estate system and encourages a disregard for the dialectic between structure and practice, for the ways structures are put into practice and practices engaged with the production of structure.

For the view that the shiki system is the core of the shōen system, see Nagahara Keiji, *Nihon chūsei shakai kōzō no kenkyū* (Tokyo: Iwanami Shoten, 1973), 28–55. Cornelius J. Kiley's article on property relations in the late Heian period leads in much the same direction. See "Estate and Property in the Late Heian Period," in *Medieval Japan: Essays in Institutional History*, ed. John W. Hall and Jeffrey P. Mass (New Haven: Yale University Press, 1974).

47. H. D. Harootunian, *Things Seen and Unseen: Discourse and Ideology in Tokugawa Nativism* (Chicago: University of Chicago Press, 1988), 20. Hans Kellner's plea (in *Language and Historical Representation*) for "getting the story crooked" echoes Harootunian's call for a re-exoticized past. Their concern is one that I share: a "crooked story" cannot only highlight the "constructedness" of historical discourse and make one aware of the ways in which history operates upon the material of the past, but it can also encompass a past that is not necessarily continuous or consistent.

CHAPTER TWO
HYAKUSHŌ AND THE RHETORIC OF IDENTITY

1. *Tōji hyakugō monjo*, FU 201, [Bun'ei 7 (1270)].8.11 Wakibukuro Noritsugu shojō (KI, no. 10667).

2. *Tōdaiji monjo*, Genkyō 4 (1324) Tōdaiji nen'yo kudashibumi an (DNK 18, 1:1104).

3. *Tōdaiji monjo*, Eiryaku 2 (1161).3.22 Tachibana Tsunemoto kishōmon (HI, no. 3144).

4. Kuroda Toshio, for example, proposes a five-part classification, with hyakushō at the center: 1) the aristocracy, 2) warriors, 3) hyakushō, 4) servants (*genin*), 5) outcasts (*hinin*). See his "Chūsei no mibun ishiki to shakai-kan," in *Nihon no shakaishi*, ed. Asao Naohiro et al. (Tokyo: Iwanami Shoten, 1986–88), 7:51–86.

5. My understanding of the medieval European serf follows Marc Bloch, *French Rural History: An Essay on Its Basic Characteristics*, trans. J. Sondheimer (Berkeley and Los Angeles: University of California Press, 1966), esp. 64–112, and his *Feudal Society*, trans. L. A. Manyon (Chicago: University of Chicago Press, 1961), 1:241–79; Georges Duby, *The Chivalrous Society*, trans. Cynthia Postan (Berkeley and Los Angeles: University of California Press, 1980), esp. 1–58, 186–215. Also of interest is Stefano Fenoaltea, "The Rise and Fall of a Theoretical Model: The Manorial System," *Journal of Economic History* 44 (1975): 386–409.

6. The forty-second article of *Goseibai shikimoku*, the Kamakura Bakufu's basic law code, specifies that absconding hyakushō were not to be arrested nor to have their possessions confiscated. See Kuroda Hiroko, "Chōsan, chōbō, soshite 'kyoryū no jiyū,' " *Minshūshi kenkyū* 33 (May 1987): 11–40, for an extended analysis of this article. The text of *Goseibai shikimoku* can be found in Satō and Ikeuchi, comps., *Chūsei hōsei shiryōshū*, 1:1–25.

7. See Fujiki Hisashi, *Sengoku shakaishi ron* (Tokyo: Tokyo Daigaku Shup-pankai, 1974), 97–105, 230–60. Isogai Fujio argues, unsuccessfully I believe, against this view: see Isogai Fujio, "Hyakushō mibun no tokushitsu to dorei e no tenraku o megutte," *Rekishigaku kenkyū* sp. ed. (November 1971): 66–76.

8. Jitō were local warriors appointed as estate managers or overseers by the Kamakura Bakufu. See Mass, *Warrior Government in Early Medieval Japan*, for an excellent account of this figure. The Jōkyū War refers to a conflict be-tween the imperial court and the Kamakura Bakufu; it arose out of an attempt by the retired emperor Go-Toba to overthrow the bakufu. Mass, *The Devel-opment of Kamakura Rule, 1180–1250: A History with Documents* (Stanford: Stanford University Press, 1979), 1–59, offers by far the best analysis of this conflict.

9. The jitō's misdeeds are recounted in detail in the bakufu's judgment of a suit brought against him by the residents of Tara: see THM *ho* 9, Kangen 1 (1243).11.25 Rokuhara saikyojō (DNK 10, 2:505–17).

10. THM *ye* 3, Bun'ei 10 (1273).3.17 Tara-no-shō Kanshin hanmyō myōshu shiki buninjō (KI, no. 11206).

11. THM *ye* 4, Kōan 1 (1278).4.21 Wakasa Tara-no-shō Kanshin myō myōshu shiki buninjō an (KI, no. 13022).

12. THM *sa* 3, Kōan 1 (1278).5.29 Tōji gusō gechijō an (KI, no. 13061).

13. See Amino, *Chūsei shōen no yōsō* (Tokyo: Hanawa Shobō, 1966), 125–35.

14. Amino Yoshihiko, *Mōko shūrai*, vol. 10 of *Nihon no rekishi* (Tokyo: Shōgakkan, 1974), 246–50.

15. In locating the source of hyakushō identity in a preexistent collectivity, Amino adheres to a well-established line in Japanese historiography. Ever since Shimizu Mitsuo argued that estates were not contiguous with "natural" peasant communities, historians have seen fit to divorce the question of com-

munity from that of the estate. Among others, Irumada Nobuo and Koyama Yasunori have argued that the "medieval village" constituted the prime referent for peasant identity and provided as well the core about which shōen were organized. As will become apparent, I have serious reservations about this view. It seems, in particular, to lack an appreciation of the complex interaction stimulated by the incorporation of peasant communities into the estate system. I wish to accord the system a much more significant role in forming this community. To say that the medieval village constituted the nucleus of the estate or of peasant identity requires a very unproblematic understanding of the village and of its situation within the larger system. The problem is not simply one of incorporation: both community and peasant identity seem to me the product of a highly problematic, conflicted, and ultimately transforming *interaction* between peasants and the estate context. To my mind, then, there is little value in arguing over which came first: the estate community can profitably be seen as an "imagined community" (in something like Benedict Anderson's sense), and the issue then becomes how that imagination was produced and reproduced. Benedict Anderson, *Imagined Communities: Reflections on the Origins and Spread of Nationalism* (London: Verso, 1983). Shimizu Mitsuo, *Chūsei shōen no kiso kōzō* (Tokyo: Kōtō Shoin, 1949); Irumada Nobuo, *Hyakushō mōshijō to kishōmon no sekai* (esp. the chapter titled "Heian jidai no sonraku to minshū no undō") (Tokyo: Tokyo Daigaku Shuppankai, 1986); *Chūsei sonraku to shōen ezu* (Tokyo: Tokyo Daigaku Shuppankai, 1987), 1–52, 156–80. Satō Kazuhiko, "Chūsei sonrakushi kenkyū no shiten," *Rekishi hyōron* 374 (June 1981): 2–5, offers a quick overview of perspectives on the medieval village.

16. Tōji: THM MU 22, Jōwa 5 (1349) Gakushū-gata hyōjō hikitsuke, entry for 5/8. (DNS ser. 6, 13:211). Tōdaiji: Jōō 3 (1224).2.16 Tōdaiji mandokoro kudashibumi an. In Gifu ken, comp., *Gifu kenshi*, shiryō-hen, kodai-chūsei (Gifu: Gifu ken, 1969–72), 3:182.

17. For Tara Estate, in 1302 and 1305, see THM YE 25–29; for the year 1334, see THM *ha* 86, Kenmu 1 (1334).8 Tara-no-shō hyakushō ra no mōshijō; and for 1357, see THM *shi* 24 Enbun 2 (1357).2.10 Tara-no-shō hyakushō ra no mōshijō, and THM *shi* 22, Enbun 2 (1357).10.23 Tara-no-shō hyakushō ra kishōmon. Reproductions of the first and last sets of documents can be found in Kyoto Furitsu Sōgō Shiryōkan, comp., *Zoku zuroku Tōji hyakugō monjo* (Tokyo: Yoshikawa Kōbunkan, 1974), nos. 97–101; and idem, *Zuroku Tōji hyakugō monjo* (Tokyo: Yoshikawa Kōbunkan, 1970), nos. 104–5. The 1334 petition is in DNK 10, 1:709–13. For Hiranodono, see, e.g., Enkyō 3 (1310).2.23 Yamato Hiranodono-no-shō hyakushō mōshijō (KI 31:240–41); for further examples involving this estate, see KI 31:257–58, 275–76, 291–92, 302–6ff.

18. THM *ya* 24, Shōwa 5 (1316).5.8 Ōyama-no-shō hyakushō uma-no-jō Ieyasu ukebumi. In Miyagawa, comp., *Ōyama sonshi*, vol. 2, shiryōhen, 95.

19. THM *shi* 36, Jōji 2 (1363).3 Tara-no-shō ryōke-gata hyakushō ra mōshijō (DNS ser. 6, 25:423–24).

20. Louis Althusser, "Ideology and Ideological State Apparatuses (Notes Towards an Investigation)" in *Lenin and Philosophy and Other Essays*, trans. Ben Brewster (London: New Left Books, 1971), 162–63.

21. *Azuma kagami* entry for Kangen 2 (1244).2.16. In *Zenshaku Azuma kagami*, ed. Nagahara Keiji and Kishi Shōzō (Tokyo: Shinjinbutsu Ōraisha, 1976–79), 4:373.

22. The phrase is found in a complaint from the hyakushō of Tara Estate: THM YE 46, Kenmu 1 (1334).6.26 Tara-no-shō hyakushō tō ukebumi (DNS ser. 6, 1:595–98).

23. Crime and its punishment have begun to attract the attention of Japanese historians. See, for example, the essays in Amino Yoshihiko et al., *Chūsei no tsumi to batsu* (Tokyo: Tokyo Daigaku Shuppankai, 1983), and Ishii Susumu, "Tsumi to harae," in *Nihon no shakaishi*, ed. Asao Naohiro et al. (Tokyo: Iwanami Shoten, 1987), 5:17–55.

24. *Kōyasan monjo*, Tenji 2 (1125).7.13 Kanshōfu-no-shō jūnin ra no ge (DNK ser. 1, 7:266–69).

25. *Daigoji monjo*, Kangen 1 (1243).7.19, in Fukui ken, comp., *Fukui kenshi, shiryōhen* (Fukui, 1986), 304–6.

26. On this, see Katsumata Shizuo, "Ie o yaku," in *Chūsei no tsumi to batsu*, ed. Amino Yoshihiko et al.; and Nakamura Ken, "Jūtaku hakyaku ni tsuite," in *Shōen shihai kōzō no kenkyū* (Tokyo: Yoshikawa Kōbunkan, 1978).

27. *Saidaiji monjo*, Jōji 6 (1367).8 Saidaiji shikichi nai kendan kishiki (DNS ser. 6, 28:744–49).

28. The incident generated a good deal of correspondence between the estate and Tōji; for a representative account see THM SA 110, Kansei 4 (1463).8.27 Niimi-no-shō sanshiki rensho chūshinjō, in Okayama kenshi hensan iinkai, comp., *Okayama kenshi*, vol. 20, iewake shiryō, (Okayama: Okayama ken, 1986), 736–37.

29. *Tōdaiji monjo*, Kenchō 1 (1249).6 Tōdaiji shūto ra kishōmon (KI, no. 7090).

30. THM *shi* 17, Jōwa 3 (1347).9 Tara-no-shō hyakushō Motoa sokujo Kuro Kamiko mōshijō. Transcribed in Satō Kazuhiko, "Jūyon-seiki ni okeru Wakasa Tara-no-shō no zaichi dōkō," (Tokyo Gakugei Daigaku) *Kiyō* 36 (December 1984): 156. A similar case is recorded in THM HA 42, Enbun 3 (1358).11 Tara-no-shō ryōke, jitō ryōgata hyakushō tō mōshijō (DNS ser. 6, 22:262–64).

31. See *Yasaka jinja kiroku*, entries for Shōhei 7 (1352).4.17 and int. 2.28, respectively, in Harada Tomohiko, ed., *Hennen sabetsushi shiryō shūsei* (Tokyo: San'ichi Shobō, 1983-86), 4:128–29. Kōfukuji also assembled such groups: see, e.g., *Kasugasha kiroku*, entry for Kōan 1 (1278).3.30 (*Ibid.*, 2:542–43). Significantly, the Kōfukuji group was composed of beggars and outcastes (hinin), while Gion Shrine called upon a group of outcast shrine attendants (*inu jinin*). Katsumata, "Ie o yaku," speculates that burning the dwelling may have served as a rite of purification, which was one of the recognized functions of these outcaste groups.

32. *Tōdaiji monjo*, Kōchō 2 (1262).9.30 Kuroda-no-shō shōke ie, hatake bosshū jō (DNK 18, 8:142–44).

33. *Ōne monjo*, Katei 1 (1235).12.15 Enryakuji mandokoro kudashibumi. In Makino Shinnosuke, comp., *Echizen Wakasa komonjo sen* (1933, repr., Fukui: Fukui ken meichō kankōkai, 1971), 592–93.

34. See, e.g., an early-fourteenth-century survey of Wakatsuki Estate and the 1295 survey of Ōi Estate: Tokuji 2 (1307).2.9 Wakatsuki-no-shō dochō and Einin 3 (1295).3 Ōi-no-shō kenchū jikken torichō and same date Ōi-no-shō kenchū nayosechō. These are found, respectively, in Watanabe Sumio and Kita Yoshiyuki, eds., *Yamato-no-kuni Wakatsuki-no-shō shiryō* (Yoshikawa Kōbunkan, 1972), 1:8–24; and *Gifu kenshi*, shiryōhen, kodai-chūsei 3:602–822. Inagaki Yasuhiko highlights the presence of equal residence plots on Ikeda Estate: "Shōen kaihatsu no ato o saguru," in *Shōen no sekai*, ed. Inagaki Yasuhiko (Tokyo: Tokyo Daigaku Shuppankai, 1973). See also Sakuma Takashi, "Kinai no sonraku to yashikichi," *Hisutoria* 109 (February 1985): 1–18.

35. *Tomobuchi Hachiman Jinja monjo*, Kannō 3 (1352).8.15 Getsuyo tō rensho gechijō and Shōhei 12 (1357).3.3 Tomobuchi sōshō okibumi, in Wakayama kenshi hensan iinkai, comp., *Wakayama kenshi*, chūsei shiryōhen (Wakayama: Wakayama ken, 1975), 1:622–24. For a more detailed analysis of the uprisings on Tomobuchi Estate, see Shimizu Hisao, "Kōyasan ryō shōen shihai to sonraku," in *Chūsei no seiji to bunka*, ed. Toyoda sensei koki kinenkai (Tokyo: Yoshikawa Kōbunkan, 1980).

36. Shōka 3 (1259).2.9 Kamakura bakufu tsuika hō (in Satō and Ikeuchi, *Chūsei hōsei shiryōshū*, 1:189, no. 323).

37. See Kuroda Hideo, "Chūsei no kaihatsu to shizen" in *Ikki*, ed. Aoki Michio et al. vol. 4, *Seikatsu, bunka, shisō* (Tokyo: Tokyo Daigaku Shuppankai, 1981), 91–130.

38. This is a consistent theme in much of Amino Yoshihiko's work. See, especially, *Muen, kugai, raku* (Tokyo: Heibonsha, 1978) and *Nihon chūsei minshūzō—heimin to shokunin* (Tokyo: Iwanami Shoten, 1980). Other works stressing the fluidity of medieval society include Ōyama Kyōhei, *Nihon chūsei nōsonshi no kenkyū* (Tokyo: Iwanami Shoten, 1978); Hotate Michihisa, "Chūsei minshū keizai no tenkai," in *Kōza Nihon rekishi*, ed. Rekishigaku Kenyūkai and Nihonshi Kenyūkai (Tokyo: Tokyo Daigaku Shuppankai, 1985), 4:167–206; and Nagahara Keiji, "Chūsei shakai no kōsei to hōkensei, in *Kōza Nihon rekishi*, 3:317–57.

39. For Yugeshima Estate, this practice can be explicitly documented from the mid-thirteenth century on, but Amino Yoshihiko speculates that it holds for the entire Kamakura period. See Amino, "Chūsei no seien to shio no ryūtsū," in *Kōza Nihon gijutsu no shakaishi*, ed. Yamaguchi Keiji and Nagahara Keiji, vol. 2, *Engyō, gyogyō* (Tokyo: Nihon Hyōronsha, 1985), 43–91.

40. This example comes from Tamataki Estate: *Tōdaiji monjo*, Hōgen 3 (1158) Sō Nōkei chinjō an (HI, no. 2947).

41. The 1243 judgment mentioned in n. 9 notes peasant involvement with a local market (at Niū); late Kamakura sources reveal the existence of a regular market at Obama, a nearby port: THM *ha* 118 Kenmu 1 (1334).[12?] Tara-no-shō zasshō mōshijō (DNK 10, 1:718–21). This document is a report of a robbery which occurred as some hyakushō of Tara were returning from market day at Obama. A revealing index of the material life of upper peasants, the stolen items included a good deal of cash (three *kanmon*), five rolls of brocade and other cloth, five small swords, and two linen kimono. See Sasaki Gin'ya, *Shōen no shōgyō* (Tokyo: Yoshikawa Kōbunkan, 1964).

42. The man is Miyagawa Jōren, a hyakushō of Tara Estate and one-time resident of nearby Miyagawa estate (hence his name). The information about Jōren's search for a bride came out in the dispute noted in n. 1 to this chapter between Jōren's daughter and a rival claimant for her holdings. The charge that Jōren had absconded was answered with the story of his journey to Echizen and thereafter dropped out of the case. See KI nos. 10643, 10667, 10685, 10708, and 10709. For an analysis of the marriage ties of Tara hyakushō, see Yamamoto Takashi, "Shōke no ikki no chiikiteki tenkai—Wakasa-no-kuni Niū gun," *Shichō* n.s. 14 (November 1983): 25–43.

43. This rather remarkable story begins in 1330, when Tokitomo bound over first his son, Tokisada, then his "hereditary myōden" to Masahiro, a prominent hyakushō (and evidently something of a moneylender as well) to clear a debt of 6 *koku* of rice. Twelve years later, Tokisada brought suit against Masahiro's heir, claiming that the fields should have reverted to him on Masahiro's death. The details of Tokisada's indenture and flight emerge during the ensuing suit. See DNK 10, 1:728–64 and Kasamatsu Hiroshi, Satō Shin'ichi, and Momose Kesao, eds., *Chūsei seiji shakai shisō*, (Tokyo: Iwanami Shoten, 1981), 2:277–81.

44. For Hine Estate, see *Kujō ke monjo*, Tenpuku 2 (1234).6.25 (*Kujō ke monjo*, 1:159–60), and for Ushigahara Estate, see *Daigoji monjo*, Chōshō 1 (1132).9.23 Kansenji an (HI, no. 2241). The latter document has been translated by Asakawa Kan'ichi in *Land and Society in Medieval Japan*, 42–45. In an intriguing reproduction of official shōen ideology he mistranslates "rōnin" as "outlaw."

45. *Nagato Sumiyoshi Jinja monjo*, Bunji 1 (1185).9.7 Minamoto Noriyori kudashibumi an (*Hennen sabetsushi shiryō shūsei*, 2:820).

46. The directive for Aki Province is *Itsukushima jinja monjo*, Jishō 3 (1179).11 Saki no Daijō Daijin ke mandokoro kudashibumi (KI, no. 1024); the Bakufu's orders to the jitō of Awa, Kazusa, and Shimōsa are mentioned in *Azuma kagami*, entry for Bunji 5 (1189).2.30.

47. One of the earliest examples is a report from the manager of Ishii Estate: Tengi 5 (1057) Echigo-no-kuni Ishii-no-shō shōshi Kanesada no ge (HI, no. 853).

48. Kōchō 2 (1262).3.1 Kantō gechijō (KI, no. 8775). On the equivalence of heimin and hyakushō, see Amino Yoshihiko, "Nihon chūsei ni okeru 'heimin' ni tsuite," in *Nagoya Daigaku Bungakubu sanjūshūnen kinen ronshū* (Nagoya: Nagoya Daigaku, 1979), and Toda Yoshimi, "Heimin hyakushō no chii ni tsuite," *Hisutoria* 47 (March 1963): 17–24. Kawane Yoshiyasu also equates the two terms in *Chūsei hōken shakai no shuto to nōson* (Tokyo: Tokyo Daigaku Shuppankai, 1984), 185–211.

49. *Mibu ke monjo*, Jōgen 1 (1207).12 Kantō gechijō (KI, no. 1709). Translated by Mass in *The Kamakura Bakufu*, 113–16.

50. In a recent article Suzuki Tetsuo goes further: he contends that the *kannō* process (an annual procedural rite observed in the spring which incorporated a number of procedures to "promote agriculture"—which is the literal meaning of *kannō*—including distributing seed and tools, apportioning fields to cultivators, assessing the tax status of individual fields, etc.) was

nothing other than a regularized (and ritualized) version of the process of inviting and settling *rōnin* on the estate. See "Nihon chūsei no hyakushō to tochi shoyū," *Rekishigaku kenkyū* 613 (November 1990): 68–77.

51. *Azuma kagami*, entry for Juei 3 (1184).2.25.

52. *Azuma kagami*, entry for Jōei 1 (1232).11.13. Faced with famine again in the Shōka era (1257–1259) the bakufu enjoined its men to aid the displaced (see Kamakura bakufu tsuika hō, no. 323). In Satō and Ikeuchi, comps. *Chūsei hōsei shiryōshū*, 1:190.

53. For a discussion of this process, see Irumada, *Hyakushō mōshijō to kishōmon no sekai*, 135–54. The estate's immunities were certified in a decree from the chancery of the retired emperor (Shōan 4 [1174] In-no-chō kudashibumi [HI, no. 3666]).

54. *Tōdaiji monjo*, Genkyū 1 (1204).9 Kuroda-no-shō hyakushō mōshijō (*Iga-no-kuni Kuroda-no-shō shiryō*, 2:247).

55. See Inagaki's excellent discussion of these developments in Inagaki Yasuhiko, *Nihon chūsei shakaishi ron* (Tokyo: Tokyo Daigaku Shuppankai, 1981), esp. 240–45.

56. The new order on the estate is set forth in *Kōyasan monjo*, Kenkyū 1 (1190).6 Banna okibumi, in Seno Seiichirō, comp. *Bingo-no-kuni Ōta-no-shō shiryō* (Tokyo: Yoshikawa Kōbunkan, 1986), doc. no. 38. Banna, a Kōyasan monk, appears to have been something of a troubleshooter for temple holdings. See also Minegishi Sumio, "Nengu, kuji to utokusen," in *Nihon no shakaishi*, vol. 4, *Futan to zōyō* (Tokyo: Iwanami Shoten, 1985), 55–92.

57. See Amino, *Nihon chūsei no minshūzō*, 76–91, and "Chūsei no futan taikei—nengu ni tsuite," in *Chūsei, kinsei no kokka to shakai*, ed. Nagahara Keiji et al. (Tokyo: Tokyo Daigaku Shuppankai, 1986), 72–102. Many estates, especially in Eastern Japan, were assessed a portion of their rents in silk or other kinds of cloth. Estates along the Inland Sea often paid in salt or other marine products. Niimi Estate, in Bitchū Province, was known for the iron it produced; Kuroda Estate delivered significant amounts of lumber.

58. THM *o* 5, Shōan 3 (1301).7 Tara-no-shō Sukekuni myō zōji ashi chūmon (KI, no. 20833).

59. Japanese scholars have recently begun to emphasize the social consequences of the shōen tax system. Tomisawa Kiyoto, for example, emphasizes the role this system played in instituting, from the late twelfth century on, a division of labor between peasants (now conceived of exclusively as cultivators) and specialized artisans—this division, he asserts, was a direct result of the *kuji-nengu* system and could not have occurred "without the intervention of *shōen* proprietors." See Tomisawa, "Shōen taiseika ni okeru sonraku to nōmin," *Rekishigaku kenkyū* sp. ed. (November 1976): 67–68.

60. For example, to the tenth-century courtier Fujiwara Morosuke, grandfather of Michinaga and author of the imperial court's calendar of annual observances (*nenjū gyōji*), kuji meant public affairs, court rites, and official matters. In a collection of rules for conduct he uses the term in precisely those senses: on kuji days, for instance, one should be at court early; in matters of kuji, one should "read the documents, and read them with detachment"; if kuji necessitate borrowing something, "one should return the item as soon as

the rites are concluded." See *Kujō ushōjō ikai*, in *Kodai seiji shakai shisō*, ed. Yamagishi Tokuhei et al. (Tokyo: Iwanami Shoten, 1977). For another use of kuji in this sense, see, e.g., Eiho 1 (1081).6.27 Wakasa-no-kami Fujiwara Michimune no ge (HI, no. 1185). For an overview of the term's history, see Amino, *Nihon Chūsei no minshūzō*, 76–91.

The role of spectacle in the operation of power structures has recently attracted considerable attention: see, e.g., Philip Corrigan and Derek Sayer, *The Great Arch: English State Formation as Cultural Revolution* (Oxford: Basil Blackwell, 1985) for an intriguing analysis of the "meaning of state activities, forms, routines, and rituals, . . . for the constitution and regulation of social identities, ultimately of our subjectivities" (p. 2). Michel Foucault has, of course, written extensively on the political uses of spectacle; see, in particular, *Discipline and Punish: The Birth of the Prison*, trans. Alan Sheridan (New York: Vintage Books, 1979); *see* especially chapter 2, "The Spectacle of the Scaffold." Stephen Orgel's explorations of the relationship between theater and the display of monarchical power are likewise of interest: *The Illusion of Power: Political Theater in the English Renaissance* (Berkeley and Los Angeles: University of California Press, 1975) and "The Poetics of Spectacle," *New Literary History* 3 (Spring 1971): 367–89. Clifford Geertz's research on the "poetics" of power in Bali similarly stresses the importance of ritual in statecraft: Geertz, *Negara: The Theatre-State in Nineteenth-Century Bali* (Princeton: Princeton University Press, 1980).

61. As this suggests, kuji fall broadly into three categories: 1) goods demanded by the estate holder for use in annual observances; 2) labor services; and 3) items to be used while attending upon visiting officials (rice and wine for feasts, lodging, etc.).

62. Kuroda Toshio stresses this aspect of kuji, see his analyses in "Chūsei no mibun ishiki," 62–65, and "Chūsei no mibunsei to hisen kannen," in *Chūsei no kokka to shūkyō* (Tokyo: Iwanami Shoten, 1975), 351–98.

63. THM *sa* 45, Kenkyū 2 (1191) In goryō chūshinjō (KI, no. 1305).

64. THM *no* 24, Shitoku 1 (1384).12, Hayashi-no-shō hyakushō rensho shitaji sarijō an. Quoted in Miura Keiichi, *Chūsei minshū seikatsushi no kenkyū* (Kyoto: Shibunkaku, 1981), 145.

65. *Tōdaiji monjo*, Enchō 4 (926).2.13 Minbushō fu (HI, no. 223); THM YU 1 (6), Jiryaku 3 (1067).6.3 Sanuki Mandaraji sō Zenbō no ge an (HI, no. 1005).

66. See Kawane, *Chūsei hōkensei*, 172–76, and Inagaki, *Nihon chūsei shakaishi ron*, 241–45, for typical expressions of this view. On Japan's twelfth-century crisis, see Ishii, "Insei jidai," and Ōishi, "Shōen kōryōsei no tenkai." Minegishi Sumio traces the source of crisis to a series of natural disasters, including an eruption of Mt. Asama: see his "Asamayama no funka to shōen no seiritsu," (Tokyo Toritsu Daigaku) *Jinbun gakuhō* 167 (March 1984): 1–23.

67. *Sanjūni-ban shokunin utaawase e*, ed. Mori Toru, vol. 28 of *Nihon emakimono zenshū* (Tokyo: Kadokawa Shoten, 1979). The illustration is found on p. 48.

68. Kuroda, *Nihon chūsei kaihatsushi no kenkyū*, 47–50, cites a parable in *Konjaku monogatari* which describes the possessions (*ie no gu*) of a peasant family; the list highlights the family's scythes, hoes, etc. See *Konjaku monoga-*

tari, ed. Yamada Yoshio et al., Nihon koten bungaku taikei (Tokyo: Iwanami Shoten, 1959–62), 25:443–45. A late Heian source defines "agriculturalists" (*nōgyō no tomogara*) as "those who wield hoes and plows": Eiryaku 2 (1161).5 Kii-no-kuni zaichō kanjin chinjō an (HI, no. 3153). Depictions of peasants bearing the signature hoe or rake can be found in *Hōnen shōnin eden* (early 14th century), ed. Tsukamoto Yoshitaka, vol. 13 of *Nihon emakimono zenshū* (Tokyo: Kadokawa Shoten, 1961), and in *Saigyō monogatari emaki* (13th century), ed. Hata Shirayoshi, vol. 11 of *Nihon emakimono zenshū* (Tokyo: Kadokawa Shoten, 1958).

CHAPTER THREE
OFFICIAL TRANSCRIPTS

1. THM TE 8, Shōan 1 (1299).11.5 Yano-no-shō reimyō jikken torichō an (reproduced, in part, in *Zoku zuroku Tōji hyakugō monjo*, no. 109); the process is discussed in *Aioi shishi*, comp. Aioi shishi hensan senmon iinkai (Aioi: Aioi shi kyōiku iinkai), 1:567–71.

2. On estate surveying, see Yamamoto Takashi, "Chūsei kenchū no igi," *Chihōshi kenkyū* 170 (April 1981): 35–50, and Tomisawa Kiyoto, "Chūsei kenchū no tokushitsu—torichō to mokuroku o tsūjite," *Nihonshi kenkyū* 233 (January 1982): 1–25. See also the works of Hōgetsu Keigo: "Chūsei kenchū ni tsuite no ichi, ni no mondai," *Shinano* 10 (May 1958): 26–32; "Chūsei no kenchū ni tsuite," *Chihōshi kenkyū* 91 (February 1968): 1–9; and "Shōen ni okeru kenchūshi no seikatsu jittai—Ogiso-no-shō no zōji chūmon o chūshin to shite," *Shinano* 37 (October 1985): 1–13.

3. The earliest extant reference to hyakushō myō is found in a provincial governor's decree: Shōhei 9 (932).9.22 Tanba no kokuchō (HI, no. 240), but it was not until the eleventh and twelfth centuries that myō become a widespread phenomenon. See Inagaki, "Ritsuryōseiteki tochi seido no kaitai," in *Tochi seidoshi I*, 140–72.

4. Among the works reassessing the viability of small-scale cultivation in the Heian era, the following are especially useful: Kawane, *Chūsei hōkensei seiritsushi ron*; Miura, *Chūsei minshū seikatsushi no kenkyū*; Kuroda Hideo, *Nihon chūsei kaihatsushi no kenkyū* (Tokyo: Azekura Shobō, 1984); Takahashi Masaaki, "Nihon chūsei nōgyō seisanryoku suijun saihyōka no isshiten," *Atarashii rekishigaku no tame ni* 148 (August 1977): 1–13; and Kimura Shigemitsu, "Chūsei seiritsuki ni okeru hatazukuri no seikaku to ryōyū kankei," *Nihonshi kenkyū* 180 (August 1977): 1–40.

5. Watanabe Sumio, *Kinai shōen no kiso kōzō*, rev. ed., (Tokyo: Yoshikawa Kōbunkan, 1969). Watanabe has reiterated this position in a more recent article: "Kōfukuji Daijōin ryō Yamato-no-kuni Yokota-no-shō ni tsuite," *Shigaku zasshi* 89 (March 1980): 1–25.

6. Nagahara makes this argument in two important essays: "Chūsei nōminteki tochi shoyū," and "Heian makki kōchi baiken no bunseki," both in *Nihon chūsei shakai kōzō no kenkyū*.

7. Nagahara, "Tochi shoyū," 147.

8. Kuroda Toshio, "Kamakura jidai no shōen no kannō to nōminsō no kōsei," in *Nihon chūsei hōkensei ron*, 165–232. In the last part of this article (pp. 219–32), Kuroda responds directly to Watanabe Sumio's assertions.

9. The earlier record, Kenchō 6 (1254).11.23 Tara-no-shō jikken torichō, is a survey of the paddy of the estate; a typical entry lists the area of the field and below that the name of the cultivator / possessor. The myō register, Kenchō 8 (1256) Tara-no-shō kannō chō an, groups fields into myō units. (KI, nos. 7825 and 7966, respectively.)

10. See the series of studies reprinted in Inagaki, *Nihon chūsei shakaishi ron*.

11. Inagaki Yasuhiko, "Chūsei no nōgyō keiei to shūshu keitai," in *Iwanami kōza Nihon rekishi*, vol. 6, *Chūsei 2* (Tokyo: Iwanami Shoten, 1975), 168–205.

12. Ibid., 198.

13. See, e.g., Inaba Nobumichi, "Kamakura ki no Iga-no-kuni Kuroda-no-shō no ichi kōsatsu," *Nenpō chūseishi kenkyū* 7 (May 1982): 1–51; Irumada, *Hyakushō mōshijō*; Yasuda Tsuguo, "Kōfukuji Daijōin ryō Yamato-no-kuni Yokota-no-shō no kintōmyō," *Shigaku zasshi* 88 (January 1979): 1–24, and "Hyakushō myō to tochi shoyū," *Shigaku zasshi* 90 (April 1981): 27–63; Hattori Hideo, "Buzen-no-kuni Kanada-no-shō kochi ni okeru chūsei keikan no fukugen—Nanbokuchō ki no myō no sonzai keitai" *Shigaku zasshi* 94 (July 1985): 63–93; and Okuyama Kenji, "Chūsei Hokusetsu ni okeru myō no kōzō to tochi shoyū keitai," *Shigaku kenkyū* 144 (July 1979): 28–47.

14. These posts, driven at the northeast, northwest, southeast, southwest corners of the estate, marked the "four limits" (*shiishi*) that defined the shōen's domain. Most posts were probably sticks of wood, although Shinto shrine holdings frequently used consecrated branches, and piles of stones or charcoal were sometimes also used. On this, see Nishioka Toranosuke, "Shōen bōji ni tsuite," in *Shōen ezu no kisoteki kenkyū*, ed. Shōen Kenkyūkai (Tokyo: San'ichi Shobō, 1973), 13–16. In any case the posts were not permanently anchored, surreptitiously moving the markers proved a convenient way of expanding a domain—and of creating disputes.

15. For Ota Estate, see *Myōhōin monjo*, Kenpo 6 (1218).10 Echizen-no-kuni rusudokoro kudashibumi, in Fukui ken, comp., *Fukui kenshi*, shiryōhen 2:420–21. The edict establishing Hine Estate is *Kujō ke monjo*, Tenpuku 2 (1234).6.25 Kan senji (*Kujō ke monjo*, comp. Kunaichō Shoryōbu [Tokyo: Kunaicho, 1971–], 1:159–60).

16. *Negoro yōsho*, Chōshō 1 (1132).12 Toba jōkō in-no-chō chō an (HI, no. 2254); I have omitted Ōe's numerous titles.

17. *Jingoji ryō Kii-no-kuni Kaseda-no-shō zu*. In *Nihon shōen ezu shūsei*, comp. Nishioka Toranosuke (Tokyo: Tōkyōdō Shuppan, 1976), 1:52; also in the color frontispiece to that volume.

18. In this context it is fascinating to note that boundary posts had only one estate's name inscribed on them, although they frequently marked the border between two or more estates. They express therefore a notion of boundaries that is inwardly directed, that marks the limits of sameness, not a line dividing two different realms. See the sample boundary post given in *Jurin shūyō* (in *Zoku gunsho ruijū*, 31, pt. 1, 354–88).

19. On this fifth boundary stake, see Kimura Shigemitsu, "Shōen shiishi bōji nōto (I)—Kii-no-kuni Kaseda-no-shō ezu o chūshin ni," (Tokyo Gakugei Daigaku) *Kiyō*, dai-san bumon, shakai kagaku 37 (December 1985): 209–31. On relations between Shibuta and Kaseda, see Hattori Hideo, "Mirai nengō no sekai kara—hizuke ni mujun no aru monjo yori mita shōen no yōsō," *Shigaku zasshi* 92 (August 1983) and Kōyama Yasunori, "Kaseda-no-shō ezu to sakai sōron," in *Chūsei sonraku to shōen ezu*, 255–73.

20. *Hōki-no-kuni Kawamura gun Tōgō-no-shō shitaji chūbun zu*. In *Ezu shūsei*, 1:67. For more on this ezu, see Kuroda Hideo, *Sugata to shigusa no chūseishi* (Tokyo: Heibonsha, 1986), 193–209, and *Kyōkai no chūsei, shōchō no chūsei* (Tokyo: Tokyo Daigaku Shuppankai, 1986), 89–98. In the latter, Kuroda offers an extended analysis of the artistic devices used in drawing maps to mark boundaries.

21. John Berger, in his *Ways of Seeing* (London: Pelican Books, 1972), 83–84, comments on the "analogy between *possessing* and the way of seeing which is incorporated in [European] oil painting." By presenting the estate as a single unit, enclosed and isolatable, ezu effect a similar transformation. They propose a way of seeing estates that renders them capable of being enclosed and possessed by a single proprietor.

22. The phrase is G.N.G. Clarke's, in "Taking Possession: The Cartouche as Cultural Text in Eighteenth-Century American Maps," *Word & Image* 4 (April-June 1988): 455.

23. William Boelhower points to this function of maps in "Inventing America: A Model of Cartographic Semiosis," *Word & Image* 4 (April-June 1988): 475–97. He speaks of Edward Wright's 1599 map of America as plotting, on the one hand, a "pilgrim's progress . . . the *peripli* of a people," while simultaneously seeking to achieve a "maximum degree of stasis in terms of total movement."

24. Although the earliest extant ezu is thought to date from 1143, the form itself may date back to the mid-eleventh century. On this point, see Okuno Nakahiko, "Shōen ezu no seiritsu to tenkai," and "Kaiden zu kara shishi bōji zu e no tenkai," in *Shōen ezu no kisoteki kenkyū*, ed. Shōen Kenkyūkai (Tokyo: San'ichi Shobō, 1984), 17–48; 81–126. Okuno's "Shōen shishi bōji zu no seiritsu," in *Shōensei to chūsei shakai*, comp. Takeuchi Rizō sensei kiju kinen ronbunshū kankōkai (Tokyo: Tokyo Daigaku Shuppankai, 1984), is also of interest.

25. Asakawa, "Some Documents Illustrative of the Development of *Shōen* Institutions," in *Land and Society in Medieval Japan*, 69–128.

26. THM *mugō* 1, Jōwa 12 (845).9.10 Minbu shōfu an, in Miyagawa, comp., *Ōyama sonshi*, shiryōhen, 1–2. A photograph of the original, with transcription and commentary, can be found in *Enshū komonjo sen*, shōen hen, 1:16–17.

27. For details of the ongoing struggles between Tōji and the provincial office, see Miyagawa, *Ōyama sonshi*, tsūshihen, and Elizabeth Sato, "Proprietor and Peasants: yama Estate in the Early Medieval Period," Ph.D. diss., University of Michigan, 1976.

28. THM HO 1, Kōwa 4 (1102).4.19 Tanba no kokushi chōsen (Miyagawa, *Ōyama sonshi*, shiryōhen, 28).

29. Ishimoda Shō, *Chūseiteki sekai no keisei*, 21–49. Sanetō's bequest (Tengi 4 [1056] 2.23 Fujiwara Sanetō shoryō yuzurijō an) can be found in *Iga-no-kuni Kuroda-no-shō shiryō*, 1:55–59. Kuroda Hideo also provides an extended analysis of the document; see *Nihon chūsei kaihatsushi no kenkyū*, 344–70.

30. *Kōyasan monjo*, Eishō 4 (1049).12.28 Daijō kanpu an (HI, no. 675).

31. See, e.g., the edict establishing Ishide Estate: *Negoro yōsho*, Taiji 4 (1129).11.3 Toba jōkō in-no-chō chō an (HI, no. 2145). HI, nos. 2248, 2249, and 2254 (all dated 1132) provide similar examples for Okada, Yamahigashi, and Yamazaki estates.

32. *Kyōōgokokuji monjo*, Jōwa 5 (1349).5 Wakasa Tara-no-shō monjo shū, in Akamatsu Toshihide, comp., *Kyōōgokokuji monjo* (Kyoto: Heirakuji Shoten, 1960–72), 1:617–24. Appended to this document is a register of the estate made in 1302: THM *o* 6, Shōan 4 (1302) Tara-no-shō jikken torichō an (KI, nos. 21269–70).

33. Irumada Nobuo, *Hyakushō mōshijō to kishōmon no sekai*, 110: "it was pratically impossible for a single shōen proprietor to claim exclusive authority over the people of a region." Yamazaki Yuriko also emphasizes the coexistence in one estate or village of many authorities, see Yamazaki, "Chūsei zenki no tochi shoyū—Tsu-no-kuni Ao mura ni tsuite," *Nara shien* 21/22 (August 1977): 23–54.

34. "The tenant who . . . ploughs the land and gathers in the crop; his immediate lord, to whom he pays dues . . .; the lord of the lord, and so on, right up the feudal scale—how many persons there are who can say, each with as much justification as the other, 'That is my field!' " Marc Bloch, *Feudal Society*, 1:116.

35. [Kenchō 5 (1263)] Namazue-no-shō hyakushō tō mōshijō (KI, no. 7680).

36. We know about this relationship from a suit over water rights that occurred during the early fourteenth century; the documents date the relationship back, however, to a "contract" settled in 1171. See THM *ko* 38, Tokuji 3 (1308).5.28 Ōyama-no-shō yōsui keijō, and THM YU 21, Tokuji 3 (1308).5.28 Ōyama-no-shō iryōden sarijō an (Miyagawa, *Ōyama sonshi*, shiryōhen, 80–81).

37. See, e.g., THM *ha* 9, Bun'ei 11 (1274).2 Tara-no-shō Suetake myō hyakushō shiki bunin kudashibumi an (DNS 10, 1:537–38).

38. See *Iga-no-kuni Kuroda-no-shō shiryō*, nos. 429–32.

39. *Zenjōji monjo*, Kōchō 2 (1262).11.17 Ōmi-no-kuni Ōishi-Ryūmon ryōshōmin wayo nikki an. In *Zenjōji monjo*, comp. Kodaigaku Kyōkai (Tokyo: Yoshikawa Kōbunkan, 1979), 35–36.

40. For the survey of Ogiso Estate in 1329, for example, a team of twenty surveyors (and four horses) was dispatched by the proprietor; they required a total of thirty-six-and-a-half days to complete their work and incurred expenses amounting to more than 63 kanmon—a sum nearing the total annual rent from some estates. See *Kōzanji monjo*, Gentoku 1 (1329) Ogiso-no-shō kenchū zōmotsu nikki meyasu chūmon, in *Kōzanji komonjo*, comp. Kōzanji Tenseki Monjo Sōgō Chōsadan (Tokyo, 1975), 4:133–41. Discussed in Hōgetsu, "Shōen kenchūshi no seikatsu jittai." The 1345 survey of Yano Es-

tate ran up expenses of more than 48 kanmon and 26 koku of rice. See THM *kyō* 51, Jōwa 3 (1347).2.26 Yano-no-shō kenchū yōdo chūmon (*Zoku zuroku Tōji hyakugō monjo*, no. 127).

41. Thus Sanenaga, a hyakushō of Yano Estate, proudly announced his father's role as scribe in the 1345 survey of the estate; see THM *yo* 66(1), Kōryaku 1 (1379).8 Yano-no-shō reimyō nai Korefuji myō myōshu Sanenage mōshijō (in Kasamatsu, *Chūsei seiji shakai shisō*, 2:306–11). And in 1384, Kōyasan ordered the cultivators of Kanshōfu Estate to "stand in the fields" along with the surveyors. See *Kōyasan monjo*, Genchū 1 (1384).12.7 Kanshōfu-no-shō nengu keijō (DNK 1, 7:303).

42. A complete survey (*shōken*), which covered the entire estate and for which the proprietor dispatched surveyors, was usually carried out only once during a proprietor's tenure. The registers and rent rolls produced from this survey established, sometimes once and for all, the extent of cultivation and rents for the estate. Informal surveys (*naiken*) were carried out more frequently. These, however, were usually limited to rough inspections of flood- and drought-damaged fields in order to adjust rents for the year; they did not rewrite the "books" for an estate. The shoken remained the authoritative account of the estate's fields. See Hōgetsu, "Chūsei no kenchū ni tsuite."

43. *Zappitsu yōsho*, in *Zoku gunsho ruijū*, 11:753–84.

44. THM KU 1, Bun'ei 8 (1271).2.28 Niimi-no-shō ryōke gata satomura bun shōken torichō an (*Okayama kenshi*, iewake shiryō, 191–208).

45. *Kyōōgokokuji monjo*, Kenchō 6 (1254). 11.23 Tara-no-shō jikken torichō (KI, 11:59–62).

46. *Kōyasan monjo*, Hōji 1 (1247).2.10 Tōji chōja migyōsho (KI, no. 6835).

47. *Daigoji monjo*, Jōwa 3 (1347) Ise Sone-no-shō hyakushō tō mōshijō. Cited in Hōgetsu Keigo, "Chūsei kenchū ni tsuite no ichi, ni no mondai," 27. The temple's desire to resurvey the estate was occasioned by dwindling rents, which it ascribed to "collusion" on the part of hyakushō and resident officials. Significantly, Daigoji sought only to bring rents back up to precedented levels, not to uncover new revenues.

48. *Hizen Ryūzōji monjo*, Bun'ei 3 (1265).6 Hizen-no-kuni gungō kenchūchō an (KI, 13:176–93). Surveys also generally avoided the period known as *doyō*—the eighteen days preceding the first day of each season by the lunar calendar—during which the earth was not to be disturbed. See, e.g., the dates of the Yano survey cited in n. 1 (summarized in *Aioi shishi*, 1:570–71) or the debate between *on'yōshi* recorded in AK, Gennin 1 (1224).12.2.

49. A hut set aside for the yomiai (*yomiai kariya*) is mentioned in a document from Suda Estate (*Suda ke monjo*, Kōan 3 (1280).11; KI, no. 14197); a yomiai at a local temple is described in *Kōyasan monjo*, ei 31 (1424) Jōban bajō torichō an.

50. *Tōdaiji monjo*, Kyūan 4 (1148).4.28 Akanabe-no-shō densū to chūmon (HI, no. 2645). The delinquent kumon is also cited for failing to assist in the survey, for not appearing on the estate between harvest time and spring, and for "not knowing where the field registers (*tabumi*) have got to."

51. The concluding lines of a survey of Mita gō in Aki Province confirm this practice of reporting the extent both of cultivated fields and waste: "In

accordance with an order of the retired emperor's chancery and with a directive from the provincial governor, we have surveyed the waste and fertile fields within the four boundaries [of the *gō*] and driven boundary markers. . . ." *Itsukushima monjo*, Ninpyō 4 (1154).10.11 Aki-no-kuni Takada gun, Mita gō rikken mon, in Gotō Norihiko, "Chōko zasshō shoshū no Itsukushima monjo (2)," *Shigaku zasshi* 88 (December 1979): 46–60.

52. See *Tōdaiji monjo*, Einin 3 (1296).6 Ōi-no-shō jikken bajō torichō an and (same date) Ōi-no-shō jikken nayosechō an, in *Gifu kenshi*, shiryōhen, kodai-chūsei, 3:602–48, 705–67.

53. Contrast the torichō for Mizuno with the nayosechō drawn up at the same time: *Itsukushima monjo*, Kangen 4 (1246).2.19 Mizuno mura sakuden jikken bajō torichō, and Kangen 4 (1246).2 Mizuno mura kenchū nayose chūshinjō (*Hiroshima kenshi*, kodai-chūsei shiryōhen, 4: 1408–10). The latter reveals that the holding paid rents in iron; the former suggests that the area is entirely agricultural.

54. The 1271 survey is contained in five registers, all dated Bun'ei 8 (1271).2.28; the 1325 survey also consists of five scrolls, dated Shōchū 2 (1325).2.22. See THM KU 1–5 and 11–15; in *Okayama kenshi*, 20:191–287, 359–475.

55. See, e.g., Amino, "Nihon chūsei no heimin to shokunin," *Shisō* 671 (April 1980): 14–15.

56. The organization of registers provides further testimony to the conventions that shaped contemporary attitudes. Different types of fields, notably paddy and dry field, were often segregated to separate parts, even separate volumes, of a register. The Niimi register of 1325 (cited in n. 54) required five volumes, two to contain the paddy and three to catalog the dry fields of the estate. In a similar vein, a survey of Yano Estate produced separate rolls for paddy and for "dry field and chestnut forest." See THM *mi* 25, Jōwa 1 (1345).12.8 Yano-no-shō nishikata denchi jikken nayose torichō (paddy), and THM RO 6 Jōwa 1 (1345).12.8 Yano-no-shō nishikata hatake narabi ni kuribayashi jikken nayose torichō (dry field, chestnut).

57. Registers commonly report areas as fractions of one *tan*: shō (small, 1/3 *tan*), han (1/2 *tan*), dai (large, 2/3 *tan*). See Yamamoto, "Chūsei kenchū no igi," 38–39. Likewise, the use of 2.5 shiro as the smallest unit on Niimi and many other registers from Western Japan suggests that twice that, or five shiro (1/10 *tan*, and the next smallest unit used), may have been the standard unit of reference.

58. Shōō 5 (1292).12.11 Ashari Jōhan Genshin rensho kishōmon (KI, no. 18067).

59. *Pace* Yamamura, there is no suggestion that estate proprietors attempted to "collect the maximum amount in taxes" or to "get the most out of the shōen." The available evidence indicates, rather, that proprietors valued stability (a safe, if smaller, return) over the possibility of garnering more. See Yamamura, "Tara in Transition: A Study of a Kamakura *Shōen*," *Journal of Japanese Studies* 7, no. 2 (Summer 1981): 360.

60. See Kuroda, "Kamakura jidai no shōen no kannō to nōminsō no kōsei," in *Nihon chūsei hōkensei ron*; Yamamoto, "Kenchū no igi"; and

Hashimoto Hiroshi, "Chūkan chiiki ni okeru hyakushō myō no sonzai keitai," *Nihonshi kenkyū* 282 (June 1986): 1–35.

61. See, e.g., the use of the 1254 field register for Tara Estate in a later dispute over the possession of one of the estate's myō: *Kyōōgokokuji*, Einin 7 (1298).3.1 Sukekuni myō tsubotsuke chūmon (KI, no. 19617).

62. For example, a notation on the torichō for Mizuno mura (cited in n. 53) reveals that the original (*shōmon*) remained on the estate in the possession of the kumon. Likewise, the newly appointed kumon of Sone Estate in Ise Province promises to forward the originals of torichō kept on the estate whenever the proprietor wished to consult them, as does the kumon of Kamikuze Estate, see *Daigoji monjo*, Ryakuō 3 (1340).7.13 Sone-no-shō kumon Tachibana Noriaki ukebumi (DNS ser. 6, 6:501), and THM *kyō* 56, Kannō 3 (1352).6.29 Tachibana Nakasada Kamikuze-no-shō kumon shiki jōjō ukebumi (DNS ser. 6, 17:512).

63. In this vein, it is interesting to note that mokuroku also established the legally recognized right of various parties to income from an estate. For example, a jitō accused by Kōyasan of withholding rents complained that he had had no choice but to take what he considered to be his due; although the estate had been surveyed in the 1250s, no mokuroku had yet (in 1274) been drawn up to verify his income rights—a situation, he averred, that was "most distressing." *Kōyasan monjo*, Bun'ei 11 (1274).7 Ōta-kata jitō tō chinjō (*Bingo-no-kuni Ōta-no-shō shiryō*, 1:132–35).

64. See the references in Tomisawa Kiyoto, "Chūsei kenchū no tokushitsu," 14.

65. THM RO 7, Jōwa 2 (1346).4.10 Yano-no-shō nishikata jikken narabi ni todai sadame nayosechō (*Zoku zuroku Tōji hyakugō monjo*, no. 128).

66. THM KU 16, Shōchū 1 (1325).4.22 Niimi-no-shō jito kata denchi shitaji jikken nayosechō (*Okayama kenshi*, 20:475–99; the entry cited is on pp. 487–88).

67. THM *ni* 40, Shitoku 3 (1386).2 Ōyama-no-shō densū nayosechō an (*Ōyama sonshi*, shiryōhen, 161–65).

68. THM *mi* 25, Jōwa 1 (1345).12.8 Yano-no-shō nishikata denchi jikken nayose torichō (DNS ser. 6, 9:548).

69. Cf. *Itsukushima monjo*, Kangen 4 (1246).2 Mizuno mura kenchū nayose chūshinjō and Kangen 4 (1246).2.19 Mizuno mura sakuden jikken bajō torichō an (*Hiroshima kenshi*, shiryō hen, 4:1408–10).

70. THM *to* 43, Einin 4 (1296).3 Shinchokushiden sontoku bajōchō, mura nayose, narabi ni kenchū mokuroku (DNK 10, 3:506–16). This document combines the three forms—field register, *nayosechō*, and *mokuroku*—into a single scroll.

71. THM KU 16 Shōchū 2 (1325). Niimi-no-shō jito kata denchi shitaji jikken nayosechō (*Okayama kenshi*, 20:475–99). The summary of rents is to be found on p. 499; for individual myō, see, e.g., the entry for Tomokiyo myō, pp. 476–77.

72. *Tōdaiji monjo*, Einin 3 (1295).6 Ōi-no-shō kenchū nayosechō an.

73. THM *ha* 3/*Kyōōgokokuji monjo* no. 60, Kenchō 8 (1256).2 Tara-no-shō kannō chō an (KI, no. 7966). The *torichō* of 1254 (see n. 9, above) makes no

mention of rents; however, a mokuroku drawn up four days later distinguishes seven levels of rents. See THM *ha* 2, Kenchō 6 (1254).11.27 Tara-no-shō jikken torichō mokuroku an (KI, 11:57–59).

74. Kuroda, "Kannō," 170–81.

75. Hashimoto, "Chūkan chiiki." Comparing a rent roll with the Bun'ei register upon which it was based, he notes that substantial reductions (up to 7 percent of the paddy and 23 percent of the dry field) for *kanryō* fields were allowed in calculating the taxable area of each myō. Kanryō usually refers to a payment made by (or exacted on) peasants in lieu of surveying, but in this instance the size of the reduction suggests another purpose: the fields served as a means of incorporating some leeway into myō areas to set them at a level deemed appropriate.

76. See Yasuda, "Hyakushō myō to tochi shoyū," and "Yokota-no-shō no kintōmyō."

77. Cf. John Barrell's comments regarding the enclosures of eighteenth-century England as an effort to control nature "by coming to know the natural landscape according to one system or another": "To enclose an open-field parish means in the first place to think of the details of its topography as quite erased from the map. . . . The minute and intricate divisions between land, strips, furlongs, and fields simply ceased to exist: the quantity of each proprietor's holding was recorded, but not along what furlongs it had been distributed. Everything about the place which made it precisely this place, and not that one, was forgotten; the map was drawn blank." The shōen surveying process rehearses an analogous mode of power: by redrawing the map so that the particulars of place gave way to the categories of a system, surveying established the terms by which space could be comprehended, and thereby controlled. Barrell, *The Idea of Landscape and the Sense of Place, 1730–1840: An Approach to the Poetry of John Clare* (Cambridge: Cambridge University Press, 1972), 84, 94.

78. *Sankain keshō.* The comment is appended to a copy of a late-twelfth-century land register for Izumo Estate: Bunji 2 (1186) Izumo-no-shō kenchū mokuroku (in *Shiryo sanshū*, pt. 37, 2:52; also KI, no. 202).

79. See, for example, THM *kyō* 66, Jōji 6 (1367).9 Yano-no-shō myōshu hyakushō tō mōshijō; THM *yo* 38, Ōan 2 (1369).3.15 Yano-no-shō myōshu hyakushō tō kishōmon; and THM *yo* 11–15 jō, Meitoku 4 (1393).9 Yano-no-shō bandō tō rensho kishōmon. The first two are reproduced in *Zoku zuroku* Toji hyakugō monjo, nos. 134–35; for the third, see DNS ser. 7, 1:428–29. Michiie was appointed myōshu of Sadatsugu myō in 1346; whether or not he still held that position in the 1360s is not known. See THM *fu* 44(6), Jōwa 2 (1346).4.10 Sadatsugu myō todai sadame kudashibumi an (DNS ser. 6, 10:333–34).

80. For appointments see, e.g., THM *ha* 9, Tara-no-shō Suetake myō hyakushō shiki bunin kudashibumi an (DNK 10, 1:537–38). Although not strictly an appointment, the following agreement about rents is also interesting: THM *na* 52, Shōan 4 (1302).4.23 Tara-no-shō hyakushō tō rensho mōshijō (KI, no. 21050). The signers all add the names of the myō they are responsible for below their personal names.

81. See *Katusodera monjo*, Bun'ei 11 (1274).1.10 Ama Jishō denchi baiken and Ōan 7 (1374).2.28 Nakamura ukon-no-jō denchi baiken. In Minoo shishi hensan iinkai, comp., *Minoo shishi*, shiryōhen (Minoo: Minoo Shiyakusho, 1968–73), 1:194 and 2:100, respectively.

82. This responsibility is mentioned in THM *ho* 9, Kangen 1 (1243).11.25 Rokuhara saikyojō an (DNK 10, 2:505–17).

83. Nagahara Keiji provides a convenient summary of this in "Land-ownership Under the *Shōen-Kokugaryō* System," 288–94. To this scheme, a third category might be added: exempt fields, which owed neither *nengu* nor *kuji*.

84. THM KU 8, Kōan 7 (1285).12 Niimi-no-shō kanmotsu chofu an (*Okayama kenshi*, 20:331–55).

85. Kenkyū 1 (1190).6 Banna okibumi (*Bingo-no-kuni Ōta-no-shō shiryō*, 1:38–42).

86. Watanabe, *Kinai shōen*.

87. See Kōnin 13 (823).12.9 Ōmi-no-kuni Nagaoka gōchō no ge, and Engi 11 (911).4.11 Tōdaiji jōza Keisen utsujō (HI, nos. 48 and 206).

88. See, e.g., the references to "*taku myō*" in Kōhō 1 (964).9.23 Iga-no-kuni Nabari gunji no ge an (HI, no. 278) and to "*kemyō*" in Manju 2 (1025).11 Iga-no-kuni Nabari gunji no ge an (HI, no. 504).

89. These are mentioned in Enchō 7 (929).7.14 Ise-no-kuni Iino-no-shō Daijingū kanjō (HI, no. 233). Ōta Inumaru myō was the precursor of Kohi-gashi Estate. For a detailed history of this myō-turned-estate, see Inagaki, *Nihon chūsei shakaishi ron*, 3–124.

90. M. de Certeau, *The Practice of Everyday Life*, trans. Steven F. Rendall (Berkeley and Los Angeles: Univ. of California Press, 1984), 117.

91. de Certeau, *Everyday Life*, 117.

CHAPTER FOUR
THE THEATER OF PROTEST

1. One need only look to the numerous descriptions of the taking of heads in medieval fiction or to the bloody head of Shinzei (posted on the gate to a jail) depicted in *Heiji monogatari ekotoba* for grizzly confirmation of the violence of medieval Japan. A scene in *Yugyō shōnin engie* shows a local lord torturing a man by firing blunt arrows at his back; for a discussion of this scene, see Kuroda, *Sugata to shigusa no chūseishi*, 125–27. And one of the most famous documents of the medieval period is a petition from the residents of Ategawa Estate in which they accuse the estate's jitō of cutting off the noses and ears of peasants and their children and wives. See Kenji 1 (1275).10.28 Ategawa-no-shō Kamimura hyakushō tō genjō jō. In *Kii-no-kuni Ategawa-no-shō shiryō*, comp. Nakamura Ken (Tokyo: Yoshikawa Kōbunkan, 1978), 2:14–16.

2. The work of E. P. Thompson and Natalie Zemon Davis has done much to question the dichotomy often drawn between violence and rites (and their implied corollaries, i.e., the political/economic and the cultural/symbolic).

See, especially, Thompson, "The Moral Economy of the Crowd in the Eighteenth Century," *Past and Present* 50 (1971): 76–136; and Davis, "The Rites of Violence," in *Society and Culture in Early Modern France* (Stanford: Stanford University Press, 1975). For a stimulating discussion of the cultural and discursive constitution of political identity and community, see David W. Sabean, *Power in the Blood: Popular Cultural and Village Discourse in Early Modern Germany* (Cambridge: Cambridge University Press, 1984). Recent work in cultural studies, by stressing the political dimensions of culture and the violence of the symbolic, also calls into question these divisions; for a good introduction to the field, see Stuart Hall, "Cultural Studies: Two Paradigms," *Media, Culture and Society* 2 (January 1980): 57–72.

3. Thus Guy Fourquin offers the following "general outline" of peasant protest in medieval Europe: "the explosion is sudden, unexpected, destructive, and almost always short-lived." Any movement that does not meet these criteria evidently falls outside the category of popular rebellion. See Fourquin, *The Anatomy of Popular Rebellion in the Middle Ages*, trans. Anne Chesters (Amsterdam: North-Holland, 1978), 132.

4. THM, *yo* 11–15 jō, Meitoku 4 (1393).9 Yano-no-shō bandō tō rensho kishōmon (DNS, ser. 7, 1:428–29).

5. Bloch, *French Rural History*, 170.

6. Michel Foucault, "The Subject and Power," afterword to Hubert Dreyfus and Paul Rabinow, *Michel Foucault: Beyond Structuralism and Hermeneutics* (Chicago: University of Chicago Press, 1982), 210–11.

7. See Aioi shishi hensan iinkai, comp., *Aioi shishi*, (Aioi: Aioi shi, 1987), 2:113–73, for a recent and detailed narrative of these events.

8. For a typical example of this line of argument, see Satō Kazuhiko's rendition of these uprisings in *Nanbokuchō nairanshi ron* (Tokyo: Tokyo Daigaku Shuppankai, 1979), 73–121, or Sasaki Hisahiko's treatment of shōen rebellions in general, "Nanbokuchō 'nairan' ki ni okeru 'shōke no ikki' no kentō," *Rekishigaku kenkyū*, sp. ed. (November 1973): 48–53. Amino Yoshihiko adopts a somewhat different perspective in *Chūsei Tōji to Tōji-ryō shōen*, 437–92.

9. THM MU 52, Eiwa 3 (1377) Gakushū-gata hyōjō hikitsuke. Two partial transcriptions of this document have been prepared by Satō Kazuhiko: "Harima-no-kuni Yano-no-shō ni okeru 'shōke ikki' ni tsuite—Eiwa sannen Gakushū-gata hyōjō hikitsuke no shōkai," *Minshūshi kenkyū* 6 (May 1968): 181–208, and "Jūyon-seiki ni okeru Harima-no-kuni Yano-no-shō no zaichi dōkō," (Tokyo Gakugei Daigaku) *Kiyō* 31 (January 1980): 157–81. The latter article corrects many errors in the first.

10. This was not the first time that Yano's residents had complained about Yūson. Within a few years of his appointment, Yūson was the target of peasant protests for his part in disputes over crop damages; in 1369, he clashed with peasants over his attempts to have Jitsuen, a hyakushō leader, banished for assault; and from 1374–77, Yūson and the estate's residents were embroiled in a dispute over the disposition of Jitsuen's holdings. For details, see *Aioi shishi*, 2:112–23.

11. Yūson became overseer of the estate in 1359 as a reward for his success a few years earlier in persuading the shugo to lend his support to Tōji's claim

over some disputed holdings; see THM NO 31 (1), Enbun 1 (1356).5.13 Tōji kakikudashi an. On Tara Estate, in the 1350s, Tōji also turned to an overseer who had some influence with the shugo; see THM HA 19, Shōhei 7 (1352).2.24 Tara-no-shō ukon-no-jō tō rensho mōshijō and THM HA 20, Kannō 3 (1352).4.5 Ozuki Kuniharu Tara-no-shō jitō kata kōyōsen ukebumi (DNS, ser. 6, 17:501–3 and 507, respectively).

12. Befitting a topic that for many years was a mainstay of medieval historical studies, the literature on this topic is immense. I refer the reader to Mass, *Warrior Government in Early Medieval Japan*, for information on jitō; and to Lorraine Harrington, "Social Control and the Significance of *Akutō*," in *Court and Bakufu in Japan*, ed. Jeffrey P. Mass (New Haven: Yale University Press, 1982), and Amino Yoshihiko, "Akutō, daikan, yūryoku myōshu," in *Chūsei Tōji*, and idem, "Akutō no hyōka o megutte," *Rekishigaku kenkyū* 362 (1970): 29–40, for studies of non-Kamakura local lords. Suzanne Gay's study of the Kawashima is informative on lordship in the late medieval period, while Mass and Arnesen provide interesting perspectives on lordship at the beginning of the medieval era. See Gay, "The Kawashima: Warrior-Peasants of Medieval Japan," *Harvard Journal of Asiatic Studies* 46 (June 1986): 81–119; Mass, "Patterns of Provincial Inheritance in Late Heian Japan," 67–95; and Arnesen, "The Struggle for Lordship in Late Heian Japan," 101–41.

13. See Satō, *Nanbokuchō nairanshi ron*, 13–43, 73–101. In this, Satō is elaborating a view first put forth by Suzuki Ryōichi in *Nihon chūsei no nōmin mondai* (Kyoto: Kōtō Shoin, 1948) and *Junsui hōkensei seiritsu ni okeru nōmin tōsō* (Tokyo: Nihon Hyōronsha, 1949) and further developed in Matsumoto Shinpachirō, *Chūsei shakai no kenkyū* (Tokyo: Tokyo Daigaku Shuppankai, 1956).

14. Satō stands in here for an important line of scholarship associated most prominently with Nagahara Keiji. See, especially, Nagahara's "Shugo ryōgokusei no tenkai," in *Nihon hōkensei seiritsu katei no kenkyū* (Tokyo: Iwanami Shoten, 1961) and the essays collected in *Nihon chūsei shakai kōzō no kenkyū* (Tokyo: Iwanami Shoten, 1973).

15. I find support for this assertion in Takano Yoshikazu's study of all the shugo's interventions on Yano estate in the fourteenth century. Takano concludes that the shugo did not act on his own authority; even in the 1377 uprising, the shugo exercised only the policing authority established as the office's purview by the Kamakura Bakufu. Yamakage Kazuo makes a similar argument with respect to Kōyasan's holdings. See Takano, "Nanbokuchō kōki ni okeru shōen ryōshu kendan to shugo kenryoku," *Nihonshi kenkyū* 270 (February 1985): 1–28, and Yamakage, "Nanbokuchō nairanki no ryōshu to nōmin," *Nihonshi kenkyū* 259 (March 1984): 23–48.

16. The classic expression of ritualized protest as reinforcing of the existing order is found in Max Gluckman, *Order and Rebellion in Tribal Africa* (London: Cohen and West, 1963). A large body of anthropological and other writings now exists to challenge Gluckman's ideas. See, e.g., Barbara Babcock, *Reversible Worlds: Forms of Symbolic Inversion* (Ithaca: Cornell University Press, 1978) and Michael M. J. Fischer and George Marcus, *Anthropology as Cultural Critique* (Chicago: University of Chicago Press, 1986). For a particularly fine exploration of the relationship between rules and transgression, see Allon

White, "Pigs and Pierrots: The Politics of Transgression in Modern Literature," *Raritan* 2 (Fall 1982): 51–71.

17. Pierre Bourdieu offers a thoroughgoing critique of this scholarly method which attempts to reduce practice to systems of rules and models. See "The Limits of Objectivity," *Outline of a Theory of Practice*, trans. Richard Nice (Cambridge: Cambridge University Press, 1977).

18. As Joan Scott notes, "the emphasis on 'how' suggests a study of processes, not of origins, of multiple rather than single causes, of rhetoric and discourse rather than ideology and consciousness." *Gender and the Politics of History* (New York: Columbia University Press, 1988), 4–5.

19. THM *ha* 86, Kenmu 1 (1334).8 Tara-no-shō hyakushō tō mōshijō narabi ni rensho kishōmon (DNK 10, 1:709–15).

20. Irumada, *Hyakushō mōshijō to kishōmon no sekai*, discusses the ritual in some detail, especially in part I of that work. See also Chijiwa Itaru, " 'Seiyaku no ba' no saihakken," *Nihon rekishi* 422 (July 1983): 1–16; idem, "Chūsei minshūteki sekai no chitsujo to teikō" in *Kōza Nihon rekishi*, ed. Rekishigaku Kenkyūkai and Nihonshi kenkyūkai (Tokyo: Tokyo Daigaku Shuppankai, 1985), 4:125–58; and Katsumata Shizuo, *Ikki* (Tokyo: Iwanami Shoten, 1982).

21. Amino Yoshihiko, *Chūsei shōen no yōsō* (Tokyo: Hanawa Shobō, 1966), 212.

22. Victor Turner, *From Ritual to Theatre* (New York: PAJ Publications, 1982), 26–27. I might note that absconding rehearses a similar strategy of the liminal. By "melting into the mountains and forests," peasants removed themselves to a space which was neither here nor there, a space just beyond the reach of authority. Mountain and forest are intrinsically sites of resistance to an authority that defined its special sphere as rice paddy and cultivated fields, that viewed mountains as "masterless waste." They comprised, in sum, the perfect space from which to challenge a proprietor or his proxies.

23. For Niimi, see *Okayama kenshi* iewake shiryō, 392. The rules for Okunoshima Estate may be found in Kasamatsu, *Chūsei seiji shakai shisō*, 1:165.

24. THM *ho* 19, Kangen 1 (1243).11.25 Rokuhara saikyojō an (DNK 10, 2:505–17).

25. *Goseibai shikimoku*, kishōmon. In Satō and Ikeuchi, comps., *Chūsei hōsei shiryōshū*, 1:29–30.

26. *Jingoji monjo*, Genryaku 2 (1185).1.19 Sō Mongaku kishōmon (HI, no. 4892).

27. THM *yo* 88, Kōei 3 (1344).2 Gakushū chū hyōjō shikimoku (DNS ser. 6, 9:196).

28. *Kōyasan monjo*, Kenkyū 5 (1194).7.7 Banna kishō sōsetsuchō. In Seno, comp. *Bingo-no-kuni Ōta-no-shō shiryō*, 1:51–53.

29. See Chijiwa, " 'Seiyaku no ba' no saihakken," 2.

30. See, for example, *Kōyasan monjo*, Bun'ei 10 (1273).8.10 Kantō gechijō an and *Tōdaiji monjo*, Kōan 10 (1287).10 Iga-no-kuni Kuroda-no-shō azukari dokoro saikyojō an (KI, nos. 11383 and 16383). See also Minegishi Sumio, "Seiyaku no kane" (Tokyo Toritsu Daigaku) *Jinbun gakuhō* 154 (March 1983): 55–82.

31. The shrine, Ōsake-no-miya, figured prominently in the spiritual and political life of the estate (for an overview, see *Aioi shishi*, 2:117–20, 294–99). Amino, in *Muen, kugai, raku*, explains the function of the shrine in terms of his theory of *muen* (lack of attachments), a property he ascribes to numerous sites in medieval Japan. According to Amino, Ōsake-no-miya could function as a focus of rebellion because it afforded a site removed from the attachments of everyday life. Umata Ayako, noting Tōji's extensive ties to the shrine, challenges Amino's interpretation. The shrine functioned as it did, she argues, not because it was a neutral site, but precisely because it afforded a direct connection to the temple. Again, the notion of liminality seems to suggest a way out of this impass. Like mountains and forests, the shrine occupied that ambiguous space between structure and its antithesis; it was both connected to Tōji and a site beyond authority's reach. See Umata, "Tōji-ryō shōen ni okeru zaichi jisha" in *Chūsei jiin soshiki no kenkyū*, ed. Kuroda Toshio (privately published, 1985), 65–71. On the functions of local temples in general, see Tanaka Fumihide, "Chūsei zenki no jiin to minshū," *Nihonshi kenkyū* 266 (October 1984): 4–23.

32. Two documents in the Zenjōji collection refer explicitly to the preparation of duplicate oaths. A report by the overseer of Ryūmon Estate (in Ōmi province) explains that the original of an agreement settling a boundary dispute with a neighboring estate is not available because "it was consumed by the residents of the estates as *shinsui*" (*Zenjōji monjo*, undated [1262?] Ōmi-no-kuni Ryūmon-no-shō zasshō Genjō jō an). An account of the agreement by the residents of the estates contains a similar note (*Zenjōji monjo*, Kōchō 2 (1262).11.17 Ōishi, Ryūmon ryōshō shōmin wayo nikki an). In Kodaigaku Kyōkai, comp., *Zenjōji monjo*, nos. 23–24.

33. Irumada calls oath swearing the "most fundamental ritual/ceremony of middle ages." See *Hyakushō mōshijō*, 9.

34. For Yugeshima, see THM *na* 78, Genkō 4 (1324).3 Yugeshima-no-shō satanin hyakushō mōshijō. In *Nihon engyō taikei*, comp. Nihon engyō taikei henshū iinkai (Tokyo: Nihon Senbai Kōsha, 1970), 1:326. For Ategawa, see *Tōdaiji monjo*, Kenji 1 (1275).10.28 Ategawa-no-shō Kamimura hyakushō tō genjō jō, in Nakamura, comp., *Kii-no-kuni Ategawa-no-shō shiryō*, 2:14–16.

35. *Genpei seisuiki*, v. 4 in *Nihon bungaku taikei* (Kyoto: Seibundō, 1938), 15:126.

36. See Genryaku 2 (1185).8.21 Minamoto Yoritomo kudashibumi; translated by Mass in *The Kamakura Bakufu*, 36–37.

37. See, e.g., THM *shi* 14, Bunpo 2 (1318).6.11 Tōji gusō-gata hyōjō kotogaki, THM *ni* 6, Bunpo 2 (1318).6.14 Ōyama-no-shō nengu todai keijō an, and THM *ya* 29, same date, Ōyama-no-shō hyakushō tō kishōmon; all in Miyagawa, comp. *Ōyama sonshi*, shiryō hen, 103–5.

38. See, e.g., THM HA 35, Enbun 1 (1356).7.4 Shimotsuke bō Zenshō Tarano-shō kumon shiki ukebumi (DNS ser. 6, 19:421); or *Tōdaiji monjo*, Engen 1 (1336).4.9 Akanabe-no-shō daikan sō Yūtoku kishōmon (DNK 18, 7:213).

39. For the first, see THM *yo* 88 Kōei 3 (1344).2 Gakushū chū hyōjō shikimoku (DNS ser. 6, 9:196) and Ryakuō 5 (1342).2 Hachimangū gusō hyōjō shikimoku (DNS ser. 6, 7:501–3); for the latter see, *Tōdaiji monjo*, Genkō 4 (1324).5.11 Tōdaiji jisō rensho kishōmon (DNK 18, 8:554–55).

40. Cf. the way in which carnival upends the normal hierarchies of power in E. LeRoy Ladurie, *Carnival in Romans*, trans. Mary Feeney (New York: G. Braziller, 1979).

41. *Tōdaiji monjo*, Genkyū 1 (1204).9 Kuroda-no-shō hyakushō mōshijō. In *Iga-no-kuni Kuroda-no-shō shiryō*, 2:247–48. The petition recounts how the oath was sworn orally before the Daibutsu at Tōdaiji.

42. THM *ha* 105(2), Kōan 2 (1362).3.10 Tara-no-shō hyakushō tō rensho kishōmon (DNK 10, 1:785–89).

43. THM *ya* 29, Bunpo 2 (1318).6.14 Ōyama-no-shō hyakushō tō rensho nengu todai ukebumi (Copy: DNK 10, 1:872–74).

44. Kurokawa Naonori, "Kishōmon no kotoba," *Nihonshi kenkyū* 119 (May 1971): 71–74, regards oaths as evidence of peasants' submission to authority and of their superstition.

45. THM RŪ 23, Shōwa 2 (1313).6 Yugeshima-no-shō ryōke-gata hyakushō tō mōshijō (*Nihon engyō taikei*, 1:288–90).

46. See *Kyōōgokokuji monjo*, Shōwa 2 (1313).7.12 Tōji jū-hachi kō gusō hyōjō kotogaki and Shōwa 2 (1313).7.22 Tōji jū-hachi kō gusō hyōjō kotogaki (both in *Nihon engyō taikei*, 1:290–91).

47. THM *shi* 13/*sa* 7, Shōwa 3 (1314).9 Yugeshima-no-shō ryōke-gata hyakushō tō rensho mōshijō (*Nihon engyō taikei*, 1:297–300).

48. THM *ye* 22, Shōwa 3 (1314).10.15 Tōji gusō hyōjō kotogaki; THM kyō 31, Shōwa 3 (1314).11 Yugeshima-no-shō ryōke-gata hyakushō tō rensho mōshijō; THM YO 203, [Shōwa 3 (1314).12.3 ?] Yugeshima-no-shō hyakushō, azukari dokoro Kukyo monchū kiroku (*Nihon engyō taikei*, 1:300–308). The date of this last document is supplied in THM *to* 75, Shōwa 5 (1316). int. 10.15 Yugeshima-no-shō monjo mokuroku (Ibid., 1:312).

49. See THM *na* 71, Shōwa 5 (1316). int. 10.18 Yugeshima-no-shō zasshō ukebumi an (*Nihon engyō taikei*, 1:313).

50. The first petition in the series does not survive, but another record gives an outline of the petitions and responses; according to this document the petition reached Tōji on 8/10/1304. See Kagen 2 (1304).9.21 Tara-no-shō hyakushō tō sonmō mōshijō chūki. In Akamatsu, comp., *Kyōōgokokuji monjo*, 1:364–65.

51. THM YE 22, Kagen 2 (1304).9 Tara-no-shō hyakushō mōshijō (KI, no. 21987).

52. THM YE 23, Kagen 2 (1304).9 Tara-no-shō hyakushō Ayabe Tokimistu ra rensho kasanete no mōshijō (KI, no. 21996). For Tōji's response, see the mōshijō chūki cited in n. 50. Appended to the petition was a detailed list of the damaged areas: THM E 20, Kagen 2 (1304).9 Tara-no-shō sonden chūmon.

53. See THM YE 25–29 (KI, nos. 22306, 22315, 22321, 22342, 22343). The experience of 1306 follows the same pattern as that of 1305.

54. THM YE 28 Kagen 3 (1305).9 Tara-no-shō hyakushō tō mōshijō (KI, no. 22342).

55. THM *ha* 40, Kagen 4 (1306).4.3 Tara-no-shō nengu chō (DNK 10, 1:604)

56. In *Power/Knowledge*, Michel Foucault puts forward a trenchant critique of what he calls the "economism" of traditional views of power. In both clas-

sical liberal theory and Marxist theory power is modeled upon the commodity—it is conceived of as "something that one possesses, acquires, cedes through force or contract, that one alienates or recovers. . . ." Against this, he asserts that power "exists only in action" and that the primary instance of the operation of power is the constitution of subjects: "It is already one of the prime effects of power that certain bodies, certain gestures, certain discourses, certain desires, come to be identified and constituted as individuals. The individual [peasant, estate, proprietor] . . . is not the *vis-à-vis* of power . . . it is the element of its articulation." Foucault, *Power/Knowledge: Selected Interviews and Other Writings*, ed. Colin Gordon (New York: Pantheon, 1980), 88–98.

57. See Hayashiya Tatsusaburō et al., "Kai jōtatsu monjo no hensen—'ge' yori 'mōshijō' e," *Nihon shigaku* 1 (April 1968): 3–23.

58. See Shimada Jirō, "Nihon chūsei kyōdōtai shiron," *Shichō* n.s. 4 (January 1979): 22–59.

59. Satō Shin'ichi, *Komonjogaku nyūmon* (Tokyo: Hōsei Daigaku Shuppankyoku, 1971), 195.

60. See THM SE 1, Kyūan 6 (1150).9.16 Yugeshima-no-shō hyakushō tō no ge; and THM SE 2, Kyūan 6 (1150).11.22 Yugeshima-no-shō jūnin ra no ge (*Nihon engyō taikei*, 1:2–5). The first full-fledged hyakushō mōshijō would seem to be one from Arakawa Estate: [Bunji 2 (1182)].4.4 Arakawa-no-shō hyakushō mōshijō an (KI 1:62).

61. See Ōishi, "Shōen kōryōsei no tenkai," 3:127–66, for a good summary of recent studies.

62. THM ri 5, Taiji 5 (1130).9 Ōyama-no-shō tato ra no ge; THM U 6, Tenshō 1 (1131).10.29 Ōyama-no-shō geshi jūnin ra no ge (*Ōyama sonshi*, shiryōhen, 52–3, 55).

63. For the first, see, e.g., the documents cited in n. 60; for the second, see THM SE 4, Chōkan 2 (1164).8 Yugeshima-no-shō geshi Taira Sukemichi no ge (*Nihon engyō taikei*, 1:6–7).

64. For example, *Tōdaiji monjo*, Tengi 4 (1056).3.27 Kuroda-no-shō kufu ra no ge, and Chōji 3 (1106).3.28 Kuroda-no-shō somaku ra no ge (in *Iga-no-kuni Kuroda-no-shō shiryō* 1:59–60, 113–14); and *Tōdaiji monjo*, Eiji 2 (1142).10 Akanabe-no-shō jūnin ra no ge an (in *Gifu kenshi*, shiryōhen, kodai-chūsei, 3:107–9).

65. THM ko 8(3), Nin'an 2 (1167).2.25 Yugeshima-no-shō jūnin ra no ge (*Nihon engyō taikei*, 1:11–12). In other examples, a petition of 1150.11.22 claims that the provincial governor's agents illegally confiscated 120 bales of salt; another dated 1164.12 complains of burdensome levies. See THM SE 2 Kyūan 6 (1150).11.22 Yugeshima-no-shō jūnin ra no ge and THM SE 5 Chōkan 2 (1164).12 Yugeshima-no-shō jūnin ra no ge (*Nihon engyō taikei*, 1:4–8).

66. *Tōdaiji monjo*, Tengi 1 (1053).7 Akanabe-no-shō shōshi, jūnin ra no ge an (*Gifu kenshi*, shiryōhen, kodai-chūsei, 3:14). This is the earliest known example of the genre. See Kawashima Shigehiro, "Shōen ryōshu shihai to 'jūnin ra no ge' no seiritsu," *Hitotsubashi ronsō* 87 (June 1982):40–56.

67. In substance and style, jūnin ra no ge resemble much more closely tenth-century petitions, such as the well-known Owari-no-kuni gunji

hyakushō ra no ge (988), than they do their successors, the hyakushō mōshijō. The text of this appeal is available in Yamagishi et al., eds., *Kodai seiji shakai shisō*, 253–67.

68. Both of these terms begin to come into currency from the closing decade of the eleventh century, precisely the period during which ge were giving way to mōshijō. See, e.g., HI, nos. 1353, 1422, 1441, 1444, 1530, and 1546.

69. This is common on Tōji's estates. On Tara Estate, for example, the organization of the hyakushō group came in the context of a dispute with a local lord. Similarly, Tōji actively fostered the formation of the hyakushō community on Yano Estate in opposition to the maraudings of the Terada *akutō* ("bandit"). The same pattern can be elicited from the history of Ōyama Estate. On Yano, see Koizumi Yoshiaki, "Harima-no-kuni Yano-no-shō no akutō," *Kokushigaku* 66 (January 1956): 44–63; Satō Kazuhiko, "Nanbokuchō nairanki to akutō—Harima-no-kuni Yano-no-shō o chūshin to shite," *Minshūshi kenkyū* 7 (May 1969): 66–77; and Uejima Tamotsu, "Kamakura jidai Harima-no-kuni Yano-no-shō ni tsuite," *Komonjo kenkyū* 7/8 (February 1975): 65–80.

70. [Bunji 2 (1182)].4.4 Arakawa-no-shō hyakushō mōshijō an (KI, 1:62).

71. Shimada, "Kyōdōtai shiron," 39.

72. Irumada Nobuo, *Hyakushō mōshijō*, 149–50, discusses this reorganization of Kuroda Estate, which took place during the first half of the 1170s. The first mōshijō for Kuroda dates from 1204, the last ge from 1169: *Tōdaiji monjo*, Genkyū 1 (1204).9 Kuroda-no-shō hyakushō mōshijō; Kaō 1 (1169).7 Kuroda-no-shō somaku Abe Sanshi ra no ge (*Iga-no-kuni Kuroda-no-shō shiryō*, 2:247–48; 2:71–4). For an extended discussion of the reorganization of Kuroda Estate, see Inaba, "Kamakura ki no Iga-no-kuni Kuroda-no-shō no ichi kōsatsu," 1–51.

73. THM E 2, Hōji 1 (1247).10.29 Kanto gechijō (KI, no. 6893).

74. Amino offers a detailed examination of these incidents in *Chūsei shōen no yōsō*.

75. THM *nu* 7, Bun'ei 7 (1270).6.30 Wakasa Tara-no-shō hyakushō mōshijō (KI, no. 10585) and THM *nu* 99, [Bun'ei 7 (1270)?].2.27 Wakasa Tara-no-shō hyakushō mōshijō an (KI, no. 10642).

76. Cf. John W. Hall, *Japan from Prehistory to Modern Times* (New York: Dell Publishing Co., 1970), 71: "In the *shōen* the cultivator . . . conceived of himself . . . as owing certain agreed-upon dues to certain superiors in return for personal benefices."

77. This obligation, known as *bumin*, is discussed at some length by Amino in *Mōko shūrai*, 32–73. Irumada, *Hyakushō mōshijō*, 232–40, also examines the concept.

78. Cf. Geertz, *The Interpretation of Cultures*, 363: "It is through culture patterns, ordered clusters of significant symbols, that man [sic] makes sense of the events through which he lives."

79. Foucault's most explicit definition of discursive formations is to be found in *The Archaeology of Knowledge*.

80. This concept of power is forcefully argued in Foucault, *Discipline and Punish: The Birth of the Prison*, trans. Alan Sheridan (New York: Vintage

Books, 1979), and in volume 1 of *The History of Sexuality*, trans. Robert Hurley (London: Penguin Books, 1979).

CHAPTER FIVE
CONCLUSION

1. Corrigan and Sayer, *The Great Arch*, 166.

2. Ibid., 3–4.

3. I take this phrase from an essay by Emmanuel Le Roy Ladurie entitled "History that Stands Still," in *The Mind and Method of the Historian* (Chicago: University of Chicago Press, 1981). The idea of a static, structural history is, of course, most closely associated with the *Annales* movement, in particular the work of Fernand Braudel. To negotiate a passage between structure and history, Braudel distinguishes three separate levels of time: that of the deep structure, which moves with (literally) glacial slowness; that of social groups, economic cycles, etc., of fifty to one hundred years' duration; and, finally, that of the very rapid time of the event. By maintaining these levels in relative isolation, Braudel's technique tends, however, to reinforce what seems to me an ultimately unproductive opposition between structure and history. What is needed, as David Carroll points out, is a means of approaching both simultaneously, a means that recognizes the inseparability of structural and historical questions. See David Carroll, *The Subject in Question: The Languages of Theory and the Strategies of Fiction* (Chicago and London: University of Chicago Press, 1982), especially chapter 5, "The Times of History and the Orders of Discourse." Braudel discusses his views on time in *On History* (Chicago and London: University of Chicago Press, 1980). For a general introduction to the *Annales* movement in general, see Peter Burke, *The French Historical Revolution: The* Annales *School, 1929–89* (Stanford: Stanford University Press, 1990).

4. As might be expected, a third group of scholars follows a middle path. As does the second group, the third holds that the system persisted into the sixteenth century; but, like the first, it considers the fourteenth century a watershed that divided the history of the system (and Japan's medieval era) into two distinct phases. The advent of the estate system in the eleventh and twelfth centuries marked in this telling of the tale the beginnings of the development of "medieval" forms of economic organization. The earlier phase, however, constituted an incomplete medieval revolution; the estate system remained deeply implicated in the political and economic framework of antiquity: the authority of absentee proprietors and the sway they could exert over local holders depended upon the place they held in the imperial state. This framework was rent by the political and economic currents of the thirteenth and fourteenth centuries. In particular, the organization of warrior power by the Kamakura and Muromachi bakufu precipitated a period of crisis and reorganization for the system, which ushered in a second stage in the history of the shōen. The system that emerged from this restructuring differed noticeably from its predecessor. Absentee authority was sharply curtailed, and far-flung estate networks were trimmed, leaving less attenuated lines of command. Instead of maintaining often tenuous interests in numerous estates,

estate proprietors of the later period focused their attentions on a few hold-ings over which they could exert firm control. If, in short, the Imperial family or the Fujiwara—proprietors of hundreds of estates throughout the realm, but only indirectly involved in their day-to-day management—provide the archetype for shōen holders of the earlier period, then the temple Kōyasan—lord of a handful of estates, most located nearby, over which it jealously as-serted exclusive authority—offers a paradigm for the later period. The shōen system, in short, survived, but only on a much reduced basis.

For a concise statement of this line of argument, see Kudō, "Shōensei no tenkai," 252–98. An abridged version of the essay is available in English: "Shōen," *Acta Asiatica* 44 (March 1983): 1–27. Although somewhat dated, Miyagawa Mitsuru's *Taikō kenchi ron*, vol. 1, *Nihon hōkensei kakuritsu shi* (Tokyo: Ochanomizu Shobō, 1959) offers another clear presentation of this view.

5. Matsumoto put forth this thesis in *Chūsei shakai no kenkyū*. Nagahara Keiji has built on and refined Matsumoto's basic proposition in a number of works, most notably, *Nihon hōkensei seiritsu katei no kenkyū* and *Nihon chūsei shakai kōzō no kenkyū*.

6. For a discussion of these economic developments, see Koizumi Yoshiaki, "Nairanki no shakai hendō," and Asaka Toshiki, "Chūsei no gijutsu to shukōgyōsha no soshiki," both in *Iwanami kōza Nihon rekishi*, ed. Asao Naohiro et al., vol. 6, *Chūsei 2* (Tokyo: Iwanami Shoten, 1975): 125–65; 208–44.

7. Ishimoda Shō is generally recognized as the progenitor of this line. His seminal work on the development of the Japanese medieval world (*Chūseiteki sekai no keisei*), first published in 1947, outlined what was until quite recently perhaps the dominant interpretation of Japan's medieval era. The conditions under which Ishimoda wrote this text seem in no small way to influence its argument: a Marxist history, researched and written under wartime prohibi-tions, then published in an atmosphere of postwar "liberation," it produces an alignment between Japan's past and Europe's that seems no accident of sources. As was the case for late-Meiji historians, this alignment allows Ishi-moda to bracket the experience of the immediate past and assert long-term congruences between Japan and the West. Even as Japan was attempting to place itself within a changed world order, this work placed Japan's past firmly within a world historical order.

8. This vein of scholarship may be traced to Araki Moriaki. In a controver-sial article published in 1953, Araki argued that the basis of the shōen system, and of the medieval economy in general, was state-supported "patriarchical slavery" (*kafuchōteki doreisei*); this configuration, he further asserted, was not overthrown until a feudal regime was instituted by Toyotomi Hideyoshi and others in the late sixteenth century. Araki first made this argument in "Taikō kenchi no rekishiteki zentei," *Rekishigaku kenkyū* 163–64 (May-June 1953). This article, slightly revised, has recently been reprinted in Araki, *Nihon hōken shakai seiritsushi ron* (Tokyo: Iwanami Shoten, 1984). Although they share Araki's views about the system's longevity, both Kuroda and Amino dispute Araki's most controversial contention—that the basis of the shōen system was patriarchal slavery, i.e., that the fundamental economic unit was the

family, commanded by its patriarch, supplemented by substantial amounts of nonautonomous labor. Kuroda sees the shōen system as basically feudal in nature, characterized by a serf-based system of production. Amino contends that peasants were neither serf nor slave, but free commoners. See Kuroda, *Nihon chūsei hōkensei ron*, esp. 345–90, and Amino, *Chūsei Tōji to Tōji-ryō shōen*.

9. Even here, one should be cautious. It is tempting to think that estate proprietors were interested solely in the rents they could garner from their holdings, that their concerns were exclusively economic (and by extension, then, that lack of rents would be *the* sign of dysfunction in the system). That nengu and kuji very commonly fell below stipulated amounts, or that Tōji in the fourteenth and fifteenth centuries, for instance, kept meticulous records of the fact that little or no rents were forthcoming from Tara or Ōyama estates for years on end (the very records that to Nagahara et al. prove the decline of the system) seems to suggest that some interest other than the purely economic was at work. Even from the proprietor's perspective, then, the estate should perhaps be viewed as a complex mixture of economic and symbolic capital, and registers that continued to record the names of long moribund estates or rent rolls, like Tōji's, that carefully remark the absence of revenues, might be seen as talismans that served to secure for proprietors recognition of their stature.

10. Raymond Williams, *The Long Revolution* (New York: Columbia University Press), 40–41.

11. Geertz, *The Interpretation of Cultures*, 144–45. Though not necessarily implicit in this definition per se, Geertz tends to regard culture as a stable, all-encompassing, agreed-upon groundwork for the production of meaning: his "ordered system" exists in a realm beyond dispute, beyond economic or political disorder (especially pertinent given the Indonesia he writes about in *The Interpretation of Cultures*). Culture is, in short, the code that unambiguously secures the meaning of human experience (and guarantees as well that human experience will be meaningful), whatever the political, class, social, or economic alignments of a particular time. In questing after this code, Geertzian interpretation invites an analysis that is resolutely ahistorical and apolitical. I would insist, therefore, that we take "order" to mean not only "organized," but something like "commanded," "regulated," or "dictated." These meanings have the advantage of recognizing, first, that orders tend to work in favor of certain groups over others, that they are not neutral dicta. In addition, they do not imply harmony or consent (one may have to obey an order without agreeing to it), and therefore recognize the violence that culture may inflict. Above all, these meanings indicate that order never exists apart from disorder, that the violation which elicited the regulation is an integral part, perpetually threatening to disrupt the "ordered system." See Aletta Biersack, "Local Knowledge, Local History: Geertz and Beyond," in *The New Cultural History*, ed. Lynn Hunt (Berkeley and Los Angeles: University of California Press, 1989), 72–96, and Vincent P. Pecora, "The Limits of Local Knowledge," in *The New Historicism*, ed. H. Aram Veeser (New York and London: Routledge, 1989), 243–76.

12. This definition is taken from Richard Terdiman, *Discourse/Counter-discourse* (Ithaca: Cornell University Press, 1985), 54.

13. Ibid., 33.

14. Peter Stallybrass and Allon White, *The Politics and Poetics of Transgression* (Ithaca: Cornell University Press, 1986), 4.

15. This is a charge frequently leveled against Foucault's works, see, for example, the essays in David Couzens Hoy, ed., *Foucault: A Critical Reader* (Oxford: Basil Blackwell, 1986), especially Charles Taylor's "Foucault on Freedom and Truth." Dreyfus and Rabinow also make this criticism, especially of the early works of Foucault. A rather more sophisticated criticism, from a hermeneutic point of view, can be found in Manfred Frank, *What is Neostructuralism?* (Minneapolis: University of Minnesota Press, 1989).

16. On this point, Pierre Bourdieu's theory of practice is of particular interest. Social structures, Bourdieu contends, are the product of historical practices, but the practices themselves are embedded in structure. Any attempt to ascribe primacy to one or the other is doomed: practice and structure, subject and social system, exist in a dialectic relationship. Bourdieu, *Outline of a Theory of Practice*, esp. chapter 2, "Structures and the Habitus."

17. According to Bourdieu, one of the most important products of culture is a "genesis amnesia," a forgetting or misrecognition that enables social agents to experience "the world of tradition . . . as a "natural world" [to be] taken for granted." The rules and structures guiding practice, he asserts, are generally invisible to the people who live them; they go without saying. Practice is guided instead by *doxa*, by a unquestioned, indeed unquestionable, common sense that allows the social world to be taken for the natural world. Much of culture takes place, therefore, in a "universe of the undiscussed," in a realm insulated from any specific institutions or institutional representation but implicit in a "whole universe of ritual practices, and also of discourses, sayings, proverbs." See Bourdieu, *Outline*, 164–71.

18. Marshall Sahlins, *Islands of History* (Chicago and London: University of Chicago Press, 1985), vii.

19. Bourdieu, *Outline*, 72.

20. Barry Hindess and Paul Hirst, *Pre-Capitalist Modes of Production* (London: RKP, 1975), 203: "To suppose that a mode of production of necessity ceases to reproduce itself and dissolves its limits is to suppose a teleological theory of history. . . . This supposes that a mode of production is a form which is historically finite, that is, that its conditions of existence are necessarily external to its structure. In any teleological history all finite portions of history, periods, modes of production, etc. are the *phenomena* of the action of a transhistorical cause."

21. On Nobunaga and Hideyoshi, see especially Elison's articles in George Elison and Bardwell Smith, eds. *Warlords, Artists and Commoners: Japan in the Sixteenth Century* (Honolulu: University of Hawaii Press, 1981); the articles by Fujiki Hisashi and John Hall in Hall, Nagahara Keiji, and Kozo Yamamura, eds. *Japan Before Tokugawa: Political Consolidation and Economic Growth, 1500–1600* (Princeton: Princeton University Press, 1981) are also informative. On *tenka*, see Nagahara Keiji, "Tenkajin," in *Nihon no shakaishi*, vol. 3, *Ken'i to shihai* (Tokyo: Iwanami Shoten, 1987), 199–231. Herman Ooms, *Tokugawa Ideology: Early Constructs, 1570–1680* (Princeton: Princeton University Press), 18–

62, offers a sophisticated analysis of the discursive refashioning of authority in the late sixteenth century.

22. *Kōgi no onbyakushō* was a mode of appellation adopted by peasant–adherents of the Ikkō sect; *hyakushō wa ōson*, literally "hyakushō are imperial offspring," appears in *Honpukuji atogaki*. See Kasahara Kazuo and Inoue Toshio, eds., *Rennyo, Ikkō ikki*, Nihon shisō taikei, vol. 17 (Tokyo: Iwanami Shoten, 1972). Passages in which the phrase appears are quoted in Fujiki Hisashi, "Tōitsu seiken no seiritsu," in *Iwanami kōza Nihon rekishi*, vol. 9, *Kinsei I* (Tokyo: Iwanami Shoten, 1975). Further testimony to the resurgence of this older, public meaning of hyakushō is to be found in the *Nippo jisho*, an early seventeenth-century dictionary: hyakushō is defined simply as "the masses" (*taishū*). By contrast, medieval sources recognize the term as specifying a special status. Thus in a thirteenth-century collection of Buddhist tales, hyakushō always appear paired with jitō, an indication that the term defined a status as distinct as that of the Kamakura bakufu's vassals. See *Shasekishū*, vol. 7, tales nos. 10–11, in Watanabe Tsunaya, ed. *Shasekishū*, Nihon koten bungaku taikei, vol. 85 (Tokyo: Iwanami Shoten, 1966), 306–9.

23. The Rokkaku were a powerful daimyo family from Southern Ōmi province. The Rokkaku code was drafted in 1567; its text is available in Satō and Ikeuchi, comps. *Chūsei seiji shakai shisō*, 1:280–307. The article cited appears on p. 284.

24. The phrase and the depictions of the nature of power in the late fifteenth and late sixteenth centuries are from Ooms, *Tokugawa Ideology*, 20–21.

25. Miyagawa Mitsuru, "From Shōen to Chigyō: Proprietary Lordship and the Structure of Local Power," in *Japan in the Muromachi Age*, 89–105. For more on village organization in the fifteenth and sixteenth centuries, see also Itō Hiroko, "Sōson no seiritsu to hatten," *Nihonshi kenkyū* 120–21 (July-September 1971): 1–12, 33–50; Harada Nobuo, "Nanbokuchō, Muromachi ki ni okeru 'sō' teki ketsugō no seiritsu," *Chihōshi kenkyū* 152 (April 1978): 69–88; Watanabe Hiromi, "Sengoku sonraku no kōzō," *Rekishi hyōron* 374 (June 1981): 77–92; Kurokawa Naonori, "Jūgo-jūroku seiki no nōmin mondai," *Nihonshi kenkyū* 71 (March 1964): 28–38.

26. The last Tōji survey is THM *to* 92, Shōchō 2 (1429).6 Tara-no-shō jitō-gata densū narabi ni hyakushō myō nayosechō (DNK 10, 1:709–19). See Amino, *Chūsei shōen no yōsō*, for a discussion of these changes on Tara in the fifteenth century.

27. In 1568 the residents of Sugaura in Ōmi Province declared the village to be a "self-policing area, to which the shugo is not allowed entry." (Eiroku 11 (1568).12.14 Sugaura sō okite bumi; *Nihon shisō taikei*, 22:200.) Sugaura's tradition of juridical autonomy, however, extends back to the mid-fifteenth century; see, for example, the village rules for the adjudication of theft—Kansei 2 (1461).7.13 Ōmi Sugaura shozata sōshō okite (*Chūsei seiji shakai shisō*, 2:180). In 1448, Imabori village adopted rules which set a fine for failure to attend village meetings—Bunna 5 (1448).11.14 Imabori gō shūgi okite (*Ibid.*, 177–78).

28. THM *wo* 225, Chōroku 3 (1458).9.30 Kuze jōge-no-shō samurai bun jige bun ra rensho kishōmon an. Signers of the oath are divided into "samurai-equivalent" (*samurai bun*) and "peasant-equivalent" (*jige bun*). Cited in Na-

gahara, "Village Communities and Daimyō Power," in *Japan in the Muromachi Age*, ed. John Hall and Toyoda Takeshi (Berkeley and Los Angeles: University of California Press, 1977), 108–10.

29. Kurushima Noriko, "Tōji ryō Yamashiro-no-kuni Kuze-no-shō no myōshu shiki ni tsuite," *Shigaku zasshi* 93 (August 1984), 22. The use of the term "myōshu" to encompass the latter group marks, Kurushima asserts, an attempt by the proprietor to contain them within the existing power/authority structure.

30. On Ōyama, the first use of onbyakushō as a mode of self-designation is found in a petition from 1407: THM *ni* 77, Ōei 14 (1407).12.15 Ōyama-no-sho Ichiidani hyakushō tō mōshijō (in Miyagawa, comp. *Ōyama sonshi*, shiryōhen, 203); thereafter, the term is used in all mōshijō (e.g., Ibid., nos. 304, 318–19, 324, 373). On Tara Estate, too, peasant petitions from the fifteenth century on are issued by the collective onbyakushō; see, e.g., the collection of petitions in *Chūsei seiji shakai shisō*, 2:285–96. Fujiki Hisashi, "'Hyakushō' no hōteki chii to 'onbyakushō' ishiki," in *Sengoku shakaishi ron*.

31. Miyagawa Mitsuru, "Sengoku daimyō no ryōgokusei," in *Hōken kokka no kenryoku kōzō*, ed. Shimizu Morimitsu and Aida Hidetsugu (Tokyo: Sōbunsha, 1967). A mid-fifteenth-century petition from the "onbyakushō" of Tara Estate offers interesting confirmation of these changes in hyakushō status. If the language of thirteenth- and fourteenth-century petitions from Tara depicts a hyakushō who is firmly linked to the structures of the estate system, here we can detect signs of the hyakushō's break from that system. The petition is addressed to Tōji, the estate's proprietor, but the petitioners invoke another authority to threaten their proprietor: "We have repeatedly requested that a representative be sent to the estate, but nothing has ever been done. The overlord [*uesama*, i.e., the shugo] will find it no small matter if [the proprietor] is at all remiss in his treatment of the onbyakushō" (*Chūsei seiji shakai shisō*, 2:293).

32. The *Seventeen Articles* (Asakura Toshikage jū-nana kajō) are reproduced in *Chūsei seiji shakai shisō*, 1:350–52.

33. The use of hyakushō here is of interest: it returns the term to a general usage which annuls the specificity that was the condition of its effect within the estates.

34. Hitomi Tonomura, "Forging the Past: Medieval Counterfeit Documents" *Monumenta Nipponica* 40 (Spring 1985), 69–96. Between the 1460s and the first decade of the sixteenth century, the Rokkaku assumed jurisdiction over Tokuchin-ho, an estate belonging to Enryakuji, and its residents, the Honai merchants. Concurrently, the value of the document by which these merchants claimed special privileges came into question. See Tonomura, "Community and Commerce in Late Medieval Japan: Corporate Villages of Tokuchin-ho" (Ph.D. Diss., Stanford University, 1986) for a lengthy and detailed analysis of this community in the fifteenth and sixteenth centuries. Her conclusion that Tokuchin-ho did not die of natural causes, but was "abolished in the course of national unification" (309) jibes with the argument of this chapter: that the demise of the *shōen* system was the effect of a rewriting of the discourses within which estates were constituted (and without which they had no meaningful place).

GLOSSARY

AKUTŌ. Literally "evil bands." A term of opprobrium that referred to a wide variety of bandit groups. *Akutō* activity becomes especially noticeable in the later thirteenth century.

AZUKARI DOKORO. Manager or custodian of an estate. The major commender of the land would often be appointed to the post. Frequently an absentee figure, in which case the duties of the *azukari dokoro* would be carried out by the *geshi*. *See geshi*.

BŌREI. Custom, customary practice.

BU. The smallest unit in the system of land measurement common in eastern and central Japan, about 3.2 square meters; 3600 *bu* = 10 *tan* = 1 *chō*.

BUMIN. "Succor the people." The medieval Japanese equivalent of noblesse oblige. This obligation influenced the actions of elites in many areas, a notable example being the court and bakufu decrees canceling all private debt in the name of "virtuous government" (see *tokusei*).

CHŌ. Unit of area, slightly more than a hectare. Also a unit of length nearly equivalent to 110 meters.

CHOKUSHIDEN. Imperial-grant fields. Lands exempted from state taxes because the income from them was to be set aside for the upkeep of the imperial family. The term also refers to undeveloped lands granted (by imperial decree) to temples or members of the aristocracy, who undertook to develop the holding for the sustenance of the imperial house. Many of the *shōen* confiscated in Go-Sanjō's reign appear to have been converted into *chokushiden*; they became something like imperially sanctioned *shōen* and foreshadow the sort of arrangement that was common in the twelfth century, when the imperial family became guarantor (*honke*) of a vast portfolio of estates.

DAI. Large. Used in land registers to indicate two-thirds of a *tan*, or 240 *bu*.

DAIKAN. Deputy. Holders of all manner of posts and offices, from provincial governors to low-level *shōen* officials, frequently appointed deputies to handle the day-to-day administrative details of the office. In the *shōen*, the deputy was typically resident, while the actual *azukari dokoro*, etc., lived elsewhere. *Daikan* also refers to an agent or agents sent by the proprietor to inspect crop damage, investigate peasant complaints, report on the condition of the estate, etc.

DOYŌ. The eighteen days preceding the first day of each season by the lunar calendar. During this period, the earth was not to be disturbed; thus, events like cremations and burials, but also surveys, were frequently postponed or suspended.

EZU. "Picture-map." Maps picturing estates (*shōen ezu*) were among the documents needed to certify the estate's propriety.

GE. A type of document originally prescribed for transmissions from inferior to superior within official ranks. Early examples include reports on tax receipts from provincial governors to the central government. By about the tenth century, the form of the *ge* was being used for any communication that followed the inferior-to-superior pattern, including petitions from peasants to estate proprietors and provincial officials. In the estate system, the *ge* was displaced by *mōshijō* from about the middle of the twelfth century. See *mōshijō*.

GENIN. "Inferior person." A servant.

GENSAKU. Fields currently under cultivation—as opposed to permanent waste (*jōkō*) and temporarily damaged fields (*sonden*).

GESAKU(NIN). Literally, "inferior cultivator." The term has occasioned much dispute, with some scholars arguing that it refers to the actual cultivator of a plot of land, others insisting that it indicates something akin to a serf. What is certain is that it marks a status inferior to that of *hyakushō*, an indicator of this being that *gesakunin* were exempt from *kuji*.

GESHI. The highest-ranking resident estate official. The *geshi*'s responsibilities included supervising lower resident officials (see *kumon* and *tadokoro*), overseeing rent collection, and reporting on disputes, etc. *Geshi* were often drawn from a prominent local family.

GŌ. A unit of volume, equivalent to about 0.18 liters when standardized in the Tokugawa period. In the medieval era, the size of the *gō* varied widely from about 0.072 liters up to the Tokugawa standard; 10 *gō* = 1 *shō*.

HAN. One-half. Used in land measurements to mean 1/2 *tan*. See *tan*.

HEIMIN. Commoner.

HININ. Literally, "not-human." The term refers to members of the lowest status groups—people regarded as ritually unclean and engaged in "defiling" occupations, such as tanning hides, executing condemned criminals, and preparing corpses for cremation.

HONKE (SHIKI). Patron or guarantor of an estate, often a high-ranking noble or member of the imperial family. The highest position in the chain of *shiki* rights, *honke* rarely had any hand in the daily management of an estate, but their influence at court served as the ultimate guarantee of the estate's immunities.

HYAKUSHŌ. The normative peasant subject of the shōen system.

ICHIMI; ICHIMI DŌSHIN. "Of one body"; "Of one body and like mind." Expressions of communal solidarity common in sworn statements.

ICHIMI SHINSUI. Shorthand for the ritual accompanying the swearing of oaths, especially communal ones. The first term is an expression of solidarity, the second refers to the sacred libation that sealed the oath. After swearing to the oath, the paper on which it was written was burned and the ashes mixed with water or wine; the swearers then each drank some of the potion, sealing the oath.

INU JININ. Literally, "dog shrine-attendants." *Jinin* were agents for Shinto shrines and performed various tasks for the shrine in return for its protection. *Inu jinin* were the lowest *jinin*, equivalent in status to *hinin* and engaged in similar tasks.

ISSHIKIDEN. Partially exempt fields. *Isshikiden* owed only *nengu* and were not liable for *kuji*. They were often assessed a very high rate.

JIDEN. "Temple fields." Fields within an estate exempted from proprietors' levies. The rents and services from these fields went instead to (frequently local) temples.

JITŌ (SHIKI). A warrior appointed steward of an estate by the Kamakura bakufu. Also refers to the post held by such a warrior.

JODEN. The general term for fields exempt from rents and other services.

JŌDEN. "Normal fields." Fields which owed both rents and *kuji*.

JŌKŌ. Permanent waste. Damaged fields which had become unsuited for cultivation and were therefore exempted from all levies.

JŌRI. Term for the land grid implemented in the seventh and eighth centuries. Great stretches of the country were organized into large rectangular blocks, six *chō* on a side. Each side was divided into six segments, and those on the east-west axis of the grid were known as *jō*, while those on the north-south axis were known as *ri*. Plots of land could be easily located by reference to the grid, thereby facilitating tax collection and land distribution to peasant households.

JŌSHI. A general designation for an agent or representative dispatched by the central proprietor to an estate. Agents sent to survey flooded fields, negotiate with rebels, put down brigands, or adjudicate an inheritance dispute were all known as *jōshi*.

JŪNIN. Generic term for residents (of an estate, village, etc.)

JŪNIN RA NO GE. A form of peasant petition common in the tenth and eleventh centuries; it was displaced by *hyakushō mōshijō* in the twelfth century.

KAFUCHŌTEKI DOREISEI. Patriarchal slave system. The phrase was made famous by Araki Moriaki, who argued that the entire medieval era was characterized by the persistence of an economy founded on unfree labor and patriarchal authority.

KAITO. A term appearing in Heian-period sources, it refers to paddy, garden plots, etc., immediately surrounding a residence. Typically, at least in well-to-do peasant households, this area, encircled by a fence or ditch, was generally recognized as the family's private holding and was therefore exempt from rents and other levies. *See yashiki.*

KANMON. Money. The *mon* was a copper coin, and one thousand of these made up one *kan*.

KANMOSTU DEN. Fields subject to public levies. *Kanmostu* are the goods, usually rice, taken as taxes by the provincial apparatus. Within *shōen*, the term could refer either to fields which for some reason still had to pay tax to the state, or simply to "regular" fields subject to *kuji* and *nengu*.

KANRYŌ. A payment made in lieu of having a holding surveyed.

KENMON SEIKA. The "influential houses and powerful families"—i.e., the imperial house, aristocratic families, temples, and shrines—who made up the central elite of medieval Japan. Used by historians to refer generally to the political makeup of the era. Each "Influential house," with its portfolio of estates, comprised a quasi-independent locus of authority, with the result that there was no one center of power, but a fluid and open-ended situation.

KINTŌMYŌ. *Myō* made equal in area to facilitate the collection of rents, etc. Found on a number of estates in central Japan.

KIROKUJO. "Records Office," short for Kiroku shōen kenkeisho, "Office for the Investigation of Shōen Records." The office was established by Emperor Go-Sanjō in 1069 in an attempt to curb the proliferation of estates.

KISHIN. Commendation, typically of land or other property, to temples and shrines. In a more specialized usage, it refers to the process that played a critical role in the vast expansion of estates after the mid-eleventh century: A local landowner ceded title to a holding to a temple, shrine, or high-ranking aristocrat, which then undertook to convert the holding into an estate exempt from state taxes and jurisdiction. The original holder often became custodian *(azukari dokoro)* of the new estate. "Commendation-type estates" *(kishin-gata shōen)* eventually became the most common form.

KISHŌ; KISHŌMON. Oath. *Kishō* refers to the process of swearing an oath; *kishōmon* refers to the written oath.

KITŌSHO. A "Prayer center." Could also refer to lands set aside for the upkeep of a devotional site.

KŌDEN. Literally, "public fields." In contrast to *shōen* lands, *kōden* fell under the authority of provincial officials and paid state taxes.

KŌGI. "Public authority." *Kōgi* referred equally to the most powerful authority in a territory and to the principles that justified the exercise of authority. The term originally indicated the imperial court and the high nobility, but by the mid-Muromachi period it was used as a synonym for the bakufu and the emerging daimyo. Elaborated further in the fifteenth and sixteenth centuries, the concept became part of a justification for rule that did not depend on traditional authorities.

KOKU. Unit of volume, equivalent to ten *to* or one hundred *shō*. The actual amount indicated by one *koku* varied widely from region to region and from time to time. *See shō.*

KOKUGARYŌ. Lands under the jurisdiction of provincial authorities and subject to state taxes. *Shōen* and *kokugaryō* were the two fundamental categories of land in the medieval system.

KOKUJIN IKKI. Bands of local warriors. *Kokujin*, meaning literally "men of the provinces," were warriors who became important local territorial lords during the Muromachi period. *Ikki* refers to groups of people organized for rent relief, religious purposes, defense, etc. The term could also refer to uprisings by such groups.

KŌMIN. "Public subjects." In mid-Heian sources the term sometimes appears in conjunction with *hyakushō*, indicating that the *hyakushō* of that era were considered subjects of a broadly conceived, public, imperial authority, and not, as later usage indicates, subjects of the specific authority of estate proprietors.

KORŌ HYAKUSHŌ. Village elders.

KUJI. Overall term for a variety of rents, labor services, etc., levied on individuals rather than on the land. *Kuji* and *nengu*, the land rent, formed the two axes of the *shōen* rent structure.

KUMON. A low-ranking estate official, whose principal duties involved record keeping. For example, the *kumon* seems to have been the official generally in charge of the estate's land registers.

KYŪDEN. Lands granted as perquisites to estate officials. The rents from these lands were paid to the official in question.

MANDOKORO. Administrative headquarters of high-ranking aristocratic families. The term could also refer to similar offices in temples, in the bakufu, on estates, etc.

MENDEN. The general term for fields exempted from rents and other dues.

MOKUROKU. Generally, a catalog or summary. With respect to land, a document summarizing information about an estate's rents and cultivated and noncultivated areas.

MŌSHIJŌ. A report or petition covering a wide variety of communications from lower-ranking persons to their superiors. *Hyakushō mōshijō* refer specifically to petitions from the residents of estates to their proprietors. From the mid-twelfth century forward, the *mōshijō* was the standard instrument of peasant protest.

MYŌ; MYŌDEN. The basic unit from which rents and other levies were drawn. *Myō*, which also means "name," consisted of fields gathered together under the name (it would appear) of the person responsible for the unit when the estate was established.

MYŌSHU (SHIKI). Person responsible for the management of *myōden*. Drawn from the upper peasantry and functioning as low-level estate officials, *myōshu* were vital intermediaries between the resident community and *shōen* officialdom.

NAIKEN; NAIKENCHŪ. An informal survey carried out annually or as needed to estimate the extent of fields damaged by flooding or insects, etc. Often conducted at the request of estate residents.

NAYOSECHŌ. Register of the fields of an estate, grouped by *myō*. The second product of a full survey, it organized the estate for purposes of taxation. Individual holdings (the particulars of which were reported in a field survey, or *torichō*) were gathered into *myō* units, and the rents due from each unit were noted.

NENGU. The annual land rent.

NENJŪ GYŌJI. The annual cycle of ceremonies, festivities, and other observances at court.

ONBYAKUSHŌ. Produced by adding the honorific "on" to "hyakushō," the term is a designation for the peasantry that becomes common from about the fifteenth century onwards. In this usage, the honorific does not suggest a rise in stature but a more abstract public status for the hyakushō.

RIKKEN. Official certificate establishing an estate; also the procedure by which this certificate was drawn up. Estate and provincial officials together inspected and verified the proposed estate's boundaries and land registers and drew up the *rikken*, which officially established the estate.

RŌNIN. Wanderers, unattached people. Generally, people who did not fit into the status categories of medieval life. In the rhetoric of the *shōen* system, the *rōnin* figured as the antithesis of the *hyakushō*.

RYŌCHI. The right to exploit and manage a holding.

RYŌKE (SHIKI). Proprietor of an estate; also the position of proprietor. The person or institution that held actual managerial rights over the estate.

RYŌSHŌ. To possess land or a *shiki*; also the right to possess and exploit a holding.

SANDEN. Fields held directly by the estate proprietor and assigned to cultivators, often on an annual basis. These fields were generally *isshikiden*; that is, they were only assessed the annual land rent.

SHIISHI; *SHISHI*. An estate's four boundaries. These were marked by boundary posts at the northwest, northeast, southwest, and southeast corners of the property.

SHIKI. Originally, official office; however, by the mid-eleventh century it had come to refer primarily to the income rights attached to office. The full development of the *shōen* saw a proliferation of types of *shiki*, so that even peasant tenures came to be expressed as *shiki* (i.e., *myōshu shiki*), and a further shift in the meaning of the term from office or function toward pure income right. The term therefore also suggests the structure that allowed for multiple "possession" and multiple interests in the same land.

SHINDEN. Fields set aside for the upkeep of Shinto shrines. Exempted from rents and other levies.

SHIRO. A unit of measurement common in western Japan, equal to one-fiftieth of a *tan* or about twenty-four square meters.

SHIRYŌ. A private landholding. The term appears frequently in bills of sale, in commendation documents, and in bequests as an assertion of hereditary possession and of the right to dispose of the property.

SHŌ. (1) A unit of volume, 1/100th of a *koku*. The amount indicated by one *shō* varied tremendously from region to region and over time. In fact, estate residents often used a local measure that differed from that used by their proprietor, and controversies about which to use or over how to convert from one to the other were common. (2) Small. Used in land measurements to indicate one-third of a *tan* or one hundred twenty *bu*.

SHŌKAN. General term for local estate officials, including the *kumon*, *tadokoro*, and *geshi*.

SHŌKEN; *SHŌ KENCHŪ*. Full survey of an estate or other landholding. Held only rarely (usually when an estate was established and when it changed hands), a *shōken* involved sending teams of surveyors to an estate to conduct a plot-by-plot inspection of its lands. The surveyors noted the location, size, condition, and quality of each plot, as well as the rents owed and the person responsible for the rents. Once these had been decided, they remained unchanged until the next full survey. Minor adjustments might be made from year to year on the basis of an informal survey *(naiken)*, but such adjustments never became part of the official rendering of the estate's lands.

SHŌMIN. General term for residents of an estate, excluding estate officials.

SHŌMON. A document with seals affixed, etc.; the original as opposed to a copy.

SHŌREI. "Custom of the estate"; estate precedent.

SHORYŌ. Landholdings. Also the right to income from a holding or *shiki*.

SHUGO. Provincial constable. In the Kamakura period *shugo* authority was sharply circumscribed by the warrior government in Kamakura and remained its agents. In the Muromachi period, however, many shugo gained extensive power over their domains and functioned more like independent military governors or overlords.

SONDEN. Damaged fields; fields rendered unproductive by flooding, drought, insects, or other causes. *Sonden* were exempted from rents.

TABUMI. A field register. *Tabumi* typically contained information about the size and possessor of landholdings. During the Kamakura period, the bakufu had provincewide "great field registers" (*ōtabumi*) drawn up. Several of these survive and provide valuable information about the extent of *shōen* and other lands.

TADOKORO. A local estate official whose responsibilities included land surveys and rent collection.

TAN. Unit of area, equal to one-tenth of a *chō* or 360 *bu*. About ten *are*.

TENKA. Literally, "under heaven." Used by Oda Nobunaga to refer to the realm, which he presented himself as uniquely capable of protecting and ruling.

TO. Unit of volume equal to one-tenth of a *koku* or ten *shō*.

TOKUDEN. A term found in land registers and rent reports, it refers to fields that were under cultivation, undamaged, and, hence, fully taxable.

TOKUSEI (REI). Literally, "virtuous government." A general term for government policies designed to promote the popular welfare, including support for Buddhist and Shinto observances. In the later middle ages, the term referred to court or bakufu decrees canceling debts or land sales.

TORICHŌ. Field registers. Sometimes composed on-site as the survey progressed across an estate, *torichō* present a virtual transcript of a field survey. They provide information about the location, size, quality, and cultivator of each plot of land in an estate; the fundamental land register from which other registers (see *nayosechō* and *mokuroku*) were composed.

UESAMA. Used in late medieval documents to refer to the shogun, shugo, dalimyo, or other (usually military) overlord.

UKIDEN; UKIMENDEN. Literally "floating fields." Early *shōen* often had only a tenuous territorial component, and the term refers to one such situation. Typically, the proprietor would be granted the income from a certain amount of land, but the precise fields constituting that amount would not be named.

YASHIKI; YASHIKICHI. The residence and adjoining fields of local elites, from *myōshu* on up. Such lands were considered private possessions and exempt from rents. The possession of a *yashiki* was also intimately connected with status: to be a *myōshu* was to possess lands recognized as *yashiki*. Some estates make the connection clear, apportioning a specific amount of residence fields to each *myō*.

YOMIAI. The quasi-ritual that concluded a survey. Local residents and estate officials together read through and verified the field register prepared by the survey. Each side appears to have had a copy of the register; these were read aloud and compared, and any errors were noted. The notations in vermilion ink one finds in surviving registers are the traces of this process.

ZASSHŌ SHIKI. A centrally appointed estate official, responsible for handling litigation with respect to the estate or for managing the holding. In the latter case, the *zasshō* was equivalent to the *azukari dokoro*.

ZŌYAKU KUJI; ZŌKUJI. Other terms for *kuji*.

BIBLIOGRAPHY

Abe Takeshi. *Nihon shōen seiritsushi no kenkyū*. Tokyo: Yūzankaku, 1960.

────. *Nihon shōen shi*. Tokyo: Ōhara Shinseisha, 1972.

Aioi shishi. Comp. Aioi shishi hensan senmon iinkai. Aioi: Aioi shi kyōiku iinkai, 1984.

Akamatsu Toshihide, comp. *Kyōōgokokuji monjo*. 10 vols. Kyoto: Heirakuji Shoten, 1960–72.

Althusser, Louis. *Lenin and Philosophy and Other Essays*. Trans. Ben Brewster. London: New Left Books, 1971.

Amino Yoshihiko. "Chūsei no futan taikei—nengu ni tsuite." In *Chūsei, kinsei no kokka to shakai*, ed. Nagahara Keiji et al. Tokyo: Tokyo Daigaku Shuppankai, 1986.

────. "Chūsei no seien to shio no ryūtsū." In *Kōza Nihon gijustu no shakaishi*, ed. Yamaguchi Keiji and Nagahara Keiji. Vol. 2, *Engyō, gyogyō*. Tokyo: Nihon Hyōronsha, 1985.

────. *Chūsei shōen no yōsō*. Tokyo: Hanawa Shobō, 1966.

────. *Chūsei Tōji to Tōji-ryō shōen*. Tokyo: Tokyo Daigaku Shuppankai, 1978.

────. *Mōko shūrai*. Vol. 10 of *Nihon no rekishi*. Tokyo: Shōgakkan, 1974.

────. *Muen, kugai, raku*. Tokyo: Heibonsha, 1978.

────. "Nihon chūsei no heimin to shokunin." *Shisō* 670–71 (March-April 1980): 1–25; 73–92.

────. "Nihon chūsei ni okeru 'heimin' ni tsuite." In *Nagoya Daigaku Bungakubu sanjūshūnen kinen ronshū*. Nagoya: Nagoya Daigaku, 1979.

────. *Nihon chūsei no hinōgyōmin to tennō*. Tokyo: Iwanami Shoten, 1984.

────. *Nihon chūsei no minshūzō—heimin to shokunin*. Iwanami shinsho, 136. Tokyo: Iwanami Shoten, 1980.

────. "Shōen kōryōsei no keisei to kōzō." In *Tochi seidoshi I*, ed. Takeuchi Rizō. Taikei Nihonshi sōsho, vol. 6. Tokyo: Yamakawa Shuppansha, 1973.

Amino Yoshihiko et al. *Chūsei no tsumi to batsu*. Tokyo: Tokyo Daigaku Shuppankai, 1983.

Anderson, Benedict. *Imagined Communities: Reflections on the Origins and Spread of Nationalism*. London: Verso, 1983.

Aoki Michio et al., eds. *Ikki*. 5 vols. Tokyo: Tokyo Daigaku Shuppankai, 1981.

Araki Moriaki. *Nihon hōken shakai seiritsushi ron*. Tokyo: Iwanami Shoten, 1984.

Arnesen, Peter. "The Struggle for Lordship in Late Heian Japan: The Case of Aki." *Journal of Japanese Studies* 10, no. 1 (Winter 1984): 101–41.

────. "Suō Province in the Age of Kamakura." In *Court and Bakufu in Japan*, ed. Jeffrey P. Mass. Stanford: Stanford University Press, 1982.

Asaka Toshiki. "Chūsei no gijutsu to shukōgyōsha no soshiki." In *Iwanami kōza Nihon rekishi*, ed. Asao Naohiro et al. Vol. 6, *Chūsei 2*. Tokyo: Iwanami Shoten, 1975.

Asakawa Kan'ichi. *Land and Society in Medieval Japan*. Tokyo: Japan Society for the Promotion of Science, 1965.

Asao Naohiro et al., eds. *Iwanami Kōza Nihon rekishi*. 2d ed. 26 vols. Tokyo: Iwanami Shoten, 1975–1977.

———, eds. *Nihon no shakaishi*. 8 vols. Tokyo: Iwanami Shoten, 1986–88.

Babcock, Barbara. *Reversible Worlds: Forms of Symbolic Inversion*. Ithaca: Cornell University Press, 1978.

Barrell, John. *The Idea of Landscape and the Sense of Place, 1730–1840: An Approach to the Poetry of John Clare*. Cambridge: Cambridge University Press, 1972.

Barthes, Roland. *Image, Music, Text*. Trans. Stephen Heath. New York: Hill and Wang, 1977

Berger, John. *Ways of Seeing*. London: Pelican Books, 1972.

Biersack, Aletta. "Local Knowledge, Local History: Geertz and Beyond." In *The New Cultural History*, ed. Lynn Hunt. Berkeley and Los Angeles: University of California Press, 1989.

Bloch, Marc. *Feudal Society*. 2 vols. Trans. L. A. Manyon. Chicago: University of Chicago Press, 1961.

———. *French Rural History: An Essay on Its Basic Characteristics*. Trans. Janet Sondheimer. Berkeley and Los Angeles: University of California Press, 1966.

Boelhower, William. "Inventing America: A Model of Cartographic Semiosis." *Word & Image* 4 (April–June 1988): 475–97.

Bourdieu, Pierre. *Outline of a Theory of Practice*. Trans. Richard Nice. Cambridge: Cambridge University Press, 1977.

Braudel, Fernand. *On History*. Chicago and London: University of Chicago Press, 1980.

Brown, Delmer, and Ichirō Ishida, trans. and ed. *The Future and the Past: A Translation and Study of the* Gukanshō, *an Interpretative History of Japan written in 1219*. Berkeley and Los Angeles: University of California Press, 1979.

Burke, Peter. *The French Historical Revolution: The* Annales *School, 1929–89*. Stanford: Stanford University Press, 1990.

Carroll, David. *The Subject in Question: The Languages of Theory and the Strategies of Fiction*. Chicago and London: University of Chicago Press, 1982.

Carter, Paul. *The Road to Botany Bay: An Exploration in Landscape and History*. Chicago: University of Chicago Press, 1989.

Chijiwa Itaru. "Chūsei minshūteki sekai no chitsujō to teikō." In *Kōza Nihon rekishi*, ed. Rekishigaku Kenkyūkai and Nihonshi Kenkyūkai. Vol. 4, *Chūsei 2*. Tokyo: Tokyo Daigaku Shuppankai, 1985.

———. " 'Seiyaku no ba' no saihakken." *Nihon rekishi* 422 (July 1983): 1–16.

Clarke, G.N.G. "Taking Possession: The Cartouche as Cultural Text in Eighteenth-Century American Maps." *Word & Image* 4 (April–June 1988): 455–74.

Corrigan, Philip, and Derek Sayer. *The Great Arch: English State Formation as Cultural Revolution*. Oxford: Basil Blackwell, 1985.

Coulborn, Rushton, ed. *Feudalism in History*. Princeton: Princeton University Press, 1956.

Dai Nihon komonjo. Iewake monjo. Comp. Tokyo Daigaku Shiryōhensanjo. Tokyo: Tokyo Daigaku Shuppankai, 1901–.

Dai Nihonshi. Ed. Gikō seitan sanbyakunen kinenkai. 16 vols. Tokyo: Yūbenkai, 1928–29.

Dai Nihon shiryō. Comp. Tokyo Daigaku Shiryōhensanjo. Ser. 6 and 7. Tokyo: Tokyo Daigaku Shuppankai, 1901–.

Davis, Natalie Zemon. *Society and Culture in Early Modern France.* Stanford: Stanford University Press, 1975.

de Certeau, Michel. *The Practice of Everyday Life.* Trans. Steven F. Randall. Berkeley and Los Angeles: University of California Press, 1984.

Dreyfus, Hubert L. and Paul Rabinow. *Michel Foucault: Beyond Structuralism and Hermeneutics.* Chicago: University of Chicago Press, 1982.

Duby, Georges. *The Chivalrous Society.* Trans. Cynthia Postan. Berkeley and Los Angeles: University of California Press, 1980.

Elison, George, and Bardwell L. Smith, eds. *Warlords, Artists and Commoners: Japan in the Sixteenth Century.* Honolulu: University of Hawaii Press, 1981.

Farris, William Wayne. *Population, Disease, and Land in Early Japan, 645–900.* Harvard-Yenching Institute Monograph Series, no. 24. Cambridge: Harvard University Press, 1985.

Fenoaltea, Stefano. "The Rise and Fall of a Theoretical Model: The Manorial System." *Journal of Economic History* 44 (1975): 386–409.

Fischer, Michael M. J., and George Marcus. *Anthropology as Cultural Critique.* Chicago: University of Chicago Press, 1986.

Foucault, Michel. *The Archaeology of Knowledge.* Trans. A. M. Sheridan Smith. New York: Harper Colophon, 1972.

———. *Discipline and Punish: The Birth of the Prison.* Trans. Alan Sheridan. New York: Vintage Books, 1979.

———. *The History of Sexuality.* Vol. 1, *An Introduction.* Trans. Robert Hurley. London: Penguin Books, 1979.

———. *Language, Counter-Memory, Practice: Selected Essays and Interviews.* Ed. Donald F. Bouchard. Ithaca: Cornell University Press, 1977.

———. *Power/Knowledge: Selected Interviews and Other Writings.* Ed. Colin Gordon. New York: Pantheon, 1980.

———. "The Subject and Power." Afterword to *Michel Foucault: Beyond Structuralism and Hermeneutics,* by H. Dreyfus and P. Rabinow. Chicago: University of Chicago Press, 1982.

Fourquin, Guy. *The Anatomy of Popular Rebellion in the Middle Ages.* Trans. Anne Chesters. Amsterdam: North-Holland, 1978.

Frank, Manfred. *What is Neostructuralism?* Trans. Sabine Wilke and Richard Gray. Theory and History of Literature, vol. 45. Minneapolis: University of Minnesota Press, 1989.

Fujiki Hisashi. *Sengoku shakaishi ron.* Tokyo: Tokyo Daigaku Shuppankai, 1974.

———. "Tōitsu seiken no seiritsu." In *Iwanami kōza Nihon rekishi.* Vol. 9, *Kinsei I.* Tokyo: Iwanami Shoten, 1975.

Fukui kenshi. Comp. Fukui ken. Shiryōhen, kodai-chūsei. 3 vols. to date. Fukui: Fukui ken, 1982–.

Furet, François. *In the Workshop of History.* Trans. Jonathan Mandelbaum. Chicago and London: University of Chicago Press, 1984.

Gay, Suzanne. "The Kawashima: Warrior-Peasants of Medieval Japan." *Harvard Journal of Asiatic Studies* 46 (June 1986): 81–119.

Geertz, Clifford. *The Interpretation of Cultures*. New York: Basic Books, 1973.

———. *Negara: The Theatre-State in Nineteenth-Century Bali*. Princeton: Princeton University Press, 1980.

Giddens, Anthony. *A Contemporary Critique of Historical Materialism*. 2 vols. Berkeley and Los Angeles: University of California Press, 1981.

Gifu kenshi. Comp. Gifu ken. Shiryōhen, kodai-chūsei. 4 vols. Gifu: Gifu ken, 1969–72.

Gluckman, Max. *Order and Rebellion in Tribal Africa*. London: Cohen and West, 1963.

Gotō Norihiko. "Chōko zasshō shoshū no Itsukushima monjo (2)." *Shigaku zasshi* 88 (December 1979): 46–60.

Grossberg, Kenneth A. *The Laws of the Muromachi Bakufu*. Tokyo: Monumenta Nipponica, 1981.

Hall, John Whitney. *Government and Local Power in Japan, 500 to 1700: A Study Based on Bizen Province*. Princeton: Princeton University Press, 1966.

———. *Japan from Prehistory to Modern Times*. New York: Dell Publishing Co., 1970.

Hall, John Whitney, and Jeffrey P. Mass, eds. *Medieval Japan: Essays in Institutional History*. New Haven: Yale University Press, 1974.

Hall, John Whitney, Nagahara Keiji, and Kozo Yamamura. *Japan Before Tokugawa: Political Consolidation and Economic Growth, 1500–1600*. Princeton: Princeton University Press, 1981.

Hall, John Whitney, and Toyoda Takeshi, eds. *Japan in the Muromachi Age*. Berkeley and Los Angeles: University of California Press, 1977.

Hall, Stuart. "Cultural Studies: Two Paradigms." *Media, Culture and Society*, 2 (January 1980): 57–72.

Harada Nobuo. "Nanbokuchō, Muromachi ki ni okeru 'sō' teki ketsugō no seiritsu." *Chihōshi kenkyū* 152 (April 1978): 69–88.

Harada Tomohiko, ed. *Hennen sabetsushi shiryō shūsei*. Vols. 1–5. Tokyo: San'ichi Shobō, 1983–86.

Harootunian, H. D. *Things Seen and Unseen: Discourse and Ideology in Tokugawa Nativism*. Chicago: University of Chicago Press, 1988.

Harrington, Lorraine F. "Social Control and the Significance of the Akutō." In *The Bakufu in Japanese History*, ed. Jeffrey P. Mass and William B. Hauser. New Haven: Yale University Press, 1985.

Hashimoto Hiroshi. "Chūkan chiiki ni okeru hyakushō myō no sonzai keitai." *Nihonshi kenkyū* 282 (June 1986): 1–35.

Hattori Hideo. "Buzen-no-kuni Kanada-no-shō kochi ni okeru chūsei keikan no fukugen—Nanbokuchō ki no myō no sonzai keitai." *Shigaku zasshi* 94 (July 1985): 63–93.

———. "Mirai nengō no sekai kara—hizuke ni mujun no aru monjo yori mita shōen no yōsō." *Shigaku zasshi* 92 (August 1982): 38–65.

Hayashiya Tatsusaburō et al. "Kai jōtatsu monjo no hensen—'ge' yori 'mōshijō' e." *Nihon shigaku* 1 (April 1968): 3–23.

Hindess, Barry, and Paul Hirst. *Pre-Capitalist Modes of Production*. London: RKP, 1975.

Hiroshima kenshi. Comp. Hiroshima ken. *Kodai-chūsei shiryō*. 5 vols. Hiroshima: Hiroshima ken, 1974–80.

Hōgetsu Keigo. "Chūsei kenchū ni tsuite no ichi, ni no mondai." *Shinano* 10 (May 1958): 26–32.

———. "Chūsei no kenchū ni tsuite." *Chihōshi kenkyū* 91 (February 1968): 1–9.

———. "Shōen ni okeru kenchūshi no seikatsu jittai—Ogiso-no-shō no zōji chūmon o chūshin to shite." *Shinano* 37 (October 1985): 1–13.

Hōnen shōnin eden. Ed. Tsukamoto Yoshitaka. Vol. 13 of *Nihon emakimono zenshū*. Tokyo: Kadokawa Shoten, 1961.

Hotate Michihisa. "Chūsei minshū keizai no tenkai." In *Kōza Nihon rekishi*, ed. Rekishigaku Kenkyūkai and Nihonshi Kenkyūkai. Vol. 3, *Chūsei 1*. Tokyo: Tokyo Daigaku Shuppankai, 1984.

Hoy, David Couzens, ed. *Foucault: A Critical Reader*. Oxford: Basil Blackwell, 1986.

Hurst, G. Cameron. *Insei: Abdicated Sovereigns in the Politics of Late Heian Japan, 1086–1185*. New York: Columbia University Press, 1976.

———. "The Reign of Go-Sanjō and the Revival of Imperial Power." *Monumenta Nipponica* 27 (Spring 1972): 65–83.

Inaba Nobumichi. "Kamakura ki no Iga-no-kuni Kuroda-no-shō no ichi kōsatsu." *Nenpō chūseishi kenkyū* 7 (May 1982): 1–51.

Inagaki Yasuhiko. "Chūsei nōgyō keiei to shūshu keitai." In *Iwanami kōza Nihon rekishi*. Vol. 6, *Chūsei 2*. Tokyo: Iwanami Shoten, 1975.

———. *Nihon chūsei shakaishi ron*. Tokyo: Tokyo Daigaku Shuppankai, 1981.

———. "Ritsuryōseiteki tochi seido no kaitai." In *Tochi seidoshi I*, ed. Takeuchi Rizō. Tokyo: Yamakawa Shuppansha, 1973.

———, ed. *Shōen no sekai*. Tokyo: Tokyo Daigaku Shuppankai, 1973.

Inoue Toshio. *Yama no tami, kawa no tami*. Tokyo: Heibonsha, 1981.

Irumada Nobuo. *Hyakushō mōshijō to kishōmon no sekai*. Tokyo: Tokyo Daigaku Shuppankai, 1986.

———. "Kubyō to bumin—chūsei ni okeru 'kō' to kihan ishiki." In *Nihon no shakaishi*, ed. Asao Naohiro et al. Vol 5, *Saiban to kihan*. Tokyo: Iwanami Shoten, 1987.

Ishii Susumu. "Insei jidai." In *Kōza Nihonshi*, ed. Rekishigaku Kenkyūkai and Nihonshi Kenkyūkai. Vol. 2, *Hōken shakai no seiritsu*. Tokyo: Tokyo Daigaku Shuppankai, 1970.

———. "Tsumi to 'harae.' " In *Nihon no shakaishi*, ed. Asao Naohiro et al. Vol. 5, *Saiban to kihan*. Tokyo: Iwanami Shoten, 1987.

Ishimoda Shō. *Chūseiteki sekai no keisei*. Rev. ed. Tokyo: Iwanami Shoten, 1985.

Isogai Fujio. "Hyakushō mibun no tokushitsu to dorei e no tenraku o megutte." *Rekishigaku kenkyū* sp. ed. (November 1971): 66–76.

Itō Hiroko. "Sōson no seiritsu to hatten," *Nihonshi kenkyū* 120–21 (July-September 1971): 1–12, 33–50.

Kasahara Kazuo and Inoue Toshio, eds. *Rennyo, Ikkō ikki*. Nihon shisō taikei, vol. 17. Tokyo: Iwanami Shoten, 1972.

Kasamatsu Hiroshi, Satō Shin'ichi, and Momose Kesao, eds. *Chūsei seiji shakai shisō*. Nihon shisō taikei, vols. 21–22. Tokyo: Iwanami Shoten, 1981.

Katsumata Shizuo. "Ie o yaku." In *Chūsei no tsumi to batsu*, ed. Amino Yoshihiko et al. Tokyo: Tokyo Daigaku Shuppankai, 1983.

———. *Ikki*. Tokyo: Iwanami Shoten, 1982.

Kawane Yoshiyasu. *Chūsei hōkensei seiritsushi ron*. Tokyo: Tokyo Daigaku Shuppankai, 1971.

———. *Chūsei hōken shakai no shuto to nōson*. Tokyo: Tokyo Daigaku Shuppankai, 1984.

Kawashima Shigehiro. "Shōen ryōshu shihai to 'jūnin ra no ge' no seiritsu." *Hitotsubashi ronsō* 87 (June 1982): 40–56.

Keirstead, Thomas E. "Fragmented Estates: The Breakup of the *Myō* and the Decline of the *Shōen* System." *Monumenta Nipponica* 40 (Autumn 1985): 21–39.

Kellner, Hans. *Language and Historical Representation: Getting the Story Crooked*. Madison: University of Wisconsin Press, 1989.

Kimura Shigemitsu. "Chūsei seiritsuki ni okeru hatazukuri no seikaku to ryōyū kankei." *Nihonshi kenkyū* 180 (August 1977): 1–40.

———. "Harima-no-kuni Akaho gun Hisatomi ho no kaihatsu ni tsuite." *Chihōshi kenkyū* 178 (August 1982): 69–82.

———. "Shōen shiishi bōji nōto (I)—Kii-no-kuni Kaseda-no-shō ezu o chūshin ni." (Tokyo Gakugei Daigaku) *Kiyō*. Dai-san bumon, shakai kagaku 37 (December 1985): 209–31.

Kishi Toshio et al., eds. *Asahi hyakka Nihon no rekishi*. Tokyo: Asahi Shinbunsha, 1986–88.

Kodaigaku Kyōkai, comp. *Zenjōji monjo*. Tokyo: Yoshikawa Kōbunkan, 1979.

Koizumi Yoshiaki. "Harima-no-kuni Yano-no-shō no akutō." *Kokushigaku* 66 (January 1956): 44–63.

———. "Nairanki no shakai hendō." In *Iwanami kōza Nihon rekishi*. Vol. 6, *Chūsei 2*. Tokyo: Iwanami Shoten, 1975.

Konjaku monogatari. Ed. Yamada Yoshio et al. Vols. 21–26 in Nihon koten bungaku taikei. Tokyo: Iwanami Shoten, 1959–62.

Koyama Yasunori. *Chūsei sonraku to shōen ezu*. Tokyo: Tokyo Daigaku Shuppankai, 1987.

———. "Shōenseiteki ryōiki shihai to chūsei sonraku." *Nihonshi kenkyū* 139/140 (March 1974): 103–19.

Kōyasan monjo. In *Dai Nihon komonjo*. Iewake 1, comp. Tokyo Daigaku Shiryōhensanjo. 8 vols. Tokyo: Tokyo Daigaku Shuppankai, 1904–7.

Kōzanji komonjo. Comp. Kōzanji Tenseki Monjo Sōgō Chōsadan. Kōzanji shiryō sōsho, vol. 4. Tokyo, 1975.

Kudō Keiichi. "Shōen." *Acta Asiatica* 44 (March 1983): 1–27.

———. "Shōensei no tenkai." In *Iwanami kōza Nihon rekishi*. Vol. 5, *Chūsei 1*. Tokyo: Iwanami Shoten, 1975.

Kujō ke monjo. Comp. Kunaichō Shoryōbu. Tokyo: Kunaichō, 1971–.

Kuroda Hideo. "Chūsei no kaihatsu to shizen." In *Ikki*, ed. Aoki Michio et al. Vol. 4, *Seikatsu, bunka, shisō*. Tokyo: Tokyo Daigaku Shuppankai, 1981.

———. *Kyōkai no chūsei, shōchō no chūsei.* Tokyo: Tokyo Daigaku Shuppankai, 1986.

———. *Nihon chūsei kaihatsushi no kenkyū.* Tokyo: Azekura Shobō, 1984.

———. *Sugata to shigusa no chūseishi.* Tokyo: Heibonsha, 1986.

Kuroda Hiroko. "Chōsan, chōbō, shoshite 'kyoryū no jiyū.'" *Minshūshi kenkyū* 33 (May 1987): 11–40.

Kuroda Toshio. *Chūsei no kokka to shūkyō.* Tokyo: Iwanami Shoten, 1975.

———. "Chūsei no mibun ishiki to shakai kan." In *Nihon no shakaishi,* ed. Asao Naohiro et al. Vol. 7, *Shakaikan to sekaizō.* Tokyo: Iwanami Shoten, 1987.

———. *Nihon chūsei hōkensei ron.* Tokyo: Tokyo Daigaku Shuppankai, 1974.

———. "Kishōmon no kotoba." *Nihonshi kenkyū* 119 (May 1971): 71–74.

Kurokawa Naonori. "Jūgo-jūroku seiki no nōmin mondai." *Nihonshi kenkyū* 71 (March 1964): 28–38.

Kurushima Noriko. "Tōji ryō Yamashiro-no-kuni Kuze-no-shō no myōshu shiki ni tsuite." *Shigaku zasshi* 93 (August 1984): 1–46.

Kyoto Furitsu Sōgō Shiryōkan, comp. *Tōji hyakugō monjo mokuroku.* 5 vols. Tokyo: Yoshikawa Kōbunkan, 1976–79.

———, comp. *Zoku zuroku Tōji hyakugō monjo.* Tokyo: Yoshikawa Kōbunkan, 1974.

———, comp. *Zuroku Tōji hyakugō monjo.* Tokyo: Yoshikawa Kōbunkan, 1970.

Le Roy Ladurie, Emmanuel. *Carnival in Romans.* Trans. Mary Feeney. New York: G. Braziller, 1979.

Makino Shinnosuke, comp. *Echizen Wakasa komonjo sen.* 1933. Reprint. Fukui: Fukui ken meicho kankōkai, 1971.

Mass, Jeffrey P. *The Development of Kamakura Rule, 1180–1250: A History with Documents.* Stanford: Stanford University Press, 1979.

———. *The Kamakura Bakufu: A Study in Documents.* Stanford: Stanford University Press, 1976.

———. "Patterns of Provincial Inheritance in Late Heian Japan." *Journal of Japanese Studies* 9 (Winter 1983): 67–95.

———. *Warrior Government in Early Medieval Japan: A Study of the Kamakura Bakufu, Shugo, and Jitō.* New Haven and London: Yale University Press, 1974.

Matsumoto Shinpachirō. *Chūsei shakai no kenkyū.* Tokyo: Tokyo Daigaku Shuppankai, 1956.

Minegishi Sumio. "Asamayama no funka to shōen no seiritsu." (Tokyo Toritsu Daigaku) *Jinbun gakuhō* 167 (March 1984): 1–23.

———. "Nengu, kuji to utokusen." In *Nihon no shakaishi.* Vol. 4, *Futan to zōyō.* Tokyo: Iwanami Shoten, 1985.

———. "Seiyaku no kane." (Tokyo Toritsu Daigaku) *Jinbun gakuhō* 154 (March 1983): 55–82.

Minoo shishi hensan iinkai, comp. *Minoo shishi,* shiryōhen. 2 vols. Minoo: Minoo Shiyakusho, 1968–73.

Miura Keiichi. *Chūsei minshū seikatsushi no kenkyū.* Kyoto: Shibunkaku, 1981.

Miyagawa Mitsuru. "From Shōen to Chigyō: Proprietary Lordship and the Structure of Local Power." In *Japan in the Muromachi Age,* ed. John Hall and

Toyoda Takeshi. Berkeley and Los Angeles: University of California Press, 1977.

———. "Harima-no-kuni Yano-no-shō no seiritsu jijō ni tsuite." *Hyōgoken no rekishi* 18 (September 1981): 1–9.

———. "Sengoku daimyō no ryōgokusei." In *Hōken kokka no kenryoku kōzō*, ed. Shimizu Morimitsu and Aida Hidetsugu. Tokyo: Sōbunsha, 1967.

———. *Taikō kenchi ron.* Vol. 1, *Nihon hōkensei kakuritsu shi.* Tokyo: Ochanomizu Shobō, 1959.

———, comp. *Ōyama sonshi.* Vol. 1, Tsūshihen. Vol. 2, Shiryōhen. Tokyo: Hanawa Shobō, 1964.

Miyamoto Tasuku. "Ritsuryōseiteki tochi seido." In *Tochi seidoshi I*, ed. Takeuchi Rizō. Tokyo: Yamakawa Shuppansha, 1973.

Mizuno Shōji. "Chūsei sonraku to ryōiki kōsei." *Nihonshi kenkyū* 271 (April 1985): 54–81.

Nagahara Keiji. "Chūsei shakai kōsei to hōkensei." In *Kōza Nihon rekishi*, ed. Rekishigaku Kenkyūkai and Nihonshi Kenkyūkai. Vol. 4, *Chūsei 2.* Tokyo: Tokyo Daigaku Shuppankai, 1985.

———. "The Decline of the *Shōen* System." In *The Cambridge History of Japan.* Vol. 3, *Medieval Japan.* Ed. Kozo Yamamura. Cambridge: Cambridge University Press, 1990.

———. "Land Ownership Under the *Shōen-Kokugaryō* System." *Journal of Japanese Studies* 1 (Spring 1975): 269–96.

———. "The Medieval Peasant." In *The Cambridge History of Japan.* Vol. 3, *Medieval Japan.* Ed. Kozo Yamamura. Cambridge: Cambridge University Press, 1990.

———. *Nihon chūsei shakai kōzō no kenkyū.* Tokyo: Iwanami Shoten, 1973.

———. *Nihon hōkensei seiritsu katei no kenkyū.* Tokyo: Iwanami Shoten, 1961.

———. "Rekishi ishiki to rekishi no shiten—Nihon shigaku shi ni okeru chūseikan no tenkai." *Shisō* 615 (September 1975): 1–22.

———. "Tenkajin." In *Nihon no shakaishi.* Vol. 3, *Ken'i to shihai.* Tokyo: Iwanami Shoten, 1987.

———. "Village Communities and Daimyō Power." In *Japan in the Muromachi Age*, ed. John Hall and Toyoda Takeshi. Berkeley and Los Angeles: University of California Press, 1977.

Nagahara Keiji, and Kishi Shōzō, eds. *Zenshaku Azuma kagami.* 6 vols. Tokyo: Shinjinbutsu Ōraisha, 1976–79.

Nakada Kaoru. *Shōen no kenkyū.* Tokyo: Shōkō Shoin, 1948.

Nakagomi Ritsuko. "Ōchō kokka ki ni okeru kokuga kokunai shihai no kōzō to tokushitsu." *Gakushūin shigaku* 23 (April 1985): 45–63.

Nakamura Ken. *Shōen shihai kōzō no kenkyū.* Tokyo: Yoshikawa Kōbunkan, 1978.

———, comp. *Kii-no-kuni Ategawa-no-shō shiryō.* Shōen shiryō sōsho. 1 vol. to date. Tokyo: Yoshikawa Kōbunkan, 1976–.

Nakano Hideo. *Chūsei shōenshi kenkyū no ayumi: Ritsuryōsei kara Kamakura bakufu made.* Tokyo: Shinjinbutsu Ōraisha, 1982.

Nihon engyō taikei hensan iinkai, comp. *Nihon engyō taikei.* 3 vols. to date. Tokyo: Nihon Senbai Kōsha, 1970–.

Nihon rekishi gakkai, ed. *Enshū komonjo sen*. Shōen hen. 2 vols. Tokyo: Yoshikawa Kōbunkan, 1980–81.

Nishioka Toranosuke. "Shōen bōji ni tsuite." In *Shōen ezu no kisoteki kenkyū*, ed. Shōen Kenkyūkai. Tokyo: San'ichi Shobō, 1973.

———, comp. *Nihon shōen ezu shūsei*. 2 vols. Tokyo: Tōkyōdō Shuppan, 1976– 77.

Ōishi Naomasa. "Shōen kōryōsei no tenkai." In *Kōza Nihon rekishi*, ed. Rekishigaku Kenkyūkai and Nihonshi Kenkyūkai. Vol. 3, *Chūsei 1*. Tokyo: Tokyo Daigaku Shuppankai, 1984.

Okayama kenshi. Comp. Okayama kenshi hensan iinkai. Vol. 20, *Iewake shiryō*. Okayama: Okayama ken, 1986.

Okuno Nakahiko. "Kaiden zu kara shishi bōji zu e no tenkai." In *Shōen ezu no kisoteki kenkyū*, ed. Shōen Kenkyūkai. Tokyo: San'ichi Shobō, 1984.

———. "Shōen ezu no seiritsu to tenkai." In *Shōen ezu no kisoteki kenkyū*, ed. Shōen Kenkyūkai. Tokyo: San'ichi Shobō, 1984.

———. "Shōen shishi bōji zu no seiritsu." In *Shōensei to chūsei shakai*, comp. Takeuchi Rizō sensei kiju kinen ronbunshū kankōkai. Tokyo: Tokyo Daigaku Shuppankai, 1984.

Okuyama Kenji. "Chūsei Hokusetsu ni okeru myō no kōzō to tochi shoyū keitai." *Shigaku kenkyū* 144 (July 1979): 28–47.

Ooms, Herman. *Tokugawa Ideology: Early Constructs, 1570–1680*. Princeton: Princeton University Press, 1985.

Orgel, Stephen. *The Illusion of Power: Political Threater in the English Renaissance*. Berkeley and Los Angeles: University of California Press, 1975.

———. "The Poetics of Spectacle." *New Literary History* 3 (Spring 1971): 367– 89.

Ōyama Kyōhei. "Medieval *Shōen*." In *The Cambridge History of Japan*. Vol. 3, *Medieval Japan*, ed. Kozo Yamamura. Cambridge: Cambridge University Press, 1990.

———. *Nihon chūsei nōsonshi no kenkyū*. Tokyo: Iwanami Shoten, 1978.

Pecora, Vincent P. "The Limits of Local Knowledge." In *The New Historicism*, ed. H. Aram Veeser. New York and London: Routledge, 1989.

Piggott, Joan. "Hierarchy and Economics in Early Medieval Tōdaiji." In *Court and Bakufu in Medieval Japan*, ed. Jeffrey P. Mass. Stanford: Stanford University Press, 1982.

Rekishigaku Kenkyūkai and Nihonshi Kenkyūkai, eds. *Kōza Nihonshi*. 10 vols. Tokyo: Tokyo Daigaku Shuppankai, 1970–71.

———, eds. *Kōza Nihon rekishi*. 13 vols. Tokyo: Tokyo Daigaku Shuppankai, 1985.

Sabean, David W. *Power in the Blood: Popular Culture and Village Discourse in Early Modern Germany*. Cambridge: Cambridge University Press, 1984.

Sahlins, Marshall. *Islands of History*. Chicago and London: University of Chicago Press, 1985.

Saigyō monogatari emaki. Ed. Hata Shirayoshi. Vol. 11 of *Nihon emakimono zenshū*. Tokyo: Kadokawa Shoten, 1958.

Sakamoto Shōzō. *Nihon ōchō kokka taisei ron*. Tokyo: Tokyo Daigaku Shuppankai, 1972.

Sakaue Yasutoshi. "Aki-no-kuni Takada gunji Fujiwara shi no shoryō shūseki to denryō." *Shigaku zasshi* 91 (September 1982): 1375–412.

Sakuma Takashi. "Kinai no chūsei sonraku to yashikichi." *Hisutoria* 109 (February 1985): 1–18.

Sanjūni-ban shokunin utaawase e. Ed. Mori Toru. Vol. 28 of *Nihon emakimono zenshū.* Tokyo: Kadokawa Shoten, 1979.

Sankain keshō. Comp. Zoku Gunsho Ruijū Kanseikai. 2 vols. Part 37 of *Shiryō sanshū.* Tokyo: Zoku Gunsho Ruijū Kanseikai, 1984.

Sasaki, Gin'ya. *Shōen no shōgyō.* Tokyo: Yoshikawa Kōbunkan, 1964.

Sasaki Hisahiko. "Nanbokuchō 'nairan' ki ni okeru 'shōke no ikki' no kentō." *Rekishigaku kenkyū,* sp. ed. (November 1973): 48–53.

———. "Ōyama Estate and Insei Land Policies." *Monumenta Nipponica* 34, no. 1 (Spring 1979): 73–99.

———. "Proprietor and Peasants: Ōyama Estate in the Early Medieval Period." Ph.D. diss. University of Michigan, 1976.

Sato, Elizabeth. "The Early Development of the Shōen." In *Medieval Japan: Essays in Institutional History,* ed. John W. Hall and Jeffrey P. Mass. New Haven: Yale University Press, 1974.

Satō Kazuhiko. "Chūsei sonrakushi kenkyū no shiten." *Rekishi hyōron* 374 (June 1981): 2–5.

———. "Harima-no-kuni Yano-no-shō ni okeru 'shōke ikki' ni tsuite—Eiwa sannen Gakushū-gata hyōjō hikitsuke no shōkai." *Minshūshi kenkyū* 6 (May 1968): 181–208.

———. "Jūyon-seiki ni okeru Harima-no-kuni Yano-no-shō no zaichi dōkō." (Tokyo Gakugei Daigaku) *Kiyō,* Dai-san bumon, shakai kagaku 31 (January 1980): 157–81.

———. "Jūyon-seiki ni okeru Wakasa Tara-no-shō no zaichi dōkō." (Tokyo Gakugei Daigaku) *Kiyō,* Dai-san bumon shakai kagaku 36 (December 1984): 137–57.

———. "Nanbokuchō nairanki to akutō—Harima-no-kuni Yano-no-shō o chūshin to shite." *Minshūshi kenkyū* 7 (May 1969): 66–77.

———. *Nanbokuchō nairanshi ron.* Tokyo: Tokyo Daigaku Shuppankai, 1979.

Satō Shin'ichi. *Komonjogaku nyūmon.* Tokyo: Hōsei Daigaku Shuppankyoku, 1971.

Satō Shin'ichi, and Ikeuchi Yoshisuke, comps. *Chūsei hōsei shiryōshū.* Vol. 1, *Kamakura Bakufu hō.* Vol. 2, *Muromachi Bakufu hō.* Tokyo: Iwanami Shoten, 1955–57.

Scott, Joan W. *Gender and the Politics of History.* New York: Columbia University Press, 1988.

Seno Seiichirō, comp. *Bingo-no-kuni Ōta-no-shō shiryō.* Shōen shiryō sōsho. Tokyo: Yoshikawa Kōbunkan, 1986.

———, comp. *Kamakura bakufu saikyojōshū.* 2 vols. Tokyo: Yoshikawa Kōbunkan, 1970.

Shimada Jirō. "Nihon chūsei kyōdōtai shiron." *Shichō* n.s. 4 (January 1979): 22–59.

Shimizu Hisao. "Kōyasan ryō shōen shihai to sonraku." In *Chūsei no seiji to bunka*, ed. Toyoda sensei koki kinenkai. Tokyo: Yoshikawa Kōbunkan, 1980.

Shimizu Mistuo. *Chūsei shōen no kiso kōzō*. Tokyo: Kōtō Shoin, 1949.

Shimizu Morimitsu and Aida Hidetsugu, eds. *Hōken kokka no kenryoku kōzō*. Tokyo: Sōbunsha, 1967.

Shōen kenkyūkai, ed. *Shōen ezu no kisoteki kenkyū*. Tokyo: San'ichi Shobo, 1973.

Stallybrass, Peter, and Allon White. *The Politics and Poetics of Transgression*. Ithaca: Cornell University Press, 1986.

Suzuki Ryōichi. *Junsui hōkensei seiritsu ni okeru nōmin tōsō*. Tokyo: Nihon Hyōronsha, 1949.

———. *Nihon chūsei no nōmin mondai*. Kyoto: Kōtō Shoin, 1948.

Suzuki Tetsuo. "Nihon chūsei no hyakushō to tochi shoyū." *Rekishigaku kenkyū* 613 (November 1990): 68–77.

Takada Minoru. "Jūni-jūsan seiki ni okeru kokka kenryoku to kokuga shihai." *Shichō* 99 (June 1967): 6–25.

Takahashi Masaaki. "Nihon chūsei nōgyō seisanryoku suijun saihyōka no is-shiten." *Atarashii rekishigaku no tame ni* 148 (August 1977): 1–13.

Takano Yoshikazu. "Nanbokuchō kōki ni okeru shōen ryōshu kendan to shugo kenryoku." *Nihonshi kenkyū* 270 (February 1985): 1–28.

Takeuchi Rizō, comp. *Heian ibun*. Tokyo: Tōkyōdō Shoten, 1963–68.

———, comp. *Iga-no-kuni Kuroda-no-shō shiryō*. Tokyo: Yoshikawa Kōbunkan, 1975.

———, comp. *Kamakura ibun*. Tokyo: Tōkyōdō Shoten, 1971-90.

———, comp. *Kii-no-kuni Kuroda-no-shō shiryō*. Shōen shiryō sōsho. Tokyo: Yoshikawa Kōbunkan, 1975.

———, ed. *Tochi seidoshi I*. Taikei Nihonshi sōsho, vol. 6. Tokyo: Yamakawa Shuppansha, 1973.

Tanaka Fumihide. "Chūsei zenki no jiin to minshū." *Nihonshi kenkyū* 266 (October 1984): 4–23.

Terdiman, Richard. *Discourse/Counter-discourse*. Ithaca: Cornell University Press, 1986.

Thompson, E. P. "The Moral Economy of the Crowd in the Eighteenth Century." *Past and Present* 50 (1971): 76–136.

Tōdaiji monjo. In *Dai Nihon komonjo. Iewake monjo* 18, comp. Tokyo Daigaku Shiryōhensanjo. Tokyo: Tokyo Daigaku Shiryōhensanjo, 1944-.

Toda Yoshimi. "Heimin hyakushō no chii ni tsuite." *Hisutoria* 47 (March 1963): 17–24.

———. *Nihon ryōshusei seiritsushi no kenkyū*. Tokyo: Iwanami Shoten, 1967.

Tōji monjo. In *Dai Nihon komonjo. Iewake monjo* 10, comp. Tokyo Daigaku Shiryōhensanjo. Tokyo: Tokyo Daigaku Shiryōhensanjo, 1924-.

Tomisawa Kiyoto. "Chūsei kenchū no tokushitsu—torichō to mokuroku o tsūjite." *Nihonshi kenkyū* 233 (January 1982): 1–25.

———. "Shōen taiseika ni okeru sonraku to nōmin." *Rekishigaku kenkyū* sp. ed. (November 1976): 64–71.

Tonomura, Hitomi. "Community and Commerce in Late Medieval Japan:

Corporate Villages of Tokuchin-ho." Ph.D. Diss. Stanford University, 1986.

———. "Forging the Past: Medieval Counterfeit Documents." *Monumenta Nipponica* 40 (Spring 1985): 69–96.

Toyoda sensei koki kinenkai, ed. *Nihon chūsei no seiji to bunka*. Tokyo: Yoshikawa Kōbunkan, 1980.

Turner, Victor. *From Ritual to Theatre*. New York: PAJ Publications, 1982.

Uejima Tamotsu. "Kamakura jidai Harima-no-kuni Yano-no-shō ni tsuite." *Komonjo kenkyū* 7/8 (February 1975): 65–80.

Umata Ayako. "Tōji-ryō shōen ni okeru zaichi jisha." In *Chūsei jiin soshiki no kenkyū*, ed. Kuroda Toshio. Privately published, 1985.

Varley, H. Paul, trans. *A Chronicle of Gods and Sovereigns:* Jinnō Shōtōki *of Kitabake Chikafusa*. New York: Columbia University Press, 1980.

Wakayama kenshi. Comp. Wakayama kenshi hensan iinkai. Chūsei shiryōhen. Wakayama: Wakayama ken, 1975.

Wakita Haruko. *Nihon chūsei shōgyō hattatsushi no kenkyū*. Tokyo: Ochanomizu Shobō, 1969.

Watanabe Hiromi. "Sengoku sonraku no kōzō." *Rekishi hyōron* 374 (June 1981): 77–92.

Watanabe Sumio. *Kinai shōen no kiso kōzō*. Rev. ed. 2 vols. Tokyo: Yoshikawa Kōbunkan, 1969.

———. "Kōfukuji Daijōin ryō Yamato-no-kuni Yokota-no-shō ni tsuite." *Shigaku zasshi* 89 (March 1980): 1–25.

Watanabe Sumio, and Kita Yoshiyuki, eds. *Yamato-no-kuni Wakatsuki-no-shō shiryō*. Tokyo: Yoshikawa Kōbunkan, 1972.

Watanabe Tsunaya, ed. *Shasekishū*. Nihon koten bungaku taikei, vol. 85. Tokyo: Iwanami Shoten, 1966.

White, Allon. "Pigs and Pierrots: The Politics of Transgression in Modern Literature." *Raritan* 2 (Fall 1982): 51–71.

White, Hayden. *The Content of the Form: Narrative Discourse and Historical Representation*. Baltimore and London: Johns Hopkins University Press, 1987.

Williams, Raymond. *The Long Revolution*. New York: Columbia University Press, 1961.

Yamagishi Tokuhei et al., eds. *Kodai seiji shakai shisō*. Nihon shisō taikei, vol. 8. Tokyo: Iwanami Shoten, 1977.

Yamaguchi Keiji and Nagahara Keiji, eds. *Kōza Nihon gijutsu no shakaishi*. 10 vols. Tokyo: Nihon Hyōronsha, 1983–86.

Yamamoto Takashi. "Chūsei kenchū no igi." *Chihōshi kenkyū* 170 (April 1981): 35–50.

———. "Shōke no ikki no chiikiteki tenkai—Wakasa-no-kuni Niū gun." *Shichō* n.s. 14 (November 1983): 25–43.

Yamamura, Kozo. "The Decline of the Ritsuryō System: Hypotheses on Economic and Institutional Change." *Journal of Japanese Studies* 1 (Autumn 1974): 3–37.

———. "Tara in Transition: A Study of a Kamakura Shōen." *Journal of Japanese Studies* 7 (Summer 1981): 360.

Yamazaki Yuriko. "Chūsei zenki no tochi shoyū—Tsu-no-kuni Ao mura ni tsuite." *Nara shien* 21/22 (August 1977): 23–54.

Yasuda Tsuguo. "Hyakushō myō to tochi shoyū." *Shigaku zasshi* 90 (April 1981): 27–63.

———. "Kōfukuji Daijōin ryō Yamato-no-kuni Yokota-no-shō no kintōmyō." *Shigaku zasshi* 88 (January 1979): 1–24.

Zappitsu yōsho. In *Zoku gunsho ruijū.* Vol. 11. Tokyo: Zoku Gunsho Ruijū Kanseikai, 1931–33.

INDEX

absconding, 72, 80. *See also* peasant rebellion
Akanabe Estate, 30, 60, 91
Althusser, Louis, 31
Amino Yoshihiko, 60, 101, 131 n. 38; on community, 28–30, 128 n. 15
Arakawa Estate, 93
Araki Moriaki, 101, 152 n. 8
archive, 18
Asakawa Kan'ichi, 3–4
Ategawa Estate, 85
attachment, 31, 37
authority, public and private, 15, 16–17, 19–20, 43, 115

Banna, 41, 84; and reorganization of Ōta Estate, 38–41
Barthes, Roland, 121 n. 7
Bloch, Marc, 56, 73, 138 n. 34
Bourdieu, Pierre, 114, 154 n. 16, 154 n. 17
Braudel, Fernand, 151 n. 3
bricoleur: *hyakushō* as, 30

class struggle, 23, 104
commendation, 11, 20–21, 126 n. 46
community, 33, 34, 36, 42–43, 93–94; and *hyakushō* status, 28–31, 128 n. 15; and peasant solidarity, 78–79, 94
Corrigan, Philip, 98
crime, 31–33, 56, 130 n. 23
culture, 98–100, 106–7; as form of discourse, 100; as system, 8, 12, 105, 153 n. 11

de Certeau, Michel, 69
discourse, 4, 18, 23, 34, 98–99, 106; as analytic tool, 110–13
discursive formations, 96–97

Eiwa Uprising (1377), 74–79, 80
English Peasants' Revolt (1381), 72
estate boundaries, 19, 22, 31, 37; disputes over, 56–57; marking off, 51–52, 136 n. 14; permeability of, 34, 54–56
estate maps (*ezu*), 19, 23, 51–54, 124 n. 21

estate system, 10, 21; decline of, 99–105, 151 n. 4; enabling oppositions of, 98–99, 107; as field of struggle, 82, 114–15; "invention" of, 3–5
estates: types of, 10–11; compared with estate system, 12–14; immunities of, 16; in medieval law, 120 n. 3

Foucault, Michel, 13–14, 18, 73, 96, 122 n. 10, 134 n. 60, 148 n. 56
Fujiki Hisashi, 117
Fujiwara Naritaka, 20–21
Fujiwara Sanetō, 20, 54–55
Fukuzawa Yukichi, 3, 119 n. 1
Furet, François, 6, 120 n. 7

Gakushū-gata (Tōji), 74, 77
Geertz, Clifford, 106, 122 n. 13, 150 n. 78, 153 n. 7
Giddens, Anthony, 8, 22, 122 n. 13, 123 n. 14
Gion Shrine, 32
Go-Sanjō, and estate regulation, 17–18

Harrotunian, H. D., 24, 127 n. 47
Hashimoto Hiroshi, 65
Hine Estate, 36, 51
Hiranodono Estate, 30
historical materialism, 104–5, 152 n. 7
Hitoyoshi Shrine, 33
Hon'iden Iehisa, 74, 75, 76
hyakushō, 22, 25–29; in medieval law, 128 n. 6; as public subject, 36–37; representations of, 44, 134 n. 68; social networks of, 35
hyakushō mōshijō, 90–94, 96–97

ichimi shinsui, 83–85
ideological closure, 43–45
ideology, 31, 52–53, 107; of elites, 43; of space, 57; of peasant rebellion, 79, 82, 86
Ikadachi Estate, 56
Inagaki Yasuhiko, 50
Irumada Nobuo, 56